TOMMY'S FIELD

TOMMY'S FIELD

love, loss, and the

goal of a lifetime

NIKKI MARK

UNION SQUARE & CO.

NEW YORK

UNION SQUARE & CO.

NEW YORK

ISBN 978-1-4549-5104-9
ISBN 978-1-4549-5105-6 (e-book)

For information about custom editions, special sales, and premium purchases,
please contact specialsales@unionsquareandco.com.

Printed in the USA

2 4 6 8 10 9 7 5 3 1

unionsquareandco.com

Cover design by Lisa Forde
Cover images: Udomsook/iStock/Getty Images Plus (ball);
Atthapol Saita/Shutterstock.com (turf), topseller/ Shutterstock.com (hummingbird)
Interior design by Rich Hazelton

For Donovan

On July 22, 2022, a visitor in my dreams told me
that "Obstacles are not meant to make us quit but
to teach us how to persevere."

No matter how impossible some obstacles appear, I have
learned that there is always a magical way forward.

Tommy's Field was mine.

PROLOGUE

ELEVEN MILES EAST OF MY HOME IN WESTWOOD SITS EXPOSITION Park, where culture and nature merge in the congested heart of Los Angeles. The 160-acre park is home to the Los Angeles Memorial Coliseum, a historic stadium and world-class amphitheater that attracts the world's brightest stars and amuses this diverse city in a way that only the thrill of competition and the sizzle of entertainment can. The park is also full of iconic museums and enchanting rose gardens, and is an urban oasis surrounded by big city problems. Walk outside its northern gates and the University of Southern California proudly radiates prosperity, good fortune, and the bright side of life. Exit the park to the south and neglected blocks of homeless encampments expose life's wounds. The park's spirit of wonder and play serves to unite its neighbors but the disparity between them only widens depending on which side of the park they live.

OPPOSITE: Tommy Mark at almost twelve years old.

I had visited Expo Park countless times. First, on painfully long school field trips as a child. Again, decades later in life, when I became the mother of a boy who dreamed of becoming a professional soccer player. "I want to play with Hispanic kids," he told me and his dad with a crackling sparkle in his eye. "They take the game more seriously than the kids in our neighborhood and playing with them will make me better. I'm ready for them." He was nine years old, the same age when his mischievous brown eyes met mine and did not flinch when he announced that he'd be moving to Europe to play soccer. "Get ready now, Mom. I'll be leaving home by the time I'm fifteen." I believed him and quietly anticipated his departure ever since. But a mother can never truly be prepared for her child to leave. He said he would leave "by fifteen." I didn't realize that would mean "almost thirteen." And when he said *leave*, I thought he meant for a while.

On this particular morning, January 16, 2020, I drove from Westwood, home of the UCLA Bruins, to Expo Park—rival USC Trojan territory—and was flooded with memories of the Expo Park train stop. My son was eleven when he started walking across the street from his West Los Angeles middle school to take the metro eastbound toward soccer practice. The Expo Station was his stop, and the train ride to it exposed him to the kind of inner-city lifestyle that he had only heard about secondhand from his favorite rap artists. The train not only educated his soul, but it also saved us an hour cutting through midtown traffic and expedited a young boy's dreams.

My logistical memories of driving from work to meet my son at the Expo Station and then transporting him to East Los Angeles so he could practice with his team were full of shades of gray. There was the charcoal-gray exterior of my SUV that weaved through the inner-city streets of South Central and attracted the wrong kind of attention. There was the light-gray fabric of my interior seats that collected multicolored crumbs from the snacks I'd pack for him to eat along on the way. There was the heather-gray practice jersey that he changed into along our route that magically transformed him from a student into a committed athlete. And there were the many shades of gray asphalt that extended the 10 East Freeway as far as our eyes could see as we sat idle on top of it and inched our way to the eastern edge of our city at a pace my speedometer could barely record. Sometimes a stiffness in my lower back and a burning in my strained eyes prompted me to test his ambitions. "Are you sick of this yet?" I would ask, full of hope. His reaction surprised and enlightened me. "No way, I love it! We eat, we talk, we listen to music. And I love my team. What could be better?" He was right. What seemed like insanity at the time was, in retrospect, perfection.

As I made my way closer to Expo Park on this winter morning, my memories skipped further back to when my son was nine and joined his first team in East Los Angeles, just as he had begged us to let him do. That's when I accepted that driving to and from practices and games in this crowded city can actually take longer than the practices and games themselves. That's when I first started calculating the time and expense that families of all kinds were sacrificing so their children could play the game they loved. That's when I stopped to question whether my husband and I were supporting my son's dreams or simply indulging them.

The analysis always led me to the same conclusion. He was the unusually coordinated toddler who kept a ball at his feet since the day he was handed one. He was the curious explorer who discovered his own talents and nourished them with love and enthusiasm to grow. He was the observant little boy who recognized that the soccer clubs in our neighborhood could not satisfy his hunger for the game. And unbeknownst to us at the time, he was the flashy sparkling spirit who was born with a much faster clock than the rest of us and had a fearless urgency to become what he loved. We could only do so much to support him, and we did all that and more. But, ultimately, he was the one who had to perform. And because he did, Europe inched closer.

Now, when I spotted the iron gates of Expo Park, I became sadly aware of how drastically my circumstances had changed. I had no one to pick up. No snacks to pack. No practice to ultimately watch. I pointed my chin straight ahead as I passed the metro station, drove through the northern gates of the park and found a parking spot in an empty lot to the south that would soon be full. I shut off my engine, stared through my front windshield and tended to the thoughts streaming in through the top of my head, which was tingling. Then I spoke out loud in the privacy of my front seat. "I know you are here with me. If you send me a sign, I will look for it." I grounded myself with a deep breath, stepped out of the car and walked toward the stocky white concrete building that had LOS ANGELES SWIMMING STADIUM in mid-century modern font neatly stuck on the front of it. In a slightly smaller font below it I found what I was looking for: DEPT OF RECREATION AND PARKS. As I approached the front door, two hummingbirds nearly grazed my left arm before landing on the tree right in front of me. *Perfect timing*, I thought. *You're here.*

I walked up to the second-floor auditorium, kissed my husband hello, hugged my younger son, and was instantly overwhelmed by the number of friends and colleagues who had taken the time to make the same trek toward downtown to support us. It was ironic that we had all driven forty minutes east in morning traffic to Expo Park to discuss a Westside park—Westwood Park, the relatively small, obscure one located only five minutes from most of our homes. But just as I had surrendered to the universe when my son departed, I had surrendered to the ways of city government. *This is all part of some carefully designed plan*, I told myself, a survival method that gave me hope.

The regularly scheduled bimonthly meeting held by the Board of Recreation and Park commissioners began promptly at 9:30 a.m. I took a seat next to my husband and prepared myself so I was ready when it was my turn to speak. *Project. Be concise. Look them all in the eye. And, by all means, do not cry.*

When my name was called, I approached a sleek black microphone that stood at attention on a slim stand directly in front of four Recreation and Park commissioners. A hundred pairs of eyes stared at the back of my head and my body temperature spiked. *You have sixty seconds to tell your story*, I reminded myself. I stopped an inch away from the microphone and stared at the commissioners who were sitting behind tables that had been draped with black linens and pushed together to form a barrier between them and us. *I just have to convince three out of four of you to vote in our favor. Three of you are women. Maybe you are mothers.* My hands dropped to my sides and I pushed my shoulders down and chest up, as yoga had consistently asked me to do ever since my son had left.

A red light sat above a large digital clock that was frozen on the number sixty and eager to count down. *"It's time to finish, Mom!"* I heard my son shout, as if I were one of his teammates heading toward goal. In a way, I was, and had prepared to finish strong. In another way, I was aware that I could be developing a mild form of schizophrenia. That thought made me smile. The clock started counting down to zero while the red light tried to intimidate me. I rushed to find my voice.

"Today is exactly one year and nine months since the day my twelve-year-old son, Tommy, went to sleep and didn't wake up. We still don't know why." My voice was already shaking and violating my game plan. The four commissioners stared back at me with what seemed like not an ounce of compassion in their eyes. Before I could process what was happening to me, an intense wave of grief crept up my throat and nearly crashed through the backs of my eyes. *Not now!* I implored. *Give me sixty seconds to get through this, please. I can feel you. Back off a little and when I'm done, come back.* I willed my emotions back down into the cracks in my heart, which caused a low tremble that spread instantly from my gut to my limbs.

The grief retreated and allowed me to continue. "Twenty-four hours after my son passed away, our community came together to create a legacy for my son that honors his passion for sports and his spirit of play." The commissioners looked bored. I had said it all before. Ten times on the record before, to be exact. Not to mention, dozens of times in between. But because the facts kept being ignored, I repeated them over and over again as if I was the crazy person in all of this.

The clock expired, the red light blinked, and neither cared less that I was a mother who had lost her oldest son. The commissioners stared back blankly at me. There was no hidden message in their eyes. No empathy. No hint on how they'd vote. Not even a "thank you" for extending this gift. The silence tried to rattle me, but my soul had come too far to let it.

The top of my head started tingling down to the bottom of my temples, and another download set me straight. *"The commissioners are like referees, Mom. Their job is to stay objective and not let their hearts influence their decisions. Don't let them throw you off your game. Trust they are doing the best they can."* Those were the same words I was pretty sure I had said to Tommy after some disappointing soccer match that he and his teammates blamed on a bad call. I appreciated the advice and was reminded that the commissioners were volunteers appointed by our mayor. *Be grateful for their service,* I told myself. *Trust they are doing the best they can.*

I turned around, walked back to my seat and prepared for my grief to return when I said it could. Tears promptly rolled down my cheeks and fell on the rim of my turtleneck sweater. *Sorry, T, that was not my best speech. But apparently it was the best I could do today.*

As I listened to over an hour of public comments and endured hisses from the row of opposition sitting directly behind me, it dawned on me that while I was trembling, I wasn't frightened. Nothing frightened me anymore. No longer was I the little girl who worried about saying or doing the wrong thing. No longer was I the friend who kept her life so private that she hid her deepest beliefs and opinions from her own self. No longer was I the businesswoman who found her niche building start-ups for inspiring visionaries and helped them manifest their dreams while ignoring her own. And no longer was I the mom who worried about the future without even feeling the present.

I sat there raw. Fully exposed but insulated by a love so indescribably vast and excruciatingly deep that not even the row behind or the decision-makers in front could penetrate it.

Sitting taller in my seat, I grabbed my husband's hand and tuned into the last few public comments until silence filled the room and the commissioners prepared to vote. The top of my head was burning. I could feel my son's enthusiasm breathing down my neck: *"Let's hurry up and finish this already, Mom!"* A cool breeze passed over me and made me shiver.

"I know, T, it's time. There's nothing left we can do or say. We have done our best."

"Don't worry, Mom. There's no way they will vote against my field. You have something that all of them combined don't have."

"What's that, T?"

"You have me."

I quickly responded, *"Yes, T, I know. I just wish you were still here."* A wave of fresh salty tears escaped my eyes until I checked myself. *"I wish you were physically here."* My heart and mind were constantly jostling for position as one foot stood firmly rooted in this reality while the other dangled in some sort of sacred world. But since I had a son in each, I was okay with it.

I looked up when the commissioners started voting and was at peace with what I knew they would say. This wasn't about winning. My family had already lost.

I had received countless messages, signs, and dreams to decipher and decode since the day Tommy departed, and my career building start-ups had taught me to interpret each one of them in the context of whatever outcome I needed to create. What I needed to do the day Tommy left was find a way to survive the unfathomable pain of losing him. Physically dying seemed much easier, but when I looked at my younger son and husband during the earliest moments of our tragedy, I knew that was not an option. So, while survival was everything, it wasn't nearly enough. I also had to create a way to transform my suffering into a joyful and meaningful life, and inspire Tommy's heartbroken younger brother, with a lifetime ahead of him, to do the same. It all felt impossible, unimaginable, and too much to be asked of me.

"Figure it out," the universe taunted.

In honor of my two sons, I knew that I could. For the sake of making the most out of this lifetime, the universe hoped that I would.

When the first commissioner voted, my husband squeezed my right hand and Tommy's spirit hugged my soul. *"This is going to be fun, Mom. I promise you."* His infectious laughter roared, and a bittersweet smile stretched across my face that startled me. Smiles did not usually come so easily these days, and this one felt premature. I wanted to take it back.

Then these words were spoken to me: *"Soccer taught me how to win at life, Mom. Now you're in training. Keep playing hard, I showed you how."*

Suddenly, something old released and something new advanced, and I was no longer just building a field or enduring a nasty introduction to local politics. I was playing a meticulously orchestrated game of life designed and manipulated especially for me. To guide my journey and make sure I didn't quit, soccer appeared—like a religion that activated my imagination, connected me to my son, and showed me how to play. And no matter what people thought, or how crazy it sounded, or how minuscule the chances were that it could be true, in my mind, Tommy was playing with me. In my heart, we were like World Cup champions, committed to building his legacy and uniting both of our worlds through the beautiful game. And in my soul, we would never stop playing until I remembered who I was and why I was here, and we lived the story that we both came here to tell.

PART 1

The Loss

CHAPTER 1

TOMMY'S FIELD HAD TWO INCARNATIONS IN THE SAME LIFETIME, just as I did. The first started in 2013 when I volunteered to be president of a Westside youth soccer club and found myself in a position where I needed to help others. The second began five years later when Tommy didn't wake up one morning and I needed to help myself. Like clever dancing twists of fate, both were complete and unwelcome surprises, and entirely dependent on the other.

It was after my second incarnation abruptly began that I started evaluating my life in the privacy of a forest-green, leather-bound journal that still sits on my nightstand and waits for me to purge my emotions. The journal was left in a pile of condolence gifts and cards, and when a debilitating darkness tried to swallow me whole after Tommy's funeral, the journal caught my eye and screamed at me for attention. I pulled it out and dumped unrecognizable anguish on its lined white pages until the cramping of my right hand tried to distract me from my throbbing heart. On good days, Tommy still hears from me every night in that journal. On bad days, he hears from me more than once. Together, as a trio, Tommy, my green journal, and I analyze this lifetime together and contemplate the depths of our relationship.

My journal and I have discussed at great length the tragedy that struck on April 17, 2018, two days before my forty-eighth birthday, and twenty-seven days before Tommy would have turned thirteen.

The prior evening was typical for a Monday. Tommy returned from soccer practice, ate dinner, showered, and made his nightly calls to friends. At around 9:00 p.m., I walked into my younger son Donovan's room and saw him pinned underneath Tommy, who was practicing one of his Krav Maga, self-defense, around-the-neck-and-squeeze moves.

"This is a new position I learned the other day," Tommy exclaimed to me. "I'm trying it out on Dono!" Laughter erupted from the bottom of his soul and immediately ignited mine, as Lionel Messi, blown up and stuck to Donovan's wall, pointed his index fingers up to the sky. Even Donovan, who was choking, howled through his tears. I unwrapped Tommy's arms by tickling under them until another dose of his laughter infected me, and Donovan was released.

Then Tommy stood up and started singing. He was always singing. On this particular evening he was rapping and turned to his brother, "My rapper name is Big T. Yours is Little D. Good night Little D. I love you."

Dressed in black dry-fit boxers accessorized with a soccer ball at his feet, he followed me out of Dono's room and stopped by our family's communal charging station to plug in his cell phone for the night and comply with my "no technology in the bedroom while we sleep" rule. I was pleasantly surprised when he didn't grumble about it, and even chuckled when he stepped back, took a few jabs at the air, and told me how excited he was for his early morning Krav Maga workout before school. He was always moving. Always squeezing in more. Always mindful beyond his years and making the moment he was in feel just as important as the one before and after it.

I made my way to the family room, sat down on the couch next to my husband with my laptop by my side, and silently reflected on how mature and responsible Tommy had become. It seemed to me that his stars were aligning and that turning thirteen really was some kind of magic number.

Tommy walked toward us with the ball still spinning between his feet and said, "Mom, my ribs are sore, I think I need an adjustment." He accentuated his point by crossing his arms in front of him and rubbing both sides of his rib cage with his palms. Tommy was a dedicated athlete whose body required constant maintenance, so I didn't think much of it.

"I'll call the chiropractor in the morning," I assured him, turning on my laptop and making a mental note of it.

My husband, Doug, promptly took matters into his own hands and stood up to examine Tommy himself. He massaged Tommy's back, lifted his long thin arms out to the side, and then embraced him from behind. With one playful squeeze, he gave Tommy the bear hug of a lifetime until his toes lifted off the ground and Tommy let out a loud grunt. When Doug released him and Tommy landed, they smiled at each other, shared one last laugh, and unknowingly said goodbye.

"Good night, guys, I love you," Tommy sang back at us as he headed toward his bedroom, dragging our cinnamon-brown pocket pit bull, Ginger, with him. It wasn't easy pulling a sixty-pound pit who hunkered down like a dead weight when she was asked to move off her luxurious fuzzy pillow-bed. Still, night after night, since the day our family rescued her, she let Tommy grab her by the collar, slide her across the living-room floor, and pull her down two short flights of stairs into his room. It was more than just a routine. It was their special game that always ended with Ginger leaping onto his bed, sprawling vertically alongside him, and smooshing her massive head into the pillow next to his as they fell asleep with their arms entwined.

"Love you, too, T-bone," Doug yelled back.

"Love you, T," I followed with an echo.

I heard Tommy's door shut, and then Donovan's, and an hour later the entire household was asleep.

The next morning, shortly before 7:00 a.m., I was in the kitchen making Tommy's favorite breakfast sandwich: a toasted bagel spread with butter and layered with one egg, a slice of Canadian bacon, and half an avocado smashed on top. He called it the breakfast of champions and said it made him stronger.

Doug was at the other end of the kitchen pouring his second cup of coffee, while Donovan was sitting at our kitchen table explaining to me that his stomach hurt. He said he had thrown up and that he was too sick to go to school. I asked Donovan to rest on the couch in the family room until I could verify his sudden illness.

Five minutes later, when Tommy's breakfast was assembled, wrapped in foil, and ready to travel with him to Krav, I glanced at the clock and was surprised to see that he wasn't up yet. Tommy was always up. Always ready. Always on time. Only mildly concerned, I strolled across the house, glanced at his cell phone that was still charging next to mine, and quietly entered his bedroom to check on him. I opened his blinds to let in some Southern California sunshine and was startled when he still didn't stir. *Maybe he's going through a growth spurt*, I thought. *Maybe he's sick. Maybe I should cancel his workout and let him sleep in.* Then I glanced over at Tommy still in bed and zoomed in closer. Something wasn't right.

"Tommy!" I shouted, racing toward him. When he didn't respond, I shouted for my husband, grabbed my cell phone, and frantically dialed 911.

Within seconds, Doug flew into the room.

"Tommy's not breathing!" I shouted.

Then I heard the sound of small feet growing louder behind him.

Donovan rushed into the room and yelled, "What's happening? What's happening to Tommy?!"

Devoid of any answers, Doug ran over to Tommy's bed and pleaded over and over again, "Wake up, Tommy!"

Seconds later, Dono and I followed Doug as he carried Tommy into our bedroom, laid him flat on our floor, and followed the CPR instructions that the operator was giving him on my phone.

I knelt next to Tommy and silently wept, *Please wake up, Tommy. We love you. Don't leave us.*

Then, for the first time in my life, I really prayed. *Please don't take Tommy. We need him here. Take me, not him.*

While Doug repeatedly pumped on Tommy's chest and breathed into his mouth, Donovan sobbed, "Please don't die, Tommy. I'm too young to lose my big brother."

Distraught that our tragedy was unfolding in real time in front of my younger son and there was nothing I could do about it, I begged my husband, "Fix him, Doug! Please fix him!"

My business instincts turned on, my mind settled, and I reassured myself: *This is just a glitch. We can fix him.*

But when the fireman arrived and looked up at me less than five minutes later, I understood that Tommy was not fixable, and it felt intentional. Overnight, while I had been sleeping, I was failing at the most important job I had ever been given, and all this morning had to say about it was that I would not be given a single chance to correct my mistake. It was inconceivable. Inexplicable. And tragically indisputable. *Mothers protect their children*, I chastised myself. *Mothers raise their children to be adults. Mothers do not let their children down like this.*

As I wrestled with my thoughts and tried to make sense of what had just happened and why, my mind got creative and presented another theory. The universe, composed of all matter and space, was fully aware of my problem-solving capabilities. It knew what I could do. It had seen what I could deliver. It did not want me to save my oldest son and disrupt the order of its ways. So it conspired with fate behind my back to take him from me in the middle of the night when my intuition was switched off, my senses had dimmed, and it knew I would be incapacitated and unable to intervene.

Whether our family was a random victim or specifically chosen, I reasoned that the result was sadly the same.

"Ma'am," the lead fireman said to me as I held Tommy and stared off into space. "He's been gone a long time. What time did he go to sleep last night?"

"Around 9:00 or 9:30," I responded, unable to look him in the eye.

"He probably passed shortly after that," he said, making me feel even worse. How could I have possibly been sleeping when Tommy was leaving?

I looked over at Dono and watched my sweet silly ten-year-old son transform into an adult before my eyes. I internally thanked him for the way he had flagged down the firemen, led them into our room, and explained the circumstances. I privately reflected on all the touching words he had shared with his big brother throughout the morning and the many reasons he had offered to convince him to stay. I quietly marveled at the way he'd shoved his own fears aside and allowed his instincts to guide when to stand by our side and when to give everyone room to breathe.

What could have been one minute or an hour later, I looked up and noticed that the door to my room was shut and Tommy and I were alone. Apparently, the bond between a mother and her child had earned me special privileges and I was grateful to the firemen for teaching my family this lesson. Suddenly, a love so painfully deep took over my entire being and urged me to wrap my arms around Tommy and speak to him before all systems shut down. *I'm so sorry I failed you, T. I love being your mom. I will always be your mom. I will always love you. I did the best I could. But I missed it, T. I'm so sorry*

I missed it. Please forgive me. These words looped over and over in my mind and bounced backward and forward until my head unexpectedly jerked up as if I were a baby who couldn't control her own neck. The jarring impact of my head against my upper back forced me to intermittently look up and search the air. *Where are you, T? I know you are here somewhere.* My mother had always warned me to live my life as though someone were watching. Only now was I desperate enough to explore what she meant. Still, as hard as I tried, I saw nothing.

Through the walls, I heard cries pouring out from the bottom of Doug's soul. I closed my eyes and wilted as my first incarnation as Tommy's mom came to a stupefying end.

CHAPTER 2

"It's mystical," I told Doug as we sat on the couch in our pajamas, sharing the pain that comes from obliterated hearts. His hazel eyes stared back at me, looking so traumatized that the natural golden flecks in them had turned bright orange, as if they were on fire.

"There's something about the way you reacted this morning that makes it seem like you knew this would happen," he responded, unable to further articulate what he meant. "I can't explain it."

I nodded and responded with the only words I could find. "This is not some random mistake. This is part of some plan." Then I went numb.

I recognized that the world I once knew and the person I once was, had changed overnight and I was certain that the universe had made a giant mistake. I was Nikki Mark. Nikki Alison Mark. The "normal" one, according to nearly half a century of girlfriends. The "stable" one, according to generations of colleagues and employers. The one who rarely got caught up in the highs and lows of life and who had taught herself at a very young age to avoid unnecessary drama at all costs. In fact, I was the one who managed drama. I fixed drama. I was a self-proclaimed master of preventing drama! No, I was not the right person for this tragedy, and had a forty-eight-year track record to prove it.

I was born into a loving upper-middle-class family in Encino, California, home of the original Valley Girl and just six gridlocked miles north of Westwood. Throughout my childhood, friends often teased that my family was like the Ingalls, referring to the family upon which the 1970's hit television show *Little House on the Prairie* was based. We trusted each other. Supported one another. Even genuinely enjoyed being together. Rarely did we raise our voices. Never would we talk behind each other's backs. Seldom did we curse. In fact, when Doug first met my family, he turned to me and asked, "What the hell is going on here?" When he saw genuine confusion spread across my face, he took the opportunity to tell me that he had been raised by wolves. That his father doted on his sisters. His mother prioritized her pills. So, he was left to fend for himself as a young child to the point where he regularly wandered over to a neighbor's house before school to get breakfast. He had never seen a family like mine before and for years thought we were putting on some kind of show . . . just like the Ingalls did for my generation and the Cleavers in *Leave it to Beaver* did in his.

My father was a dentist, and my mother managed his dental office, our home, and their various entrepreneurial projects. Together they gave me and my older brother a childhood full of travel, music, sports, and, most of all, love. While they were models for what it meant to be honest, disciplined, and full of humility, they also passed down a singular family trait that we never discussed but all learned to perfect. Our family was exceptionally private. We did not cause problems. We rarely talked about our problems. Unless invited, we rarely inserted ourselves into other people's problems.

My brother was the smart one, I the artistic one, and, for whatever reason, I decided that I could only be one or the other. Not both. By the time I entered middle school, I had suppressed my creative passions and dedicated myself to becoming smart, whatever that meant. I felt my deepest joy singing, dancing, playing guitar, and writing short stories and poetry on the side, but I prioritized school and friendships, and became a dedicated student who forgot almost everything she learned after achieving the grade point average that college applications and employment resumes required. I wasn't brilliant. I didn't have to be a genius. I just wanted to be smart enough.

After college, I went to business school. My guitar came with me and sat in my apartment while I applied my business studies to the music industry and reasoned that if I didn't have the courage to be a true artist, then I would apply my growing smartness and help those who did.

I spent the next twenty-two years working for entrepreneurs with big personalities and inspiring visions, and helping them build their companies from the ground up. While they focused on revolutionizing their respective industries, I developed their business operations and was given an executive title that put me in charge of them. I flourished working in highly creative and fast-paced environments where instruction was vague and timelines incredibly unrealistic, and quickly developed a strong mindset that nothing was impossible. No deadline was too soon. No problem too complex. There was always a solution, and I developed a weird obsession and knack for finding it.

I had conveyed all this to Tommy when I drove him to San Diego for a league match the weekend before he departed. He had asked me, "Mom, what exactly do you do?" I explained the trajectory of my career and the many challenging projects that I had brought to fruition across three industries: music, hospitality, and professional soccer. Then I took the opportunity to impart some wisdom that I never imagined I'd need myself just four days later. "There's always a way, T-bone. An honest way. You just have to be creative, believe in yourself, and trust that the universe will help you."

Well, only days after I had genuinely complimented it, my so-called "universe" pushed me too far. It took my son and put forth an unbearable challenge for which there was no solution. My mind shut off and without asking for my permission, some other consciousness switched on.

I sank into the couch, descending deeper into darkness until my body forced me to take a gulp of air and snap back into the real world in front of me. As if some small crack opened in time, a recent memory broke through. *My life has been too easy.* That's what I had told myself no less than twice the week before. When it entered my mind the first time, I labeled it a random thought and questioned whether I had failed to show enough gratitude in my life. When it entered my mind the second time, a nervous anxiety permeated my system. It wasn't until Tommy was gone and my first incarnation as his mother abruptly ended that I realized there was nothing random about it. *My life has been too easy* was an intentionally placed message advising me to be grateful for the last forty-eight years because my turn to get whacked was imminent.

CHAPTER 3

BY THE TIME THE CITY'S HOMICIDE INVESTIGATORS WALKED INTO our home and sat down across from me and Doug to ask routine questions, a textbook version of shock had attacked my entire body. The past was no longer relevant. The future had just blown up. All that registered was the present moment that I desperately wanted to end.

The two investigators asked a number of questions, but a piercing high-pitched ring in both of my ears muffled their voices. I attempted to read their lips, but a thick fog had invaded my brain and disconnected all relevant circuits. I couldn't process anything beyond the second I was in and with every passing second less of me was in it. My soul, which I couldn't remember ever acknowledging before, was frantically chasing after Tommy and trying to bring him back where he belonged. Periodically, it glanced back at me sitting on the couch next to my husband and saw a terrible actress starring in the worst movie of all time. The scene was my living room, and the homicide officers were questioning me about a terrible crime. I was innocent, as far as I knew, but could not string together a coherent sentence. My mind was unable to process their questions. *Guilty* flashed in front of my eyes. Fortunately, my husband covered for me by answering the investigators' questions while I sat there realizing that it's impossible to speak or act like the sane person you once thought you were when tragedy blindsides you and smashes you inside out with terror.

As Doug and the officers conversed, fragments of Tommy's medical history surfaced in my mind and made me question what I might have missed.

There were the respiratory illnesses that Tommy suffered no less than twice a year. They clogged up his ears, nose, and throat for months at a time and produced a relentless dry chest cough that woke us both up in the middle of the night and required an adult dose of NyQuil to calm.

There were the late-evening gushing bloody noses every winter and summer that resulted in us spending multiple hours together in the middle of the night pinching his nostrils and reading books until the blood dried up and he eventually fell back to sleep.

There were the allergies to grass, dust, and walnut trees that required one-minute allergy shots that often took us an hour to get to and from every week in Santa Monica.

There were the physical sports-related injuries, including sore heels, swollen ankles, and overused muscles that required constant maintenance, including weekly acupuncture and chiropractic treatments administered by practitioners who squeezed in early-morning appointments before school and on weekends, not only because they enjoyed Tommy's company, but because they were the special ones being called upon to help a young boy achieve his dreams.

Lastly, there were the panic attacks and nightmares that woke him up in the middle of the night every evening for the first nine years of his life. At two or three in the morning he would run out of his room into mine, and crawl in between me and Doug before promptly falling back asleep until morning. Nothing could keep him in his bed. Not threats. Not punishments. Not even therapy. "He came into this lifetime with this fear," a child psychologist once told me, leaving her final diagnosis at that.

It suddenly seemed to me, sitting in front of those officers in my home, that Tommy's soul knew his clock was ticking, and his body kept finding clever new ways to maximize our time together and make up for the precious years we were destined to lose.

But there was nothing in his medical history to suggest there was anything seriously wrong with him. As if the female officer had been reading my mind, she said, "Don't beat yourself up. There's a lot we don't know about the human body."

After the officers left, my head jerked up and I saw my parents and closest friends entering our home. An inner voice spoke to me and advised, *"Let people help you. . . they want to . . . they need to . . . this is not just about you."*

As I watched our inner circle come together in some sort of tribal way to support the needs of our family, and each other, I thought to myself, *I'm grateful for whatever they want to do for us for as long as they want to do it. I wouldn't know what to do for them if they were in my position, so I don't expect them to know what to do for us. They're here. They're trying. That's a lot.*

As if my thoughts had been heard, an inner voice advised me further. *"Tell them what you need. They need help, too."*

Curled up on our couch sinking before everyone's eyes, I became lost in an internal dialogue that was impossible to rationalize or explain. *"I surrender,"* I spoke telepathically to the nebulous entity that I called the universe. *"Just tell me what you want me to do, and I'll do it."*

I had never committed to a particular god. So, when life handed my family the most extreme of all tragedies, I held each and every possible deity accountable. I did not know their names or care about their stories. I simply lumped them all together with the rest of all matter and space and called it the "universe." To me, the universe was far more powerful and inclusive than any one god, and I blamed it for executing the perfect tragedy.

"Keep your enemies closer," Tommy used to tell me when I marveled at his ability to forgive others so quickly. I followed his advice and accepted that if was ever going to understand this unfathomable plan, I had to strengthen my connection to the top where important decisions are made. The universe was my new boss now, and as with every entrepreneur for whom I had ever worked, I had to figure out how to collaborate.

My head jerked back again, and a voice reminded me to check on Doug and Donovan. *"You are still a mother and a wife. Take care of them."*

I stood up and shuffled toward the dining room where friends had congregated around a buffet table of food. *I will never eat again*, I thought. As I looked around for Donovan, Doug suddenly grabbed my hand and squeezed it tight, as if he had his own voices talking to him at the same time. I gazed up and saw his lips moving but couldn't follow them.

"Huh?" I asked, the ringing in my ears and the increasing volume in our home making it difficult to hear him. Close friends and family huddled nearby.

His voice grew louder. "This is not our fault. We watched Tommy like a hawk," he shouted.

My head, which felt as heavy as a brick, nodded in agreement.

"We will not be a tragic family," he continued, grabbing both of my shoulders, and forcing me to look in his eyes. "We will get through this together. Do you understand me?"

"Yes, I understand," I whispered. "I agree." The last thing I knew Tommy would want is for his family to fall apart. *This is a plan*, I reminded myself. *There is a reason we are experiencing this tragedy together.*

I turned and started heading back toward the couch when I heard my name being called in the distance. I looked over and saw Dono running up to me with the father of one of Tommy's best friends by his side. I tried to stand up straight.

"Mom!" he yelled with an urgency that held my attention and popped my ears. "There is a huge brown hawk staring at us from a tree across the street. I think it's Tommy watching everything going on and reporting back to God." Donovan and I had never spoken about God before, but since I had been speaking to the entire universe of gods and goddesses that morning, I wasn't one to judge. The two of them proceeded to describe the position of the hawk, the intensity of its stare, and the way it fixated on our home that entire afternoon. They were convinced that the hawk had something to do with Tommy. As much as I wasn't a god person, I was even less of a bird person. Still, I couldn't deny finding comfort in Donovan's spiritual impressions, for as life unraveled before my very eyes, his explanations were the only ones that made any sense.

CHAPTER 4

By evening, word had traveled around the city with Tommy Mark speed, and our home was filled with a community that I didn't even know we had. Earlier that morning, Doug posted a picture of Tommy on his Facebook page with the caption underneath, "We were lucky to have him." The response was immediate. From teachers to coaches to friends, teammates, and business colleagues, it seemed that everyone who had ever known Tommy or a member of our family had shown up from all corners of our city to share our grief.

My memory of that day is scattered.

I remember Donovan consoling his father, whose cries were bouncing off our walls and scaring him.

"Dad, control yourself," Dono advised through his own tears. "Or you are going to have a heart attack, too." We didn't know what had happened to Tommy that morning, but both the firemen and the homicide detectives thought his exit likely had something to do with his heart.

I remember my stepson, Ethan, who was twenty-five at the time and almost thirteen years older than Tommy, running through our front door pale as a ghost, falling into Doug's arms and struggling to comprehend how the little brother he had picked up from school and driven to soccer practice the week before was suddenly gone.

"I was finally becoming an involved big brother," he cried to Doug within earshot. "I still had so much I wanted to teach him."

I remember looking up and seeing Ethan's mom at one of our sides. Consoling. Organizing. Supervising.

I remember Donovan appearing on the couch next to me at some point and asking, "Why wasn't I taken instead of Tommy? He was the special one." My girlfriends sitting on the other side of me simultaneously squeezed my hand and gasped, while their tears drenched their faces.

"Oh, Dono," I responded, forcing my voice to connect with my thoughts. "You are just as special as Tommy. Do not ever think this should have happened to you instead of him. If anyone had to go, it should have been me."

I remember Dono spending most of the day in our backyard, sitting in the middle of the synthetic lawn where only a day earlier he and Tommy had played soccer. Now this was where Tommy's teammates from the east side of our city mourned with Tommy's Westside friends, sharing stories and trying to console one another. This was also where our nanny, Estela, watched Dono from afar and deferred her own grief to tend to our home and manage our guests. I wanted to tell her not to work. To help support Dono. To simply sit with all of us and grieve. But the universe had shown me that I was not in control, and, ultimately, she made it clear that helping others was how she processed her own grief best.

Dono acknowledged to me that day how important Estela was to him. He asked if it was okay to call her his *abuela*. He had recently learned the words for family members in Spanish and wanted to give the one meaning "grandmother" to her. While she had helped raise Ethan and was considered part of the family even before my boys and I entered it, I understood that Dono needed to make the relationship formal that day and help make up for the family member who had that very morning disappeared.

Just when I thought there couldn't possibly be anyone else we knew who wasn't already in our home, I looked up and saw my friend and fellow soccer mom, Linda, walking toward me in slow motion with a potted red rosebush in her hands. "This rosebush is for your front yard," she said, pulling me into another room and sitting down next to me. "Plant it and when it blooms it will represent all the love that you and Tommy share, forever." I was speechless and couldn't understand how she had already found the perfect symbol for my son. Red roses were on his favorite socks. They were embedded in the posters and stickers on his bedroom walls. They were on the Guns N' Roses T-shirts that he wore. They were even in the title of a filthy rap song on his favorite playlist. A red rose embodied everything Tommy. Bold. Special. And full of love. Red roses would grace our home, both inside and out, from that day forward.

Tears of gratitude drained from my eyes and released pressure from my pounding head. "Nikki," Linda said, with my anguish reflected in her blue eyes, "let's create Tommy's legacy. You have been wanting to build a soccer field for this community. Let's build that field and honor Tommy and his love for the game. Everyone wants to do something to help. No one knows what to do."

I could barely digest her words.

"This will be the perfect project to pour our hearts into," Linda continued, repeating herself multiple times until she saw her idea sink in. "This field will benefit so many generations of children, Nikki. Tommy would love to know that his life is continuing to impact others and inspiring them to play." She pushed her blond hair away from her forehead and offered to make the first donation.

Despite my present state, Linda knew me well enough to know that if I committed to getting something done, I would. She was a fellow board member when I volunteered to be president of Tommy's first Westside soccer club and was fully aware of my plans to build an athletic field for the community in our neighborhood park, Westwood Recreation Center. She was a supportive friend when just four months prior to this tragic day I paused my career to focus on my boys and give thoughtful consideration to my next job. She was a thorn in my side during that mini-retirement period, pushing me to do fundraising for the new athletic field and bribing me with wine and home-cooked dinners until I agreed to finish what I had started. And she was a passionate soccer mom who not only helped dozens of talented players from underserved communities apply for and earn college scholarships, but also cheered when I, a woman, was hired by one of our city's Major League Soccer clubs to help establish its youth development program and consult on special projects. Linda, I would soon realize, was the chosen one who pulled the loose ends from the first field incarnation and securely tied them to Tommy's Field.

When Linda suggested that we build Tommy's legacy, she triggered a recent memory.

"Just a few days ago, Linda, I drove Tommy down to San Diego for a soccer game." My voice was quivering, and the rhythm of my words deviated from their normal cadence. "During that drive I told him that I was planning to build a soccer field for the community." His sparkling brown eyes and handsome face looked over at me from the passenger seat and he flashed a giant smile. "He said, 'Really? That's so cool, Mom. Our part of town doesn't have anything like that. Everyone will want to play on it. I can't wait!'" As the memory spilled out of me, I connected Linda's idea to Tommy's reaction and knew that she was right. Building a soccer field to honor Tommy was the perfect legacy. I told him I was going to do it. He wanted me to do it. Therefore, I would.

Doug joined our conversation and immediately agreed. He suggested we name it "Tommy's Field," and, within minutes, members of our growing tribe huddled around us and formulated a plan. The operator in me began to manifest a clear vision and a dedicated bank account so that we could announce Tommy's Field at his memorial and immediately start collecting charitable donations. I had never been challenged to survive and function at the very same time, but this was for Tommy. I would die for him if I could but since I wasn't given that opportunity, I would build his field and share his spirit of play with our entire city.

First, I had to do the near impossible. I had to find my voice, call our city's Department of Recreation and Parks, and explain to someone I barely knew what I didn't even yet believe—that my oldest son had unexpectedly passed away overnight. And during that same unfathomable conversation, I had to remember how to be the businesswoman I was the day before and ask if the city would give our family naming rights in return for donating 100 percent of the funding to build the field. Thinking that far ahead made my head pound harder.

As Tuesday, April 17, 2018 came to an end and Tommy's Field was officially born, Donovan, Doug, and I stumbled back toward our bedrooms for the very first time since morning. I looked over at Donovan and could feel how acutely lonely a family of three already felt to him. When we entered the hallway that led to our bedrooms, I glanced to my right and peeked at Tommy's room at the very end. Movement under his closed door made me pause. I turned his doorknob and for the first time since that tragic morning, peered into his room. His television was on. When I looked closer, I saw that it was turned to some random channel that Tommy would have never watched. I looked back at Donovan and cautiously asked, "Did you happen to turn on Tommy's TV today?" I already heard the answer. *No one would have entered Tommy's room after what happened in there this morning.*

"No," Donovan confirmed. "The door has been shut all day and no one else has been in this part of the house. I was outside in the backyard with Tommy's friends but when I went into my bathroom a few hours ago I heard the TV was on and wondered why." *"Is this my sign, T?"* I looked at Doug, who had spent some time in Tommy's room earlier that morning, but he had no answers. I found the remote and felt a spark of energy from Tommy's fingerprints on it. I turned the television off and closed the door.

I whispered in my mind, *"Good night, T. I love you."*

I thought I heard him respond the way he did every night since he learned to speak: *"Good night, Mom, I love you, too."*

It was 3:00 a.m. when the three of us all climbed into bed together and turned off the lights. We all wished we'd never wake up. But by 5:00 a.m. Doug was already in the other room wailing and by 6:00 a.m., I was awake, thinking what I knew I'd think every day for the rest of my life. *It's still true. He's gone. And he's not coming back. Not ever.* As if I weren't being tortured enough, instincts warned that I was only at the middle point of my life. I would live to be ninety-six years old, just like my grandmother, Mama, had. Whether I wanted to or not, I would carry on the legacy of a long life in my family and endure the reality of losing Tommy for another forty-eight years.

Before that thought was able to annihilate me, Donovan sat up next to me in bed and said with tears stuck to his little face, "I saw how heaven works last night in my dreams." His blue eyes, shaped round and large like mine, began changing colors.

"Really, D? Explain." The word *heaven* was as foreign to me as the word *god*. And yet, while his comment surprised me, I was also intrigued.

"So, this is what happens," he continued. "We all agree to come down here together to be a family but each time our roles change. This time you're the mom and Tommy and I are your sons, but after you die you might come back one day as the daughter and I may be your father. We all agree before we are born which family member we will be and then at some point, after we all die, we regroup and change it all up again. We just aren't always here at the exact same time."

"That feels right," I acknowledged, noticing that my sentences were getting shorter and harder to articulate. His tears had transformed his eyes into a stunning shade of turquoise that distracted me.

Irritated that I was losing focus, he raised his voice. "I'm telling you, Mom, this is what I learned in my dreams last night. I'm not making this up."

"I believe you, Donovan," I said, staring into the shiny windows of his wise eyes. "I have heard that when you dream, you can connect to the spirit world. It seems like that happened to you last night."

"But if we all agreed to come into this lifetime together, why would we agree on Tommy dying and leaving us so early?" he asked with visible pain spreading across his lightly freckled face.

"I don't know," I responded, fighting for every breath. "Maybe we were told up front that we could only have him for thirteen years and we all agreed that having him for such a short time period was better than not having him at all." Struggling to process my own words, I rephrased them. "If the universe asked you if you want Tommy as your brother for the first ten years of your life or not at all, what would you say now that you know the pain of him leaving?"

"I'd say I still want him," Dono replied with agony permeating his naturally scratchy voice.

"Me, too," I whispered, trying to sound strong. "That's what we have to keep remembering—that we are grateful we got him for the time that we did. Maybe one day we'll understand why we couldn't have him longer."

I got out of bed not knowing what to do next except tap my fingertips against my bedroom walls to maintain my balance. Overnight,

I had disconnected from my own body and could no longer feel the ground beneath my bare feet. My dreams had warned me that this would happen. During the few hours of sleep that I had gotten thanks to half a Xanax that was placed in the palm of my hand the evening before, my feet slid across the world at uncontrollable speeds until my big toes reached the edge of a sharp cliff and some invisible force stopped me short and woke me up. Modified versions of this same nightmare would torture me in the year ahead and show no mercy. I would slide across ancient cities, mountains, and valleys at violent speeds before nearly crashing into walls, falling from giant peaks, and skidding down steep flights of stairs leading to nowhere. I would sit in the passenger seat of convertible sports cars that raced up and down winding mountain roads and whipped me around hairpin turns until my body flew out while my hands stayed glued to every chrome emblem and door handle they could find. Sometimes I was dressed. Other times, I was naked. My conscious and subconscious states of mind were in constant torture and my nightmares would not let me forget it.

Tapping my way to the bathroom, I took a shower, got dressed, and brushed my teeth. I saw no purpose in any of it, but the oxygen mask rules on airlines reminded me that I needed to take care of myself in order to take care of Donovan. He was watching me. Donovan needed me. And he was priority number one. Plus, I had a call to make, Tommy's Field to build, and both a funeral and a memorial to plan. Love for my husband and two children flooded my entire system and convinced me to live another day.

CHAPTER 5

WHEN I ENTERED MY LIVING ROOM AROUND 7:00 A.M. ON THAT first post-Tommy morning, my fair skin was white as chalk and my slim body, bundled in black sweats, a black sweatshirt, and black Converse sneakers, had already shrunk. Without my standard checklist for the day or my son, I panicked. *What am I supposed to do now?* Fortunately, friends had already started arriving and came prepared to scoop me up, calm me down, and manage whatever the day might bring.

The fear I felt that morning had a certain similarity to the way I felt on May 15, 2005, one day after Tommy was born. His arrival had changed life as I knew it, and when we walked through our front door together twenty-four hours after his birth, I had no idea what to do with him. All of my years of education had never taught me how to begin a life, much less end one, and as far apart as both experiences registered on my emotional spectrum, I was eternally grateful to those who showed up in the early moments to help me navigate.

I made my way to the oversized sectional couch in our family room where Donovan had played sick just minutes before we had discovered what had happened to Tommy. I found a spot in the corner where I could tend to my inner world while staying visible when needed in this one. Funeral arrangements were underway around me, with a former middle school friend of Doug's being well-versed in such matters and taking the lead. I had no capacity to think or plan. I could only feel, and all I felt was how much I loved and missed Tommy.

My physical condition was rapidly deteriorating. I could hardly breathe past the back of my throat and my voice wheezed like a whisper with no volume control. I knew I did not have the mental strength to call the Department of Recreation and Parks and say, "My son passed away," without breaking mid-sentence. So, I had to feel my way toward a solution. *"Play simple,"* I heard an inner voice say, as though the thought were my own. That's what Tommy's coaches used to yell at him from the sidelines of his games when he got too tricky with the ball. "Simple Tommy! Play simple!" But simple was not Tommy's middle name. Flashy was. Still, I remembered that even he learned the value of playing simple when his touches were off, his moves weren't working for him, and he needed to reset.

I downloaded the advice and allowed the game of soccer to start guiding my life. *"Play simple."* If I couldn't speak, then maybe I could write. I opened my laptop and waited for my brain to fire up, which it proceeded to do at low capacity for only seconds at a time. It took sheer will and nearly half the day to type three overly detached-sounding sentences to Valerie, my contact at the Department of Recreation and Parks, with whom I had spoken over the previous four years about building an athletic field at Westwood Recreation Center.

"I'm in the unfortunate position of having to tell you that my twelve-year-old son, Tommy, unexpectedly passed away. We don't know why. Our community would like to honor Tommy with this field, and we are ready to activate." I threw in some closing words and copied my friend, Linda, the originator of Tommy's Field, so she could follow up in the very likely event that I further plummeted and could not. Then I pushed SEND.

I didn't even try to predict how Valerie would respond. It wasn't possible. Something just told me that she would.

The following day she did. When I answered her call, I confirmed the unimaginable and felt her heart snap. My pain was contagious, even across the phone line. She searched for the right words to say but knowing there weren't any, I let her off the hook and got down to business before I lost my composure. "My family and our community need something to pour our hearts into that will honor my son and benefit others. Will the city approve naming rights in return for funding the field? We will raise the money within the next twelve months."

"I'll ask," she said, her voice sounding softer and gentler than I remembered from our previous conversations.

A few days later, a time frame that I would soon learn is comparable to seconds in city government time, she called me back to say what my gut already told me she would. "There is precedent for projects like this and the city would be honored to call it 'Tommy's Field.'" This was great news, considering that we had already set up a charitable bank account, had a number of pledged donations from family and close friends, and were waiting for marketing materials to be delivered from the printers, which had been designed by the mother of one of Dono's friends. We still had many more details to work through, but none of them mattered until we raised the money, which I knew from prior conversations with Valerie would be in excess of $1 million. As for public messaging, we kept it simple and flexible. "Tommy's Field will be a full-size soccer/multipurpose field with lights in a West Los Angeles public park. It will be for everyone and honor Tommy's love of all sports." Friends and family began to work on the details while I survived Tommy's funeral and prepared for his memorial the following weekend.

The day of Tommy's funeral, the details of which I transferred from my memory to the darkest pages of my green journal, I knew I needed help and gravitated toward the most spiritual kind. I wanted to talk to a medium. I had never spoken to one before, but remembered that my Midwest mom once had. I was twenty-three years old when she announced that her grandmother's spirit had started visiting her.

As ludicrous as it sounded, my mother—who never told a lie, as far as I knew—disclosed it as fact and questioned what to do about it. She had loved her grandmother. She was partially raised by her. But waking up to her spirit standing next to her bed and holding her hand every morning was scaring her.

My mom believed her grandmother was trying to convey a message to her, and at the suggestion of a close friend, made an appointment with a medium to see if he could help communicate it. At the time, this particular medium was not well known. He worked out of his small apartment, charged $75, and had not yet exploded on television or become a best-selling author. My conservative father, whose very practical mind had trouble believing anything he could not see or scientifically explain, grudgingly accompanied her at the last minute. He sat by her side and listened as her grandmother communicated through the medium and complimented her favorite pictures on our walls, described the barstool where she sat and watched my dad eat breakfast, and communicated her message of unconditional love to my mother. She wanted to say hello. To tell my mother that she loved her. To make it known that she was still there. My father, still with arms crossed and eyes rolling, was stunned when the spirit of his late best friend announced himself by name. The medium not only knew his name, but he described subtleties of his friend's personality and even delivered a personal message that only my father would understand, making him laugh and shed tears at the very same time. This was over forty years ago, when there was no internet and no access to instant information. By the end of the hour-long session, my mother was a believer, my father was less of a skeptic, and the spirit of my mother's grandmother was fulfilled. She never reappeared and my mother never tried to connect with her or any other ancestor ever again.

My memory of my mother's first and only medium experience inspired me to try my own. I didn't know if it was possible to connect with Tommy's spirit a week after his departure, much less at all, but after the funeral when our home was full of friends and family, I turned to my best friend from college, the most spiritual and resourceful person I knew, and confided, "I'd like to speak to a medium." Two days later, she handed me a yellow Post-it and said, "Call Pamela. This is her number. You are scheduled to talk to her later this week on the day and time that I've written down for you. I will call you a few hours before to remind you. I spoke to her a few years ago after my father passed away. She's amazing. She knows your first name. That's all." Just the idea that someone might be able to connect me with Tommy's spirit and tell me what had happened to him gave me enough hope to survive until that day.

The morning I called Pamela, I lit a candle, opened my green journal to take notes and sat on the silver-gray shaggy rug that covered the floor in Tommy's bedroom. After a warm introduction and intention-setting prayer that instructed me to breathe and was already worth every penny she hadn't yet asked me to pay, Pamela said, "First of all, when I tune in, I see a child. Is this your son?"

"Yes," I said, beginning to relax.

"There is a grandmother over there with him. Starts with an *M*. Who is that?"

"My grandmother. We all called her Mama." *She lived to ninety-six, just like I will.*

"She was there to greet him," she said, as if it were fact.

"He tells me there was no pain, it happened very quickly. I sense something burst in his chest area and it was very sudden. I'm not a doctor but it was something with the heart. Check that," she directed. "He says there wasn't much anyone could have done about it. If you went to the doctor, they would have missed it. Even if they found it when he was born, he says it would have been too risky to do anything about it." My thoughts rewound. *I took him to the doctor on our way down to San Diego the weekend before all this happened. He said his chest hurt so I made an appointment to get him checked out and put our minds at ease. The doctor said it was growing pains. He missed it. We all missed it. The autopsy should tell us more soon.*

"Oh, gosh," she continued. "He's very mature and hardly feels or sounds like a child. He communicates better than many adults. Does that sound right?"

"Yes." Tommy could talk to anyone about anything.

"He came here to make a difference," Pamela announced. "He's a humanitarian. Someone who really has heart. Sorry for the pun. He just showed me athletics, sports. He really wanted to touch souls."

"Did he ever discuss wanting to be a professional ballplayer?" Pamela asked me.

"Yes," I responded, both surprised and optimistic about the possibility of her talking to my son.

"That's what he's showing me," she said, making it clear that she not only interpreted messages audibly, but also visually.

"He thought he could be a professional athlete but wasn't sure he could make it as a rock 'n' roll musician." *How would she know about Tommy's passions for music or that at one time he actually thought about quitting soccer to pursue music? Maybe she's just guessing. After all, becoming a professional athlete or a famous rock star are fairly typical childhood dreams, especially in this town.*

"Later," Pamela continued, addressing my silent skepticism, "after he was successful in sports, he planned to give back. He thought he'd have a child or two. He thought he would coach a team and then be a broadcaster. He thought he'd go further in these ways when he was too old to play sports. He had big dreams."

That was his exact plan. He told me all about it during our drive to San Diego. "Remember my plan, Mom," he said taking off his shoes, resting his feet on the dashboard and exposing his favorite charcoal-gray socks, patterned with red roses wrapped around silver knives. First, I'm going pro in Europe. Then I'll have a few kids, maybe coach a lower-level professional team in Europe and then I'll be a broadcaster. I'll also probably have a fashion line at some point." Impressed by the clarity of his vision, I said, "That sounds like a great plan, T." Then deeper thoughts invaded my mind. I looked over at Tommy in the passenger seat and said, "I love how committed you are to soccer and your dreams. If you follow your heart and stay committed to everything that you're passionate about, it can only lead you somewhere great. Even if it's somewhere different than you originally imagined." I was surprised by my own words and wondered where they came from.

Not privy to the discussion Tommy and I had just three days before his passing, Pamela continued her reading. "The sports didn't kill him by the way. Ultimately, the sports made his heart stronger." The guilt that had seized my entire body since the day Tommy left, began to ease. Between his morning trainings before school, his afternoon practices, weekend games, and very active social life, maybe it was too much. Maybe I was supposed to slow him down. Maybe if he had been less active, he would have lived longer. The maybes were endless.

"He says he's fine and not to worry about him," Pamela said. "He's sorry he put you through this and feels like he betrayed you by leaving, but he didn't know! There wasn't anything that could've been done about it. I keep hearing the word *congenital*."

As I ferociously took notes, Pamela said, "He's saying he was in a dreamlike state when it happened and was given a choice. But the choice was a bad one. It was a life full of surgeries and no sports. 'It was boring, Mom, and you would have spent your whole life taking care of me. That wasn't the life I came for. I came to have an impact.'"

I'm not happy about that choice, I admitted to myself, *but I understand it.*

"Tommy the personality didn't consciously make the choice to leave his family, by the way. It was his soul's decision," she assured me, as if I understood the difference.

"Was this planned before we arrived in this lifetime?" I interrupted, following up on Donovan's explanation of how the soul system works.

"It was one of the potential plans," she responded. "He says he knows that now but didn't when he was in his body. He says, 'You don't remember, Mom, but you agreed to this.'"

Before I could process that thought, Pamela said, "Nikki, I want to give you time to ask questions, but your son is very excited and keeps talking very quickly so I'm just going with what he wants to talk about. I hope that's okay."

"Yes, that's fine," I answered hopefully. *Tommy was a fast talker in life, so why wouldn't he be in spirit?*

Pamela continued. "He says he had trust with you. He felt like you supported him living his dreams. You gave him what he needed. You believed in him. He knows dad loves him. He had his back. That's what he needed. He's grateful you volunteered to be his mom." Tears of gratitude rolled down my cheeks while inklings of hope tried to blossom. *She sounds like Tommy. She's using his words. Tommy would always tell me, "Dad has my back."*

"Does he have a sibling nine or ten years old?"

"Yes, a brother ten years old."

"That's what he told me. He keeps going to his little brother. 'Tell him I'm here with him, I'm never going to leave him. I'm his big brother, always. And his guardian. But he's spending too much time on the video games.'" I feel like he told him that before he died. "He wants him to go out and have a life. He likes him playing sports."

"He did tell him that just a few days before he passed away," I acknowledged, hardly believing my ears. I was there when Tommy walked by Dono's room and told him that he played too many video games and needed to get outside and play more soccer.

"Your son's friends are having a hard time, by the way," she went on. "Who's Molly?"

"One of his best friends at school," I said.

"He says, if it's okay with you, that his friends can have some of his stuff to remember him by. Does he have a keyboard?"

"Yes."

"He wants his brother to have that. There is no pressure for him to use it."

She moved on. "Did you already have a funeral service of some kind?"

"Yes," I answered.

"Who's Gregg?" she asked.

"Tommy's uncle and my older brother. Tommy loved him."

"Who's Jane or Janie?" she continued.

"One of Doug's two sisters," I responded, rather shocked to hear her name.

"Did both of them speak at the funeral?" she asked.

"Gregg did," I confirmed. "Jane attended, which was surprising because we hadn't seen her in years and Tommy had always wanted to meet her."

"I think your son is trying to convey that he was at the funeral," Pamela surmised, piecing together information as it came to her. The possibility made sense to me because there was no other reason that my brother's name would be mentioned in the same conversation with Doug's sister's. They had never met each other. Did not know each other. Could still not tell you each other's names.

As Pamela shared some of the most intimate details about Tommy's funeral, my memory took a quick scan of the day. The shock. The disbelief. The darkness I felt sitting among a hundred or so friends and family as sunlight poked at me through chapel walls made of windows. There were the live music performances that opened and closed the ceremony. The display of my favorite photos of Tommy. And the six of us who spoke, including my brother, Gregg, who described what it was like to be Tommy's uncle with all the genuine warmth and kindness that Tommy loved about him. Ethan also spoke, and his edgy sense of humor and articulate tongue weaved together stories about his brother that made the room both erupt in laughter and descend in pain. They skateboarded. Bantered about music. Swam at the beach. Followed each other on social media. And, of course, they played soccer. Argued about soccer. And watched soccer. It dawned on me, sitting in the front pew that day, that Ethan had already taught Tommy so much. It was no wonder he was the person Tommy looked up to the most.

While Tommy's funeral embodied many signs of a meaningful life, it was not a day that I wanted to remember.

"If you already had his funeral," Pamela interrupted my thoughts, "Why is your son talking about a memorial coming up?"

"Because we are planning another one for all of his friends and our larger community."

"Oh, okay. He's excited about that. He'll be there. He says everyone is going to be there except for one teammate but that's okay because he has something important that he has to do."

Oh my gosh, Doug just told me earlier this morning that one of his closest soccer friends can't make it this weekend. He's the only one who has told us he can't be there.

"He says to watch your dog. Do you have a dog?"

"Yes."

We had Ginger. When Doug found her for adoption online, she was one year old and already built like a tank. Tommy, who was nine at the time, took one look in her soulful golden eyes and sized her up in less than two minutes. "She's the best dog ever! We have to take her." Ginger slept in Tommy's bed almost every night since the day she arrived and became his security blanket, not to mention one of the biggest loves of his life. With Ginger by his side, he began sleeping through the night, feeling safe and secure as her heavy breathing and powerful heartbeat calmed his nerves. His decade-long nightmares were frightened off by the sight of the sweetest pit bull in the world who helped the entire family get some much-needed rest.

"He talks to the dog," Pamela emphasized. "She can sense when he's around. Watch for signs she makes. And you can talk to him directly, he really does hear you. He still has his dreams and a mission over there. He says he's not sitting around playing a harp." She laughed, and I laughed. "Your son is very funny by the way. I don't mean to be disrespectful, he's just funny."

I know.

"He says to tell Dad he loves him but he's not sure Dad will believe all this."

"He also says you are going to do something important because of this. I don't know what that is yet, Nikki. Otherwise, he says you'll be in disbelief your entire life that this happened and have a hard time finding meaning in it."

I didn't know what to say.

"I'm so sorry this happened, Nikki, but your son is doing fine. He doesn't want you to worry. I hope this helps you."

By the time we hung up an hour later Pamela had communicated the essence of my son's personality and so many names and details associated with his funeral and short life, that I felt like I had actually spoken to my Tommy.

Doug started crying when I recapped my notes from the conversation. "How did she know all that?" he asked, wanting to believe.

I wasn't sure. All I knew was that the conversation ignited my interest in the relationship between this world and the next and inspired me to live another week until his memorial.

CHAPTER 6

BY THE MORNING OF TOMMY'S MEMORIAL, I HAD SURVIVED twelve days. Weak, frail, and unable to digest anything beyond liquids, I put on a long black silk floral sundress, black Converse sneakers, and large, rimmed black sunglasses, and walked outside my home for only the second time since Tommy's departure. Still unable to feel the ground beneath my feet, I clasped Doug's hand and shifted my weight into it. Not only could I barely walk, but I hardly recognized my own planet. The air was crisp and clean, and smelled like it had been purified and sweetened in my absence. Birds in the neighborhood had multiplied and were chirping at octaves that overwhelmed my ears. Trees were swaying with stunning grace while a fairy-tale-blue-colored sky looked down from above and tried to make me smile. The world was different now, and my senses were on fire.

"Let's be clear," I told the universe as it tried to dazzle me with its wonders of nature. *"I don't want any of this. I'm being forced to view life through a lens that I never wanted, and I'm going along with it because you have given me no choice. There is something I am supposed to do with all this, and I will figure it out."*

I walked up the street to UCLA's soccer field with my family by my side and imagined that Tommy's spirit was waiting for me there. That field was where he used to ride his bike to train before school. It was where he jumped the locked fence on weekends to play with friends. It was where he called his dad on his very last Monday morning to ask if he could stay longer to play with a former Mexican pro-soccer player named Carlos instead of getting ready for school.

When I entered the field, all of his favorites in life awaited. Candy, lemonade, and popcorn stands were positioned at one end. Teammates from across six city Los Angeles counties were playing soccer at the other end. Tommy's beloved community of coaches, teachers, doctors, friends, and family—all one thousand of them, minus one—gathered in between, while his favorite hip-hop and pop songs played overhead and attempted to lift the underlying sorrow that filled the air.

Donovan was our extension to Tommy's friends. He had taken over Tommy's cell phone the day after he left and started an Instagram account named "cinimantoastcrunch" [sic] in honor of Tommy's favorite cereal, which I would never buy but that his dad would purchase in extra-large boxes. The cinimantoastcrunch Instagram account was where Dono connected to Tommy's community. That's where he united them. That's where Dono posted his first cry for help:

> The dog needs someone to sleep on.
>
> I need a new brother.
>
> My mom needs half her hart [sic] back.
>
> And my dad just needs Tommy.

As I walked across the field questioning whether or not the day was real or simply a passing nightmare, I stared at the community that had shown up for Tommy and froze when I saw not only the quantity and quality of connections that he had made during his short lifetime, but also their diversity. From local Westside girls like Skyla, Daisy, and Jaya to teammates like Diego, Adriel, and Rafa, and coaches like the Brazilian Beto and African Lassan, the melting pot on the field that day strongly reflected the demographic makeup of our city. I wrapped my arms around one of Tommy's former teammates who had not only stayed with us for weeks at a time during winter and summer holidays, but whose family regularly invited Tommy into their home, two hours away, and introduced him to their culture, their homemade Mexican ceviche, and, to Tommy's delight, a number of essential curse words in Spanish. Soccer had united them and now we were family.

Every connection I saw at his memorial that day carried me back to a particular memory, and one after another, a review of Tommy's life flashed before my eyes.

"My teammates and guy friends at school are the same," Tommy once told me after returning from being with one group and heading out to be with the other. "It doesn't matter where we live or are from. We talk about sports, music, video games, and girls."

His openness to all kinds of people and his propensity to connect over similarities shouldn't have surprised me. He was blessed with physical features, including his olive-colored complexion, that allowed him to move swiftly between large groups of people and seamlessly blend in with them. Tommy was barely four when his preschool director named him "the mayor." She watched him banter back and forth with the school janitor; flutter up to teachers and school administrators with a giant smile; and hover in front of parents and classmates to share a laugh on his way to the playground. To him, they were all the same.

The community I saw on the field that day verified what I would later say to everyone who was there. "Tommy Mark did not like boxes. He sought out and surrounded himself with teachers, coaches, and friends—regardless of age, race, culture, or class—who challenged him to learn at the highest levels and who believed in him, inspired him, and laughed with him. If you didn't, he'd find someone who would."

In between the hundreds of hugs and thousands of teardrops that greeted me that morning, I looked everywhere for Tommy. I wasn't the only crazy one, by the way. Dono was the one who told me in no uncertain terms that he could hear Tommy and that the two of them spoke regularly. Doug was the one who said that a distinct scent flew under his nose multiple times throughout each day that he could only describe as Tommy. Ginger was the one who showed us when she saw Tommy by tilting her head from side to side and raising her pink nose high while she stared at the air and trembled. "Between all of our senses," Dono concluded, "we know when Tommy is here. I hear him. Dad smells him. You feel him. And Ginger sees him."

Doug, Donovan, and I didn't expect anyone else to understand what was happening to us, but whenever the universe surprised us with its supernatural powers, we checked in with each other to test our sanity. Most of the time it was Donovan and me playing this game, but on the day of Tommy's memorial, I was prepared for anything. If anyone's spirit could pull through with a trick or two and make its presence known, it would be Tommy's.

When the memorial ceremony was about to begin, I sat down next to Dono, Doug, and Ethan on the grass and turned around to see behind me the tiered stadium bleachers that were already fully occupied. Faces from every stage of Tommy's life stared back at me. *"Everyone showed up for you, T. You are so loved."*

Directly in front of me was a wooden podium, where at least a dozen of us would soon speak, and next to that a jumbo LED screen that waited to play the story of Tommy's life. Hundreds of Tommy's friends surrounded us on the grass, which was perfectly green and practically sparkling for the occasion. When I got settled, the music stopped, as if it had been watching me. Everyone was watching me, and yet all I was doing was searching for Tommy. When I finally looked straight ahead at the podium and prepared for the ceremony to begin, I saw a heavy black metal speaker case sitting near the podium fall over as if it had been pushed. The top and bottom of the case clanked together as they smashed to the earth and boomed like a gunshot. I jumped. Our guests rumbled. And an echo reverberated throughout the outdoor stadium. I found it strange that the other speaker cases lying in the same position nearby had not fallen. I glanced up at the trees, which were still and confirmed that there was no wind. Then I looked at Donovan, who was already staring back at me. Our eyes locked. To everyone else, it may have been a prop error. To the two of us, it was Tommy.

The ceremony began, and I quickly learned what it was like to be Tommy's friend.

"He always told me he loved me," said a tall, slim brunette with loose long curls whom Tommy called the "easygoing one," and with whom he had gone thrift shopping the day before he left.

"He told me to believe in myself," said a sweet, edgy-looking girl with a diamond stud in her nose, who Tommy once told me was the "coolest."

"He would call me in the morning before school to say he loved me and to wish me a great day," our next-door neighbor with the dyed purple hair said, which was fairly remarkable since he and his family had only moved in next to us a year earlier. I turned to Doug and whispered in his ear, "I heard him make that call on the way to school last week. He was in the car with me."

Then Molly, his best girlfriend from his middle school, spoke. "He told me not to care what other kids think, that he liked me for who I was and that's what mattered." She took the opportunity to reveal that she had been struggling that year with the girls at school. That Tommy was the only classmate who stood up for her. That he would play instruments and sing silly songs to her in the music room during lunch to lift her spirits and ensure that she didn't have to eat alone.

Doug leaned in and said loud enough so my clogged ears could hear, "While we were begging Tommy to shut down FaceTime and do his homework at night, he was doing something far more important, like connecting with friends, telling them he loved and believed in them, and growing his community." I nodded, increasingly convinced that my son was some sort of highly evolved spirit who had visited us on a very important mission.

I continued to listen as multiple groups of girlfriends from different middle schools across the city wept over the boy who, to my surprise, had either been their first kiss or best friend. Soccer teammates from competing clubs across the city rose up in unity to acknowledge the beauty in his game, the passion in his soul, and the unforgettable joy and humor he brought to their highly competitive lives. Local coaches, many of whom came from different countries, expressed their awe of Tommy's commitment to his dreams and the way his bright smile, cheeky humor, and genuine flair for the game deeply connected with their adult hearts. Following speaker after speaker, Donovan got up and hugged each one; somehow they knew that touching him was the closest they would ever physically get to their friend again. *Tommy was here to teach*," a voice said to me out of nowhere. "*Connect the dots. Figure it out.*"

After an hour of speeches, it was my turn. I walked up to the podium with Donovan by my side and looked out at everyone, feeling as hollow as I must have looked. *This is the most important speech you will ever make*, I told myself, knowing no one would judge me if I didn't get through it.

"*You can do it, Mom*," I heard Tommy whisper.

I squeezed Donovan's hand and—although I did not see it—at that moment, a majestic brown hawk promptly flew in overhead and circled. It was as if he had specifically arrived to record the moment and report back to some other world. Multiple friends texted me video footage of our familiar messenger with wings, and both Donovan and I were thrilled to learn that Tommy had celebrated his life with us that day, just as Pamela had said he would. It would be two years before it crossed my mind to ask Google what hawks symbolize in the spirit animal world. When I finally clicked SEARCH, I wasn't the least bit surprised by the first answer I read: "Hawks are messengers of the spirit world." Dono's intuition at ten years old was as sophisticated as Google's search engine.

The hawk circled high above me and Dono, waiting for our final words: "We will build a new multipurpose field in a public park in Tommy's memory. It will be called 'Tommy's Field' and it will be a place for generations of kids to play the sports he loved. But that's just the beginning. Our steps will get bigger and, like Tommy, we will make sure to process joy in each one. We hope we make him proud. I love you, T." Without missing a beat, I thought I heard him respond, *"I love you, too, Mom."*

Dono ended the speaking portion of the ceremony by comparing his brother to the smooth but "bumpy" and imperfect healing stone that he chose to put in his pocket that morning. "My brother wasn't perfect," Dono said with the kind of blunt honesty that only a young child can possess. "But he was the best brother for me. And what was most bumpy about him are the things I already miss the most." The hawk departed and then a video that Ethan's mom miraculously produced in less than a week, summarized Tommy's life in four minutes, and drained every eye on the field. Another round of hugs ensued for an hour and then the event ended. As I headed toward the exit, I heard Tommy whisper the same words that he used to say after every one of his birthday parties: *"It was perfect, Mom. Thank you so much."*

As hopeful as I was that Tommy's spirit was there with us that day, by the time I got home I recognized that my mind could be playing tricks on me. The black speaker case could have fallen by accident.

Hawks may have circled over UCLA's soccer field all the time. And, as for the voices in my head, maybe my mind had not yet accepted that Tommy was gone. Maybe it was speaking for him. Acting like him. Trying to comfort me by making me feel like he was still here.

As the morning wore off, the rest of my body switched back on as if it had been set to an automatic timer. Emotions slammed my system. Thoughts fired at me. And feelings viciously attacked my mind. *What did we do to deserve this? Were we bad parents? Are we horrible people? Was I too busy to see all the signs? Why Tommy? He had so much to offer our world. Why not me?* Self-pity hit me with a vengeance and replaced every ounce of spirituality that had gotten me through the last twelve days. Even the voices that had been guiding me like angels went silent. I wept like a baby and told my green journal all about it.

When I awoke the next day, I was aware that life was just supposed to resume, someway, somehow. My husband made coffee, put on the Grateful Dead, and got dressed for work, as he would have done before Tommy left. I woke up, checked on Donovan, and committed myself to getting him to school for the first time in two weeks. None of us hurried. Time no longer mattered. Just standing up and looking into each other's eyes was a lot.

Before heading to school, I convinced Dono to take a walk. We were already two hours late. One more wouldn't matter. "We have to get our bodies moving, Dono," I said, trying to convince both of us. "The sunlight will be good for us."

Like a pair of old snails, we strolled around our neighborhood leaving a slimy trail of tears on the sidewalk behind us. We reached the park down the street and sat on two lonely swings, side by side. Our bare feet dug into the cool sand beneath us, and hardening shells of grief hunched both of our backs and protected our fragile bodies from the air itself. We barely moved.

The park was empty. Only the maintenance crew, another extension of Tommy's community, were there. When they approached us with clueless smiles, I told them what had happened to Tommy and watched them break down crying. The rest of the community was in school or at work. Time had only stopped for us.

"Dono must be with friends," a familiar voice whispered to me. Parents and teachers had organized lunches for him through the end of the school year and a lot of love was going into each one. He needed to start digesting some of it. I got the message and walked him down the street.

Once we neared the entrance to his elementary school, Dono stopped to ask a reasonable question: "What's the point? School means nothing now. School doesn't teach us about life; I know more about life than school does now." Then he broke what was left of my dying heart. "I'm not just an only child. I'm now a lonely child, too."

Tears sprayed out from behind my sunglasses. "I'm so sorry, Dono," I responded, kneeling down and resting my hands on his slumped shoulders that were bonier than I remembered. We were both walking skeletons who never cared if we ate again. "I understand everything you are saying, and I wish I had answers for you. I would do anything to change what has happened to Tommy and our family. Let's just keep moving the best we can; otherwise, we will die, too, and that won't help Tommy."

"I miss Tommy so much," Dono said, as he reluctantly shuffled into school as if his feet were trudging through snow.

"I know. Tommy should be here with us," I commiserated.

"He is here," he replied, looking up at me with frustration.

I quickly corrected myself, "I mean he should be here with us physically." Donovan's belief system was continually challenging my own.

When the gate closed behind him at school, I turned to walk home. There was no reason to hurry. No checklist to tend to. No job to which I had to report. *"Keep it simple,"* a familiar voice reminded me just before panic could set in. *"One foot in front of the other. That is all you need to do right now."*

By the time I got home, I accepted that my only responsibility for the day was to survive it. If Donovan had the strength to sit in school for a few hours, the least I could do was be there to greet him when he got home. I just wasn't sure how. Basic human needs of survival, like eating and drinking, were meaningless to me, so I had to create my own. *From this day forward,* I vowed, *I will do one thing every day, no matter how small, to honor Tommy and build Tommy's Field. It doesn't matter what it is. It can be one email. Or one phone call. Or even just one small thought. But I will strive to honor Tommy every single day, and simultaneously survive for Donovan.*

That was my entire checklist. Once I committed to it, I lit a candle, crawled into bed with Ginger by my side and did the only thing that helped me forget how much I wanted to die. I began to write.

PART 2

The Recovery

CHAPTER 7

MY GREEN JOURNAL AND I HAVE TRACED THE ORIGINS OF THE first field incarnation back to the day when Tommy was seven years old and joined his first competitive club soccer team. Although he was two when he started kicking the ball against the walls in my bedroom; three when he took his first toddler group lesson; four when he played in his first park league; five when he asked for his first skills trainer; and six when he started playing on teams with kids two and three years older, it was when he was seven that he declared that soccer was his favorite sport and that I probably needed to learn a thing or two about it.

So, I did what all real soccer moms do. I bought a blue folding polyester chair with an attached canopy, planted myself on the sidelines of his practices and games, and sat there for ninety minutes watching my son play. As I studied the game and tried to make him proud, the start-up girl in me grew distracted by the chaotic and inefficient business around it. Parents shouted at their kids from the sidelines even though most had never played the game themselves. Children played nervous and tight, and unknowingly compromised their soccer dreams by looking up at their parents from the field instead of at their coaches. And beyond all the human relations issues that struck me as antithetical to the concept of team sports, what confused me the most was the product itself. I saw no club-wide vision. No distinct style of play. And no youth development plan across age groups. Dozens of teams shared the same field space and proudly sported identical uniforms, but they all operated as independent units in nearly every other way. Not even the $2,500 a year that parents paid the club could guarantee that their child got a "good" coach and the definition of *good* depended on who you asked.

As I processed this data from the comfort of my blue chair and compared it to the European matches I watched with my family on television, I began to understand why America has struggled to develop the kind of world-class men's superstar that Tommy aspired to be. Europe had a vision. Europe had cohesive development systems. Europe had one favorite sport, and like nearly every other country in the world outside of America, Europe lived for it. Europe bled for it. And Europe called it football.

As for America, I didn't know what the top of this professional sport thought it had at the time, but, from the bottom where I was sitting and watching its future develop, I could tell it had a long way to go. Although the women's side of the professional sport was dominating and ranked among the best in the world, America didn't invest in men's soccer, as Europe did. America didn't understand it, as Europe did. America didn't teach, much less appreciate, the nuances of it, as Europe did. To be fair, America was busy prioritizing and conquering other sports, like baseball, basketball, and American football, and paid hefty salaries to attract its top athletes. So, while the countries of Europe developed their individual styles of play and collectively advanced the beautiful game for which Europe stood, America embraced its independence, changed the foreign sport's name from football to soccer, and left it up to its fifty states to figure out.

The bright side, I decided, was that my son had joined one of the better-run clubs in our city and its field space was adjacent to Westwood and a mere two miles and twenty minutes in rush-hour traffic from our home. The other bright side was that Tommy was thriving. His trademark style of playing with a smile on his face grew exponentially during his first season with the club and I was so grateful for the experience that when I heard the club was looking for its next president of the board, I threw my name in the hat and didn't think twice. "I want to give back," I told my husband, my biggest supporter who wisely ignored the relationship between the dark circles under my eyes and the length of my daily checklist. I was stretched beyond thin, juggling my roles as a mother of two young boys and the executive in charge of operations for a growing hospitality company whose restaurant, nightlife, and hotel brands operated nearly 24/7. When I asked myself, *How hard can it be*? I told myself what I wanted to hear—*Not that hard.* If the speediness of my election was an indication of the enormous and thankless job ahead, I was far too busy to notice.

The evening I was sworn in as president, my predecessor disclosed that the club's most precious asset, its field space, was in a tenuous position. Loads of weight lifted off his shoulders and were transferred to mine as he divulged the messy details. A class-action lawsuit, he said, had been filed against our field's landlord, the federal government. As part of settlement discussions, all third-party leases operating on this massive federal property located in the middle of the Westside were being terminated. When he walked out the door and flashed me a congratulatory grin, I suddenly realized that I had become president of a local nonprofit youth soccer club about to lose its field space.

Although Tommy was only seven when he joined the club and I soon after became its president, our family had been exposed to the youth soccer circuit long enough for me to know that fields across the city were already operating well beyond capacity. Tommy had grown up on the sidelines of Ethan's games with a sippy cup in his hands and a soccer ball at his feet. On weekends, we'd load up the

64

car with game-day essentials, including snacks, drinks, sunscreen, and multiple layers of clothing, before traveling across Southern California to watch his brother play. Game after game, Tommy darted around the teams playing on the pitch, dodged the ones warming up on the side, and scurried among the siblings running around in between. Eventually, he would lay claim to an open inch of field space where he and his ball could get acquainted and maybe even make a new friend.

That was until Tommy became a preschooler and took it upon himself to find his own field-space solution. That was the day I lost him. Couldn't find him. Was sure someone had taken him. Unbeknownst to me, Tommy had packed a plastic bag full of extra T-shirts and shorts that closely matched Ethan's home and away kits. When we arrived at the field and he saw which uniform Ethan's team was wearing, he changed his outfit as quickly and discreetly as a superhero. Then, without asking, he snuck onto his sixteen-year-old brother's team bench and sat among the players coming in and out of the game. Tommy did not care that the players were five times his size and weight and sporting facial hair. He had no clue that it was a championship match and that college scouts were there recruiting. He was not at all aware that the rest of his brother's team was Hispanic and that white boys had to earn their place next to them both on the bench and on the field. He believed he belonged there. He recognized that the shade of his skin was like that of his brother's teammates and hoped the team's Guatemalan coach might mistake him for one of them. He later admitted that he just wanted a few minutes on the field. Some action in the game. A chance to prove he was a difference-maker. That was the day Ethan's coach, Julio, met Tommy. It was the day Julio shook his head in disbelief when he watched Tommy line up on the field with the coach's nationally ranked players and shake hands with the opposing team. It was the day Julio told us that our son was "delirious." "Insane." "Out of his mind." And also the day Julio admitted that he couldn't wait for Tommy to grow up so he could coach him.

By that time, youth soccer was already exploding. The city's burgeoning Hispanic community was pouring its passion and expertise into the game. Our Southern California sunshine was accommodating a highly sought-after year-round season. And local soccer associations were supporting a massive influx of new families by sanctioning dozens of new leagues and accepting hundreds of new clubs, thousands of teams, and more than 200,000 players, coaches, and referees combined.

Needless to say, field space became a problem. Public fields, originally designed for American sports like football and baseball, quickly became overrun, overcrowded and over-politicized. The quantity of fields left over for soccer was severely limited. The quality was even worse. Some fields sloped. Most were the wrong size. Those that were made of natural grass got quickly torn up by cleats, scorched by the sun, and reduced to weeds or dust, while those made of synthetic turf quickly lost their infill and became as slippery on top as they were hard on the bottom. Our public park system could not supply enough fields to satisfy the demand. Nor could our schools, which had athletic programs of their own to accommodate. The soccer community became so desperate for places to play that it even scoured the city for empty parking lots. Unfortunately, Los Angeles has always loved its cars more than all its sports combined, so those were completely full, too. The soccer community took what it could get, but was always scavenging for more.

By the time Tommy's first club season had nearly ended and his own younger brother was on the sidelines of his games watching, nearly half a million children in the city were playing soccer. This was more than any other youth sport and only a hundred thousand or so less than American's beloved baseball and football combined. And those numbers were an estimate. They didn't factor in the tens of thousands of other children whose families couldn't afford the system. Who didn't have the transportation to travel within the system. Whose parents didn't even know that the system existed.

As the president of a West Los Angeles club about to lose its field space, I quickly understood that even if our organization had the resources to move somewhere else, there was literally nowhere in the city to go. The predicament was a soccer club's worst nightmare. Without a field, there'd be no club. Without a club, players would immediately lose their team, their after-school activity, and, for many high schoolers, their chance to be scouted for university scholarships and even professional opportunities. While players could try out for other clubs across the city, assuming they had the financial means and transportation to do so, the season was underway, and there was zero chance that every other club combined had enough field space to accommodate such a large influx of players. Clubs were already playing tricks and pulling favors to access field space outside of their neighborhoods, and they were fighting each other over scraps.

Looking back on it now, the situation seems silly. Almost trivial. But, at the time, I was just a regular person with regular problems who didn't understand the luxury of being blindsided by challenges that were fixable, someway, somehow. All I knew was that I had a title that made me responsible for hundreds of families who didn't even know my name, and that failing before I had even gotten started was not how I was wired. So, I did what my career trained me to do best. I searched for a solution. When I couldn't find one, I did what Tommy and the European soccer players that he most admired did best. I created my own.

I called the Los Angeles Department of Recreation and Parks to ask if there was a West Los Angeles public park that could accommodate a new full-size soccer field with lights. I didn't know much about the politics behind our city's parks but my experience helping to build three start-up companies across three disparate industries convinced me that the less I knew, the further I would get. Like the trajectory of Tommy's performance on the field, the advancement of my career and the level of joy I derived from it had been directly proportional to the amount of freedom I was given to create, explore, and find my way.

"My name is Nikki Mark," I said when Valerie, the woman in charge of partnerships and fundraising, first answered my call. "I'm calling on behalf of two brother-sister nonprofit soccer clubs in West Los Angeles that cater to boys and girls, respectively."

A long sigh greeted me on the other end of the line and indicated that the last thing Valerie, my listener, needed was yet another field-space complaint to add to her list.

Too desperate to be deterred, I explained that our clubs had been leasing and maintaining federal property in Westside for nearly fifteen years. We were honorable tenants. We had served tens of thousands of children and families from all parts of our city. And, in case she didn't know, we were in the much-needed business of developing the future of soccer in our country.

When Valerie asked how she could help, I briefly explained the lawsuit and the ramifications of it across our entire city.

Although she empathized with our situation, she made it clear that her department and the City of Los Angeles had no control over federal property.

Unwilling to let her take the easy way out, I pressed on. "I would like to work with your department to build a full-size soccer field with lights in a Westside public park for the benefit of the entire community."

Professionally trained to only present problems when armed with viable solutions, I suggested that "Westwood Recreation Center would be an ideal location for a new public athletic field." It was the closest park to our club's current field. It had an empty dirt field sitting in the middle of it. And the park was underutilized and desperate for attention.

Before she added my request to the bottom of her lengthy to-do list and at some point presented it to her under-resourced department, I closed with what I knew any city representative would want to hear, "We are not asking for money." The soccer clubs, along with the West Los Angeles community living in and around Westwood, had the means to do fundraising for a new field and donate it to the city. Land was the problem. Not money.

To my surprise, the soccer gods aligned. The head of her department supported it. The council member in charge of Westwood gave his conceptual approval. And over the next two years, designs would be created, a budget prepared, and Westwood Rec Center's local advisory board would give the green light to start fundraising—something I had neither the time nor the experience to do.

In the meantime, Tommy continued to play. Smile. And advance. So much so that in the middle of my discussions with the Department of Recreation and Parks, he switched clubs and started playing with a mostly Hispanic team based in East Los Angeles. I never told him about the lawsuit. Not once did he see me stress about the future of the land on which he had at one time so joyfully played. He did not know about the eviction notice I received on behalf of his club and the countless sleepless nights I endured because of it. All he knew was that his mom sat in her blue chair after work and on weekends and loved watching him play.

Relieved to have a long-term solution for the field on track, I began frantically searching for a short-term one. Without substantial knowledge of government protocols or time to comply with complicated chains of command, I finagled my way in front of the representative who had been sent by Washington, DC, to implement class-action settlement terms. This was the guy. He was the one who determined which tenants got to stay and which ones had to go. By the time I sat down in front of him, I was fried. I missed my blue chair. And my real job, the one that paid me for my time, was clamoring for more attention.

"Can the nonprofit clubs and children continue playing on the field until such time as the land is further developed and actually used?" I asked, sensing the finish line.

Fortunately, this representative was passionate about soccer, cared about kids, and was as receptive as he was blunt. "The children can stay for now, but find another field because it's only a matter of time before you will need to leave."

I knew that could take years. I also knew that my job was done. In 2017, four years after I had become president, I handed over the position to a well-intentioned and capable father, and felt the weight on my shoulders transfer to his. "Field space is the priority," I told him, before practically throwing him my files, deleting my club email, and reinstating my formal position as a working soccer mom as quickly as I could. But it didn't matter where I sat or what fancy title I had. The seeds of Tommy's Field had taken root and were patiently waiting to sprout.

CHAPTER 8

IN THE WEEKS FOLLOWING TOMMY'S MEMORIAL, I REACHED OUT to Valerie to ask if Westwood Recreation Center was still the most viable park for Tommy's Field. I told her that my family was open to other neighborhood parks in the area, and while we believed that Westwood Recreation Center was an ideal location, we were prepared to follow the city's lead. She said she'd pose the question to decision-makers in the department, while my husband and I turned our attention to fundraising.

We were not professional fundraisers by any means, but we had a genuine tragedy and were committed to sharing it with anyone who would listen. Doug and I often reminisce that even those who didn't ask about it got an earful. It was as if the weight of our grief was far too heavy for us to bear by ourselves, so a community of friends and strangers showed up to help carry it. The more we shared our pain, the more support we received in ways we never could have imagined we'd need.

The financial support we received for Tommy's Field was as tangible as it was overwhelming. In less than two months we reached nearly 25 percent of our ultimate fundraising goal. Young children sold lemonade and asked for Tommy's Field donations instead of birthday presents. Teens made clever donation amounts that included the digits of Tommy's jersey numbers. Business colleagues donated. Companies matched. Friends and family told other friends and family until nearly every person our family had even known at some point in our lives made some sort of monetary contribution and gave us a piece of their heart with it.

One day, without warning, our fundraising efforts advanced significantly. LA's two Major League Soccer clubs, the LA Galaxy and Los Angeles Football Club, called and said that they wanted to support our efforts to honor Tommy, and they wanted to do it *together*.

Unlike many American youth players with large dreams and signs of talent, Tommy really didn't have his sights set on playing soccer in America at either the professional or the college level. The American version of the world's game that prioritized physical strength and size wasn't the same European game he fell in love watching and didn't match the style of play that he thought best fit his long, slender physique and the talents he had to offer. After being told by an American coach everything that was wrong about him as a player—without appreciating his technical skills, mental quickness, and creative flair for the game that multiple European coaches had told him overseas were right—Tommy told me that he wanted to play where the skills he excelled in were prioritized and more seriously developed, and that he had no desire to play like anyone but himself.

But until he fulfilled his professional dreams, and there seemed to be no doubt in his young mind that he would, Tommy was desperate to train with the strongest teams that we could find and he could make, and was honored to be selected as the starting center attacking midfielder for both Major League Soccer youth academies in his city, Los Angeles Football Club and the LA Galaxy. Tommy chose to play back-to-back seasons for these rival hometown teams and while he pursued the art of being an effective trash talker against the one whose badge wasn't on his chest, he ultimately gave his heart to both in exchange for a lifetime of meaningful experiences and friendships that he never sacrificed over wins and losses.

Crushed by the news of Tommy's passing, LAFC and the LA Galaxy organized tributes that furthered what Tommy hoped to achieve in his lifetime. The LA Galaxy organized a moment of applause during its first home game after Tommy's departure, knowing that Tommy was the kind of spirit who would want applause upon exiting this world, not silence. An image of Tommy dribbling a soccer ball in his black LA Galaxy warm-up jacket was frozen on the stadium's Jumbotron while the Galaxy's professional team stood shoulder to shoulder on the field wearing black armbands with white TM initials printed in the center of them. I sat in the stands with Dono, Doug, and Tommy's entire soccer team, wondering how Tricky Tommy, a name he gave himself at six years old, had managed to make his way into a professional game and onto the scoreboard. Surrounded by nearly 26,000 cheering fans, I sat in my seat wearing Tommy's LA Galaxy jersey, looking like everyone else but feeling like an alien who had just descended from outer space and was struggling to process the touching spectacle in front of me.

Earlier that same afternoon, 2,800 miles away in Montreal, Canada, LAFC played a match against Montreal's MLS team. LAFC was down by two goals when chants of "Tommy Mark" filled the visitor section in the twenty-third minute of the game to acknowledge Tommy's jersey number, twenty-three. When our family heard that the player wearing jersey number twenty-three scored for LAFC in the twenty-third minute of the game while supporters lit smoke bombs and chanted Tommy's name, Dono looked up and asked me nonchalantly, "I wonder if that player even thanked Tommy for his goal." I was thinking the same thing but took the opportunity to ask Dono how Tommy had the time to be at both games on the same day. He told me without missing a beat that Tommy was like a superhero and could be everywhere he wanted to be at the exact same time.

When my husband and I met with both clubs soon after Tommy's departure, I felt Tricky Tommy behind the scenes pulling more strings. We all gathered at Westwood Recreation Center on a bright sunny Los Angeles morning and stood on top of a massive piece of open land situated in between the park's eight tennis courts and its recreation center. The field had been long abandoned and sat empty during the decade that Tommy had frequented the park. As I walked across it to meet our guests, I was surprised to see how much further it had deteriorated since I introduced the first field incarnation to the city in 2014.

As the presidents of both organizations peered out over the land with their respective decision-makers by their side, Doug and I explained that the field had looked the same way Tommy's entire life. Its compact dirt surface had clumps of weeds growing in between dead grass, wide cracks, and deep divots, and just walking across its crunchy surface made dust swirl from head to toe. When it rained, or sometimes for no apparent reason at all, parts of the field turned into a thick, wet, sticky mud that made walking across, much less playing on it, impossible. The field was such a liability that when Tommy was five years old and joined a soccer team that practiced at that park, his coach moved practice over to the cement. To the MLS executives who provided pristine natural grass fields for their professional teams and well-maintained natural and synthetic turf fields for their youth teams, improving the desert wasteland in front of them was a no-brainer.

We reminisced about Tommy and exchanged words of disbelief before addressing our vision for his legacy. Tommy's Field would be designed north to south, following the natural line of the existing landscape and minimizing any threat that the sun might pose to goalkeepers at each end. It would have lights to maximize hours of play, just like the tennis courts and recreation center that sandwiched both sides of it. The surface would be made of synthetic turf with a natural infill, so it could accommodate high usage, conserve water, and minimize maintenance costs. Its dimensions would be the largest adult-size soccer field that could possibly fit, and it would accommodate all age groups and multiple field sports. Lastly, we were hopeful that the city's permit process would provide free play hours for the community to ensure that kids could gather after school and on weekends to play with their friends and not be intimidated by fences or need to jump them as Tommy always had.

After about twenty minutes, the president of LA Galaxy—who had never met Tommy or any member of our family—turned to me and my husband and said, with tears filling his kind baby blue eyes, "If Tommy's Field brings the kind of joy and enthusiasm that Tommy brought not only to the game but to our entire organization, then we want in." The president of LAFC and his general manager, both of whom personally knew Tommy and appreciated the passionate images he provided their marketing department during his tenure playing for the club's youth academy, expressed their organization's full support and said that both LAFC and the LA Galaxy agreed that the time had come to collaborate for the benefit of youth sports. An image of both of their logos on Tommy's Field flashed before my eyes and a small chuckle silently escaped beneath a strained breath of air. Only Tricky Tommy could find a way to connect two of the most meaningful organizations in his life and make sure his name was placed on prominent signage between the two of them.

Just as the Incredible Hulk manifests out of anger, Tricky Tommy was triggered by an active imagination and a childlike desire to create a world as entertaining as the one in his head. Like when he dressed up as Taylor Swift for Halloween and strutted around the neighborhood in a leopard-print onesie, black thick-heeled ankle boots, red lipstick, and a blond wig, feeling so comfortable with his own gender that he thought it would be fun to defy expectations and try out another. Like when he regularly excused himself from class to dance in the doorway of the one next door where his best friends waited for his daily dose of entertainment to break up the monotony of their day. Tricky Tommy was a certifiable trickster, born with two toes crossed in a jinxed position to prove it. He pushed limits, crossed lines, and challenged norms that not only got him in a lot of trouble, tested my patience, and rattled my nerves, but also rarely failed to make me laugh.

As our meeting with LAFC and the LA Galaxy came to a close, I stopped to take pictures of the existing field, one with and one without the lone homeless neighbor who was sleeping in the middle of it. I told myself that after Tommy's Field was built, the photos would remind me of the gift that Tommy had given his community. I would frame the best one. Hang it on my wall. And decades later, show it to Dono's children, my grandchildren, and tell them all about the uncle they never got to meet but would always carry around with them in their genes.

When my husband and I walked back to our car an hour later and looked into each other's eyes, we each saw a flicker of happiness staring back. But happiness, at least as we once knew it, was something we didn't think we could ever truly feel again. Every dollar raised to support our effort only reminded us of the tragic reason we needed that dollar in the first place. There was something, though, about the impact Tommy's life was having that kept knocking us over the head again and again and cranking our hearts open wider and wider until we accepted that what we thought was happiness was actually gratitude and we started to realize that we could feel grateful and sad at the same time. Like Tommy, who learned how to receive a ball and place it exactly where he wanted to with a smile on his face, we were learning how to receive from others and smile at the same time.

While our fundraising efforts took off, my physical condition worsened. My body produced its own cocktail of grief that viciously attacked my chest and wreaked havoc throughout my body. As if the universe could feel me slipping away and sensed the risk to my family, a flood of support started coming at us from multiple directions.

One morning, after I dropped Dono at school, I received a text from Joan, my favorite yoga instructor, whose class I had regularly taken when I was pregnant with Tommy. I hadn't seen Joan or practiced yoga in years but was relieved to hear from her.

"I heard what happened to Tommy. Tell me what I can do to help."

"*Tell her,*" one of the voices that spoke through me insisted. "*You have to tell people what you need so they can help you. It helps them, too.*"

"Come over and let's do yoga," I texted back. "I need to move energy through my body. I can't breathe."

Joan arrived that afternoon. She gave me a hug and with it a dose of energy to get through the next sixty minutes. When she asked me to balance on two feet, hip distance apart, and reach my emaciated arms straight out to the side, she confirmed what I already knew.

"You are weightless." She flapped my arms in the air despite my effort to resist her strength and then she confirmed, "A good portion of your soul is literally outside of your body. It will take some time for you to come back down to the physical world."

I knew part of my soul had flown somewhere. The problem was that I wasn't so sure where I wanted it to land.

Then, she smiled and said, "I can feel Tommy."

The second she finished saying the word *Tommy*, the television turned on right in front of us and flashed a bright blue screen. I looked up at her hopefully and pointed to the remote that was sitting on top of a cabinet across the room.

"The TV in Tommy's room turned on by itself the day we found him gone," I told her. "I feel like he's here and tries to communicate with us by turning on the television."

Joan smiled in agreement and led me into a gentle restorative pose. As I held that position for the rest of the class, she asked what my perspective was on life and death.

I had to be honest. I still didn't have one. I believed in something beyond this world, but I wasn't sure what.

"What kind of professional support are you getting?" Joan asked.

"None," I responded. Friends had insisted I see a grief therapist, so I tried. The first one told me my pain was "forever and would never go away." The second listened closely to my story and then asked, "How can I help you? There's nothing wrong with your head. You are simply heartbroken." When it became clear to me early on that traditional therapy was not what I needed, I began searching for other solutions.

Joan suggested that I start reading books about life after death. As I held my poses, she texted me a number of book titles and informed me that some were written by doctors. Others by well-respected authorities on death. "Start with these," she suggested. "See what resonates with you, Nikki. You will know."

Fortunately, I could afford to prioritize my health and was blessed that my husband gave me both the financial support and emotional freedom to do so. By the time Joan returned two days later for my next class, I had a stack of books piled high on my nightstand and was burying myself in at least one a day. Each book led me to another and during rare breaks of time, I stepped outside of my pain, glanced back at myself, and saw a student learning how to live the rest of her life.

As Doug and I continued to open up and receive, more support kept coming. One day, we were offered an unusual gift from a man I had never met, and my husband barely even knew. His name was Skyler, an actor/comedian with a big personality. He invited us to attend the Comedy Store on Sunset to watch his regular Thursday-night show. I told Doug I couldn't make it. I had dumped a whole new layer of sorrow into my green journal that day and couldn't just tell my emotions to take a break for Hollywood. Besides, comedy was too dark for me. My days were dark enough. And I didn't want to laugh. Not then. Not ever. But Doug said we had to go. As if I were a young child who needed to be bribed, he said we could leave early and practically carried me to the car.

When I met Skyler, he peered into my eyes like I was still a human being. We followed him toward what he said was his favorite booth, and I was relieved to see it perfectly hidden in a dark corner with a straight shot to the exit.

When the first comedian came out onstage, he surprised me with a gift that I never expected. Laughter. The physical relief I felt was immediately replaced by guilt. *How could I be laughing when Tommy is gone?* But then a voice stepped in and insisted, *"You will laugh again. Tommy laughed more than anyone. To laugh is to honor him."* I acquiesced, and by the time we returned home two hours later, I was covered in gratitude. Gratitude for Skyler's invitation. Gratitude that my husband forced me to receive it. And gratitude that my body remembered how to laugh, even if I didn't want it to.

Skyler followed up a few days after the show with another generous offer. He said he wanted to host a special comedy show to raise money for Tommy's Field. "Say yes!" I told Doug. Yes! A comedy show would raise money for Tommy's Field. Yes! It would share Tommy's spirit of laughter with others. Yes! If Tommy's own mother could laugh, it gave others permission to as well. This was the message I wanted Dono and Tommy's friends to receive. So, we gave Skyler the green light.

By the evening of the show, hundreds of people had bought tickets and proceeded to honor Tommy with two straight hours of laughter. At the same time, Tricky Tommy's ambitious little spirit found a way to achieve the top spot on the Comedy Store's marquee signage on the Sunset Strip and make his mother weep, yet again.

Six months later, Tommy visited me in my dreams. He gave me a big hug to make up for the one we didn't get to give each other before he left. When I studied his face, I was relieved to see the twelve-year-old boy I so desperately missed. His skin was flawless, just the way I remembered it. The single freckle on his left check was positioned exactly where I last saw it. His curious eyes twinkled, and his thick dark curly hair was buzzed short on the sides and styled high on top, just the way he and Cristiano Ronaldo, one of his idols, liked it. We began talking, but our exchange was promptly erased from my memory until I asked, *"T, are you the only one there with a great laugh?"*

He flashed me his signature Tommy Mark grin, and said very specifically, *"There are three others who have it."*

As if he could hear my thoughts, he answered a question that I didn't recall asking. *"Yes, it's special."* That prompted me to ask, *"Are you the most special soul there?"*

I expected an immediate "Yes!" from the child whose mantra in life was "Yes!" But when I asked my question, his humility surprised me, *"No, I'm not overly special."* He told me that *"All souls are special and shouldn't be compared."* I woke up, recorded our exchange in my green journal, and promptly fell back to sleep.

I learned by watching Tommy play soccer that receiving done well looks easy, and that the easier it looks means the more practice it takes. It took practice to learn how to open my front door and receive daily home-cooked meals without telling families I didn't even know that they shouldn't have. It took practice to receive a weekly playdate schedule from parents who wanted to make sure Donovan would never be alone after school if he didn't want to be. It took practice to receive texts, letters, and emails full of condolence messages stamped with heart and prayer emojis, and to allow each one of them to fill me up. The practice of receiving was an essential part of Tommy's game, and to honor him it became a part of mine.

By the time Doug and I had exhausted the majority of our own relationships, approximately 75 percent of our fundraising budget had been raised. That's when Tricky Tommy started working overtime and gave us the gift of music. Tommy and his father were both music fanatics. While Doug was a music attorney and a walking encyclopedia of everything music, Tommy sang it, played it, and wrote it. Together they listened to and debated over all kinds of music.

When Doug's colleagues in the music industry came together to produce a benefit concert for Tommy's Field, some of Tommy's favorite artists volunteered to perform. Every company involved in the show, from merchandising and marketing, to ticket sales and radio promotions, either volunteered their services or contributed their proceeds from the evening to Tommy's Field. Every seat in the theater was sold out, and, together, a full house honored Tommy by singing and dancing and allowing the power of music to heal and unite. Veterans in the music industry looked at one another after the show and reported back to my husband, "Imagine how much good we could do in the world if our industry treated each other like this all the time."

I have often asked myself why our family was so blessed to receive so much in so many ways. Yes, our roots ran deep in Los Angeles. Yes, Tommy had a knack for making special connections like the center midfielder that he was. And, yes, it was possible that Tricky Tommy's relentless spirit was breathing down everyone's neck and forcing them to pony up and get involved. But I've also come to believe that our openness to receiving further encouraged our community to give, and that the collective energy targeted at Tommy's Field simply generated more until both the project and our family advanced to a degree that could not have otherwise been achieved on our own. Community could not replace Tommy or make our pain go away, but it could help build Tommy's legacy and teach us purpose along the way.

After nine months, we were done. Tommy's Field had the vision. It had the community. And it had the love. It also had the money. Doug had spearheaded our fundraising efforts while I managed city relations and the field's design details, and together we raised $1.2 million, just as I had promised Valerie from the outset that we would. More one-off donations and creative fundraising offers continued to trickle in and frequently reminded us that we were not forgotten. The time had come to reenter the real world, visit with Recreation and Park decision-makers, discuss field designs, talk gift agreement terms, and advance overall discussions. The businesswoman in me was being called on to dust herself off and manifest the most meaningful project of her life.

Stepping into the real world was like entering a separate but parallel dimension. I could see it. Touch it. Feel it. But was no longer calibrated for it. Real-world energy was too busy and intense for me. Loud noises made me jump. Clutter made me dizzy. And my senses were so open that the energy of real-world people walking by or standing too close literally threw me off balance.

Life in my new dimension was slower, gentler, and more forgiving. The more I acclimated to it, the more I noticed the way real-world people could visit me in my dimension and then quickly transition back into their regular lives. I could not go back and forth as easily. My grief could not simply be turned on and off. And I could not pretend that what interested real-world people still mattered to me. But like two atoms that shared a common element, Tommy's Field united us and kept us functioning in our respective ways.

One morning, Doug and I found Donovan lying on his bedroom floor succumbing to the emotional pain that was ravaging his little body. He was still struggling to understand why school mattered and took the opportunity to point out more real-world differences. "To everyone else it feels like weeks or months since Tommy left. But to us, it feels like yesterday," he said, adding that he yearned to go be with Tommy. After I made a mental note to tell my green journal about Dono's quote, he fed me another. "I feel like teachers and everyone around me are going to say, 'Stop making excuses. Tommy died a long time ago. Focus and get back to normal.' But I'll never be normal."

I told him that no one would ever say that to him, despite knowing that real-world people would soon think it, if they hadn't already. I said that it no longer mattered what teachers thought or what grades they gave. We were beyond all those real-world concerns and it was clear that his soul had already achieved a PhD level in love. And I agreed that *normal* would probably never again be part of our vocabulary, even though it was the foundation on which my first incarnation thrived. But Tricky Tommy wasn't normal, either, I assured Donovan. And if this dimension is where we needed to be to connect with him and fulfill our mission, then I never wanted to be normal again.

CHAPTER 9

AFTER THE BENEFIT CONCERT FOR TOMMY'S FIELD, I CALLED Valerie to let her know that we had officially reached our fundraising goal and were ready to finalize the design and all other outstanding details for Tommy's Field. As our conversation commenced, my mind flickered and I assumed the position I had played and enjoyed the most throughout my career. It was the facilitator role, similar to the center midfield one that Tommy played.

Like every position in soccer, center midfielders have unique skills and dispositions. First and foremost, they are a collaborative breed looking for the most efficient and effective connection, period. Whether it's their first pass that changes the momentum of the game or their last that puts the ball into the net, center midfielders strive to control the middle of the field to push their team forward and create pathways to the goal that no one else can see.

When I took my position and discussed next steps with Valerie, I naturally established myself as the hub through which my family and the city connected. Valerie advised that the next logical step in the process was to update the field drawings that had been produced four years earlier when I was still president of Tommy's Westside soccer club. She promptly connected me to Jimmy, who referred me to Joe, who I remembered from the first iteration of Tommy's Field. Joe was a kind, elderly fellow who consulted for the department for many years and had designed and project-managed dozens of its athletic fields. Joe's no-nonsense manner, combined with his frank opinions about city policies, confirmed that he knew the ins and outs of the city's ways and had successfully developed dozens of athletic fields in spite of the bureaucracy.

Joe and I proceeded to visit the only two Westside parks that I was told had the potential to accommodate an adult-size soccer field. Joe measured and evaluated both sites while I stood off to the side eyeballing trees that looked like obstacles and trying to feel where Tommy's spirit belonged.

Valerie reported back that Westwood Recreation Center was the only option. The other park Joe measured ran a successful baseball league and did not have enough land to support the dimensions of Tommy's Field. Additional parks separately evaluated by the city were also deemed to be overprogrammed or unable to accommodate the lighting and parking that Tommy's Field required. The city's analysis sounded reasonable to me.

When Joe emailed me the first official Tommy's Field design at Westwood Rec Center, it looked exactly as I envisioned it would. We were so close to our goal that I boldly told Doug we were only a few months away from having formal approval and starting development.

"Everyone tells me that it can take three to five years to get anything done with the City of Los Angeles," Doug said, his tone both complimenting and challenging me at the very same time. As much as my husband's brain has always impressed me, I had learned over our eighteen-year relationship that it could frustrate me even more. Doug has the kind of brain that hears only snippets of a story and then accurately predicts its ending. The most frustrating part about his brain, I had found, was that it was usually right.

"Well, that's not my experience," I said, feeling a bit miffed that he and his brain were at it again.

But the game of soccer is a game of inches and it's virtually impossible to predict how a match will end. No matter how close a ball gets to the back of the net, all that matters is when it does. Just when I thought it was game over and that our team had performed master-fully, considering our circumstances, my weaknesses became seri-ously exposed and the universe reminded me that I was not the kind of person who got hired for easy projects.

Out of nowhere, Valerie notified me that the city's planning department, which I didn't even know existed, revised Joe's original designs because there were park-wide policies and procedures that Joe hadn't taken into consideration. I found this news perplexing, given how many fields Joe had already successfully designed for the city. When I called Joe to ask about such design changes, he sounded as confused as I was. I felt his shoulders shrug when he told me there was nothing he could do. He worked for the city. So did Valerie. And the planning department was a member of their team. For the first time I saw disconnects between departments of city government that had the potential to derail Tommy's Field.

Deciding to take a simple step forward, I explained to Valerie, one center midfielder to another, that the revised field designs were problematic. Our family did not have many design stipulations but the few we did were important to us, and from what I could see, they had been ignored.

First, the planning department's drawings showed Tommy's Field with a fifteen-foot locked fence around it, which was a deal-breaker. "Tommy's Field will be for everyone," I reminded Valerie. No locks. No high fences. No divisions. She confirmed that these details had all been communicated to the planning department but that high fences were part of citywide design protocols. There appeared to be no one I could speak with who had the authority to explain those design protocols or reconsider them.

The second problem with the drawings was that the field was too short. Valerie told me in no uncertain terms that an adult-size soccer field at Westwood Recreation Center was "impossible" and that there was not another Westside park that could accommodate the dimensions of Tommy's Field. A familiar portal inside me burst open. I had underestimated how much that word, *impossible*, had driven me in my former incarnation and was surprised by the extent to which it still fueled me in my new one. Dots formed in front of me like teammates on a field and when I tried to connect them, new obstacles pushed back like defenders and got in my way. I didn't know which way to move. Did I work this out with Valerie, who had supported me every step of the way . . . or did I create new ways to the goal by circumventing her?

I was stuck. And, not only that, my grief was worsening. I did not recognize myself. I did not know myself. And I could not console myself. While the Department of Recreation and Parks stayed busy with its growing list of projects across the city and waited for me to make the next move with field designs, my mental and physical health took a turn for the worse, and I sought help.

Since traditional talk therapy commonly endorsed by Western medicine had not resonated with me early on, I desperately turned to Eastern medicine for support. Like a mad scientist, I searched off the beaten path for an effective way to heal a grieving mother.

I started by scheduling more time with Joan. Twice a week. Talking. Practicing yoga. Debating life and death. After she told me how she came to terms with her mother's death at a very young age, I told her about the conversation Tommy and I had while we were driving to San Diego.

"Is it possible to go to sleep and not wake up?" Tommy had asked me almost forty-five minutes into our drive.

I took my eyes off the road, lifted my large black-rimmed sunglasses, and looked over at him before responding: "Only if you're really old. Your piano-playing grandma, Dad's mom, passed away in her sleep, but she was in her late eighties. That's the perfect way to go. No pain and no drama. Totally unlike her to have made it so easy on everyone, by the way. But that doesn't happen to healthy kids and young adults. You don't just go to sleep and not wake up without some sort of warning." I sounded so confident.

"Why?" I asked.

"Because I had a nightmare the other night that I went to sleep and didn't wake up. When I got up in the morning, I was so relieved that it wasn't real."

"You never said anything about it," I answered.

"I forgot all about it until now," he said, unconvincingly.

"You probably didn't die in your dream," I said. "I don't think that's possible. I think you probably thought you died and then woke up."

"No, Mom, I died in my dream."

It wasn't until after Tommy was gone that I remembered he died in my dreams, too, maybe on the exact same night he died in his. But when I woke up in a panic on the very morning I had that dream, I was so relieved to hear Tommy's voice shouting in the hallway that I forgot all about the entire nightmare. It was hard to believe that Tommy's own description of his dream during our drive hadn't triggered the memory of mine. I would like to think that if it had, I would have connected the dots and driven straight to the nearest hospital.

"The dying will always give you clues when their time has come," Joan said, paraphrasing an author named Elizabeth Kübler-Ross whose books she had recommended I read. "You just have to look closely at the signs and listen." Reflecting on the dream both Tommy and I had of him dying and the conversation we had about it, I knew the signs had been given to me. I simply missed them.

"Your souls were talking, and on a soul level, you both knew he would be leaving," Joan continued.

"That's what I'm starting to believe," I said, appreciating the way her words resonated with me.

It was difficult for me to distinguish between my personality and my soul. I did not understand how one could be engaged in one activity while the other might be plotting something quite different. I was grappling with the idea that while Tommy and I were having one very live hypothetical conversation on our way down to San Diego, our souls were having a private one.

When both Joan and my body made it very clear that I could not run from my emotional pain without new physical ones chasing me down, I forced myself to reenter the real world in a bigger way. I had to keep moving. That's what Tommy would do.

So, I began taking beginner-level hot yoga classes, the gentlest kind I could find, where my tears and sweat mixed without being judged. I also started taking group meditation classes. I had never meditated before, and was never one for groups, but dire circumstances required dire measures. I started slow. Lying down on a flat black mat while vibrations from crystal bowls massaged my brain, popped my ears, and made space so my spirit could delicately reenter the earth's atmosphere. When I felt ambitious, I ventured into a breathwork class and when the instructor encouraged the class to laugh, I cried. When they told us to shout, I cried some more. I kept moving from healer to class and class to green journal, and back to class again, day after day, until I no longer felt like the lead in a horror film. I had become the star of my very own tragicomedy and was learning to laugh at myself.

Finally, to address my wandering soul, I started seeing alternative healers. Lots of them. Every week, for at least one hour, sometimes two. Joan recommended the first one, which led me to the next, and soon enough I was indoctrinated into the world of spiritual healing. I didn't know if it was possible for anyone else to actually heal me of a loss so deep and permanent, but each one sparked my curiosity, gave me something to compare and contrast in my green journal, and inspired me to survive week to week until my next appointment.

My exploration into the alternative healing world had its glitches. Early on, a friend of a friend recommended a medium to me who nearly destroyed my developing faith. She was in town for only two days. She was a celebrity medium and a best-selling author. She was in such high demand that she even had a closed waiting list. Given my dire situation, however, she was able to open up a slot the very next morning for little old me. My first medium reading with Pamela after Tommy's funeral was so positive and uplifting that I graciously accepted the offer from a friend of a friend and made the appointment.

The minute I sat down in front of this celebrity medium, however, I felt duped. My chest tightened, my stomach churned, and a loud voice inside my head told me to run. It didn't matter that she had a reputation as being one of "the best." She spent more time boasting about her best-selling book and her rising fame than focusing on the job for which she had clearly earned such accolades. I wanted to tell her that I grew up in Los Angeles. That celebrities were part of daily life in this town. That I was a grieving mother and incapable of being impressed. But I sat there listening because I did not know who to trust more—the voice in my head or her.

After she closed her eyes and said she had connected to Tommy's spirit, she proceeded to speak about him and his passing in a way that told me she had heard way too much about us from the friend of a friend. Her messages were inconsistent and disjointed and felt overly prepared rehearsed and fake. When I walked out of the appointment, I cried the rest of the day. I would have cried all day anyway, but my tears after seeing her were laced with something new. Hopelessness.

Fortunately, I was scheduled to see Joan later that afternoon. When I told her what had happened with the celebrity medium and she saw how distraught I was, she kneeled down in front of me, pulled her long brown hair behind her ears, and looked through me with her makeup-free eyes.

"On some level of your being, you already know all the answers that you seek," Joan assured me. "When you speak to me or any kind of healer for support, you are trying to get confirmation of what feels right to you. It doesn't matter how prestigious anyone's record is or how many testimonials they have. It's gotta feel right to you. Your inner being always recognizes the truth."

That philosophy had served my former self well. I had a strong gut. A reliable gauge. An intuition that reinforced a deeper knowing. But now I was too overwhelmed by shock and grief to determine what to believe and when to trust myself.

"What I believe," Joan continued, "is that a person who transitions, regardless of their age, is always when they are meant to go. It may not make sense to us a lot of the time but from the perspective of a spirit and the nonphysical world it's about that individual being's mission and purpose, and sometimes there is a lot of purpose not just in their life, but also in their passing."

As I stared at the red rose tattooed above her right ankle and followed its swirly green vine to the top of her foot, she added, "Tommy's passing is waking people up. Maybe because of him people will appreciate their families more. Their connections more. Even their own lives more."

The frequency of the ringing in my ears began rising and the darkness in the pit of my stomach lifted.

"As for your healing," Joan continued, "this experience is forcing you to strengthen the inner connection to yourself. Are you taking any medication?"

"Yes," I said. "I take half a tablet of Xanax at night to help me sleep for a few hours."

"When you feel ready, try to wean yourself off it," Joan suggested. "Medication dulls pain and creates a barrier between you and your heart. The sooner you allow yourself to feel the depth of your grief, the faster you will move through it. Otherwise, the pain can resurface in unexpected ways over time and prolong the healing process."

When she explained that the medication might also make it more difficult for me to connect with Tommy's spirit, I committed to reducing my dosage to one quarter of a pill and throwing away all refill prescriptions once the bottle I had was empty.

"Trust yourself, Nikki," Joan encouraged. "Process your grief in whatever way feels right to you. If you wake up one morning and feel like you can't get out of bed, do what you need to do, but reach for the thoughts that you know to be the highest truth. You know the truth. Stay true to yourself, Nikki, and you will find your way."

As honest as I had always been with others, life was now forcing me to be honest with myself.

I started by confronting the growing guilt I felt about not working. Unlike Doug, whose law practice had become like a healing sanctuary where he could detach from his grief for hours at a time and find comfort, I was still very much unemployed and in no shape to start job hunting. When Doug suggested that going back to work might help me move forward the way it was helping him, I explained that resurrecting my career, even part-time, was not an option, regardless of how uncomfortable I felt about it. Tommy's departure was impacting us in different ways, and, as per Joan's advice, I could not pretend otherwise. For Doug, it affected who he wanted to *be*. For me, it changed what I wanted to *do*. Life expected something different from me now, and I felt driven to figure out what that was.

In terms of *what* I wanted to do, all I knew for sure was that I was passionate about building Tommy's Field and did not feel any pressure, internally or externally, to do so. My entire being wanted to do it. It felt right to do it. I just had to find a way to do it. As if Tommy started feeding me memories of watching him play soccer, it dawned on me that he committed to the game because of the way it made him *feel*, and that getting stuck between two players and figuring his way around them was all part of the fun. I immediately applied this teaching to Tommy's Field. The project was at a standstill—that much was clear. But suddenly, a fence designed too high and a field designed too short looked like nothing but opportunities to strengthen both my feet and find the joy in learning new ways to turn.

CHAPTER 10

FEELING MORE IN TOUCH WITH MYSELF AND CAPABLE OF GETTING Tommy's Field back on track, I met with the president of Westwood Recreation Center's advisory board to gauge how he and the park board felt about Tommy's Field. The board was composed of elected community members who made local park recommendations on behalf of the greater community. He reminded me that he was also president of the same board when I proposed the field's first incarnation and that a year before that time the board had already approved a master plan incorporating a synthetic-turf athletic field in the exact area where we wanted to build Tommy's Field. This type of field had always fit in perfectly with the park's long-term plans. Still, he warned that working with the City of Los Angeles could be slow and agonizingly difficult, and that my experience getting Tommy's Field approved was destined to be unlike any project I had ever managed in the start-up world.

To emphasize his point, he walked me around the park until we reached the front of the recreation center. "You see this flagpole?" he asked, already knowing that I could.

"Yes," I said, curious where his story was headed.

"It used to be located three feet from here. It was smack in the middle of this walkway where we are standing. I wanted to move it back three feet so we could add drinking fountains and make a proper ADA-compliant walkway into the recreation center. Seems totally reasonable, right? I wasn't even asking the city to pay for it.

The nonprofit that I serve in Westwood that supports local schools, our library, this park, and even our local fire station, had the funds to pay for it. Still, it took me ten years to get the city's approval."

"Wow," I responded, silently questioning his business skills and feeling increasingly confident about mine.

Then I updated him on the trajectory of Tommy's Field in hopes that he could offer some advice. "I have no idea what to do next."

The board's president proceeded to surprise me with his knowledge of the park, the inner workings of Westwood, and the ways of city government.

"You see these trees over here?" he asked, as we continued our tour around the park.

"Yeah," I responded, gearing up for the punch line.

"They are all dead. I have been trying to get them removed for years. "If you want to move Tommy's Field along," he said, "I recommend that you hire an independent arborist to evaluate the situation. Otherwise, it could take the city years to do it, if they do it at all." I stared at the flagpole and got his drift.

By the time we parted ways an hour later, two things were very clear to me. First, I needed this guy on my team. He was built like the perfect center back—sturdy and full of so much city knowledge and park history that he would be difficult for any opposition to get around. Second, I had to find a way to work with the City of Los Angeles. It was the biggest and strongest player in the game and despite its clumsiness and lack of speed, there was no way to build Tommy's Field without it.

A week later, I walked the park with an arborist. Three weeks later, I reviewed his thirty-six-page report that verified that all the healthy trees affecting the length of the field could be moved elsewhere in the park and all the dead and diseased ones should immediately be removed for safety reasons. I forwarded the report to Valerie.

We no longer had a tree issue, I assured her. Joe's design would work. If she could pass the report on to the city's planning department, I was confident that they would agree.

When a few weeks passed without any feedback from Valerie, I barely noticed. I was busy breathing, stretching, and grieving, while attempting to be a stable and present mother to Donovan in between. But when almost a month passed and I still hadn't heard back from her, I realized that a year could easily go by without the city even noticing, and that Doug's annoying prediction of a three- to five-year project might actually prove to be accurate. The thought of either one happening made my stomach drop. I called Valerie again and pressed her for an update. Unable to disclose whether the report had been opened, much less read by her team, she advised that the city wasn't prepared to fight tree preservationists, period.

I was not happy, which was saying a lot given that I had already died once, was in my second incarnation, and was as miserable as a human being could be. I was reminded that I did not like being told something definitely could not be done that potentially could. Grief may have strained the muscles in my back, produced asthmatic symptoms in my chest, and drained every ounce of fat from my body, but my heart kept pumping out new strains of will that refused to succumb to the kind of rigid and outdated rules that I had spent my entire first-incarnation career defeating.

"What would Tommy do?" I asked myself.

I thought back to when Tommy was in the fifth grade and complained, "I can't learn like this anymore, Mom. I can't sit in a classroom with thirty-five kids and have a teacher talking at me for eight hours a day and then go home and memorize facts all night that I don't care about. I want to go to a middle school where learning is creative and interesting. I need something different." He was articulating who he was and what he needed and challenged me to defy universal odds by helping him find a middle school experience that would not stink.

Since his frustrations in the classroom were starting to negatively affect his behavior on the schoolyard, I had him tested to see how he learned best and what kind of middle school would help him reach his goal. That's when I learned that he had acquired a part of his father's brain—the visual-processing part that tested at the top of standardized tests and enabled him to observe and evaluate his environment while simultaneously reacting to it in mid-flight. It was the part that enabled him to dribble a ball at high speed with his feet as he lifted his head, swiveled it from side to side, checked over his shoulder, and kicked the ball forward so it landed precisely where he estimated a teammate's cleat on the run would meet it. It was also the part that loathed math. That refused to break down his answers and show his work. That caught all the details but did not have the time or desire to explain them.

I wasn't born a center midfielder like Tommy. My skills took an entire first incarnation to identify and refine. I attempted to be Wonder Woman the way Tommy aspired to be Cristiano Ronaldo, but he flashed and sparkled while I worked and worked and enjoyed helping others shine.

Despite our stylistic differences, connections were our specialty, and we came from a long line of them. Upon taking his first breath, Tommy became a third-generation Angeleno on *both* sides of his family. Doug and I learned six months into our relationship that our families were deeply connected two generations before us. My grandmother, Mama, had been best friends with Doug's favorite aunt, and the two of them always hoped someone in the family would marry so they could become sisters. When Doug and I discovered that this lifetime was not the first time the universe had miraculously connected our families in the second most populated city in the United States, we surrendered ourselves to fate and got married. A year later, we produced Tommy. This city was the perfect place for a boy with big dreams and the courage to pursue them.

By the time Tommy turned eleven, he had been fortunate to play both with and against teams in Europe enough times to gauge whether his development was on track. He played abroad every chance he got and became increasingly serious about moving to whichever European country wanted to develop him the most. But there was a major glitch in Tommy's plan that had to be addressed. FIFA, the worldwide governing body of the sport, prevented foreign youth players under the age of eighteen from playing in Europe without proper citizenship. The word *impossible* flashed before my eyes, toggled my start-up switch, and challenged me to find a solution. "Let's make the impossible happen, T," I told him, rationalizing that, soccer or no soccer, living in Europe for a period of time would be a great cultural experience for our entire family.

Knowing there had to be a way to reach this goal, I suddenly remembered that my grandmother, Mama, had narrated a detailed documentary about her life a few years before she passed away. After digging it out of a drawer and watching the initial five minutes of it, I learned for the very first time that I had a great-great-grandfather, who immigrated to the United States from Hungary.

I promptly researched Hungarian immigration laws and learned that Hungary was the only EU country that allowed for dual citizenship if a direct connection to Hungarian ancestors could be proven, regardless of how far back those Hungarian roots were established. If I could prove my Hungarian roots, my boys and I would qualify for citizenship and be able to live and work in any European Union country we wanted. It was as if fate had scheduled a very important appointment to connect some obscure dots and start making destiny happen.

Excited about the possibilities, I hired immigration experts in Budapest who told me that I needed to produce my great-great-grandfather's birth record in order to qualify. They also advised that, given the Austro-Hungarian region where I believed my great-great-grandfather was born in 1867, his birth record would be found in present-day Slovakia, somewhere.

To my surprise, it took me about a minute to find a reputable genealogist in Slovakia who would take on my project. It took about three weeks for him to confirm that he had searched the records of every church where babies were born back in my great-great-grandfather's day, and had indeed found his birth record. My mind could hardly grasp what my gut never doubted. A few weeks later, I had notarized copies of his birth record in hand and, after striking gold, I proceeded to track down every birth and marriage license that connected me to him. Poring over my family's history after work and on weekends, I took over our dining-room table and replaced family dinners with growing piles of pictures, timelines, and certified documents.

In the meantime, I started learning Hungarian. The citizenship process required me to speak basic Hungarian, submit my application in Hungarian, and pass a verbal conversational test in Hungarian with the consul general in my city. For six months, while I worked full time, every open minute of every day was filled with something Hungarian. I listened to Hungarian language CDs while driving Tommy to and from soccer. I scoured online immigration databases and libraries during lunch breaks. I connected with immigration experts in Budapest during the middle of the night when Los Angeles was asleep and Hungary was awake. Meanwhile, all Tommy could do to help was play his little heart out.

When the Hungarian immigration experts in Budapest verified that my documents were complete, I turned my attention to the lives of my ancestors. I was curious about who they were and what genes and traits they may have passed down to me and my children. The more I got to know them, the more my dining-room chandelier started flickering. For months I sat under dancing light bulbs while tracing the lives of ancestors I never knew. As the lights competed for my attention, hints of spirituality arrived unannounced and prompted me to look up and say hello. I wondered if my ancestors were trying to tell me something. Their presence motivated me to dig deeper into my past until one revelation made me question if I had gone too far.

Census records from the 1900s revealed what my grandmother's documentary confirmed: that my Hungarian great-great-grandfather, married to my American great-great-grandmother, had lost a son at the age of twelve or thirteen years old. Sitting all alone under a chandelier that shimmered like stars, chills traveled up from the base of my spine until I was overcome by an intense sadness for the ancestors I never knew. The emotional imprint that this child's death left on me was palpable.

I called my father and asked, "How did the memory of this child not get passed down through our family?"

"No one really talked about those kinds of things in our day," he responded.

Suddenly, my family had scars. I felt vulnerable. And more spirituality began to surface from within.

In December 2017, approximately six months after I embarked on my journey for Hungarian citizenship and less than four months before the day Tommy did not wake up, I was scheduled to take my verbal exam with the consul general. That morning, with dozens of perfectly organized certified documents in hand, I stopped on my way out the door to address the flickering lights that had been following me from room to room. I turned around, looked up at them, and quickly whispered so Doug wouldn't hear, "Please help me pass this test. At the very least, wish me luck. Thank you."

Approximately one hour later, I was bantering back and forth with the consul general in Hungarian and imagined my ancestors huddled around me, translating and feeding me words. After about ten minutes, with Doug by my side, the consul, who had graciously slowed her pace and enunciated her words, gave me a pass on the verbal exam and told me all of my documentation was approved. Tommy, Dono, and I would soon become Hungarian citizens. Doug could apply if he ever decided to learn the language. I privately thanked my ancestors and shivered when I thought I heard them cheer.

On the drive home, I felt different. No longer was I confined to achieving other people's visions. I had started believing in my own.

Looking back, I now see that two different plotlines had been developing at the same time. While I was consciously supporting Tommy's dreams and motivated to give my entire family the gift of living abroad, I was subconsciously reaching back into my family's history and innocently tugging on a loose thread that had been dangling in my lineage for generations. Unaware of the consequences, I pulled on it, dragged it through the modern world, and then innocently tied it to my future. Finding my grandmother's documentary in a drawer. Stumbling upon my Hungarian ancestry. Learning about the death of a child in my family the same age as Tommy. None of it was luck. It was all a setup. Destiny in progress.

When I returned home from the consulate, I broke a family technology rule that I had put in place and texted Tommy at school. I was unaware that Tommy, the Trickster, had been breaking my "no cell phone use during school" rule for a while, and also had his laptop programmed to receive texts.

"T, I passed. We should have formal approval and passports in a year."

Tommy immediately texted back multiple rows of colorful emojis expressing gratitude for my gift, while I promptly celebrated the most personal and meaningful project of my life by booking two tickets for me and Doug to Budapest that New Year's Eve.

By the end of 2017, my Hungarian citizenship process was complete, and I stopped working. I was tired. Ready for a short break. I wanted to spend more time with my family and friends. I started contemplating what my next project should be and wondered what could possibly be more meaningful than the personal one I had just completed for my own family.

"What will you do next, Mom?" Tommy had asked me.

"I think I need some time to just 'be,'" I told him, feeling somewhat directionless. "What would you do, Tommy?"

"Stay in soccer, Mom. The sport in America needs you."

"I don't know, Tommy. Soccer is your dream. I think I'd rather watch you play it than try to fix it."

Neither of us ever suspected that fate would step in four months later and dictate an answer. What would I do next? I would mourn. And when it was time to do something else, I would continue to ask myself, "What would Tommy do?"

That was the same question I asked when Tommy's Field got mired in political bureaucracy. "What would Tommy do?" The answer came in fast and clear. He would stay on his toes. He would keep looking up. And he would never give up.

"Life is all about the details, Mom," he had once told me. Even though he never stopped to explain them, they rarely passed him by. I applied his message. It was time to stop focusing on the goal and to start concentrating on how I played the game.

Not wanting to disrespect Valerie, who was clearly stuck in the inner workings of city bureaucracy, I reached out to a former colleague named Tina, who was a political consultant. I asked for her help navigating our city government and getting to the table with the right decision-makers. I recognized that I didn't have the time or stamina to weave my way through the system and promised that the favor wouldn't cost more than a few phone calls.

Less than a week later, I was downtown in City Hall sitting beside Tina and across from the general manager of the Department of Recreation and Parks and the chief of staff for Westwood's council member. They immediately humanized local government for me and reminded me how efficient it could be at the top. They asked me to share my story. They told me they were sorry for my loss. They cried when they heard about all the love behind Tommy's Field. They expressed genuine gratitude for our gift and apologized for any confusion. Then they asked a question that I thought was silly and made me feel like they hadn't listened to a word I'd said.

"Do you have community support?"

Without hesitation I exclaimed, "Of course! This is a community project. The community helped my family raise the money for Tommy's Field."

To test me, they threw out the name of one particular activist who—although I did not know it—had a history of fighting new projects in our neighborhood. Not only was she a Tommy's Field donor, I said proudly, but she was also a friend. *Bam!* I applauded my team. *This is what happens when our city government deals with second-generation Angelenos, and especially my husband.* He was raised in Westwood. He could tell you who lived in what home, on what block, and for how long. He rarely forgets a name or a face, and his community spans wide and deep, going all the way back to elementary school. I was very confident that there would not be many Westwood residents against improving a public field and honoring the life of a young child who left us all too soon.

When we reconvened a few weeks later, the planning department had generated new Tommy's Field designs and the GM responded to my design requests with Valerie sitting by his side. The low fence without a lock was not only acceptable, but a good idea, he assured me. Our desire to build a donor wall would not be a problem. Meaningful community hours would be designated so kids could enjoy free and unstructured play. Tommy's Field signage was acceptable. And while he pointed out that the city attorney's office had become increasingly opposed to logos in its public parks, the idea that LAFC and LA Galaxy crests might both share the field was a legitimate consideration.

Just when it seemed like we were all on the same page, the GM threw in an unexpected twist. He repositioned Tommy's Field from north to south to east to west, eliminating two existing tennis courts to do so. My gut started pulsating. He explained that the tennis courts were underutilized and that with this new design there would still be six courts remaining, two of which would be renovated at the city's expense. I reminded him of the arborist's report that no one seemed to have read and pointed out that we could move some trees and still make the field fit north to south without disrupting tennis. But he and his team preferred preserving more open space than tennis courts and believed it was better overall planning for the park. The operator in me disagreed, but who was I to doubt his expertise? I didn't design parks. I wasn't a civil engineer. I was a grieving mom trying to give a gift. I left City Hall feeling grateful for his support and hopeful that Tommy's Field was back on track.

As we waited for next steps, Doug scheduled a phone appointment with a British medium named Robert, who had been strongly recommended to him. After Tommy passed, a friend of Doug's privately divulged that he, too, had lost a child, and that the only thing that had helped him even remotely recover was talking to a medium. As skeptical as Doug was of the path he had seen me pursue, his spirit needed a boost and he was ready to do some exploring itself.

The morning we called Robert, our cordless, landline phones were plugged in, charged, and ready to go. Robert didn't know that I would be joining the call but didn't seem to mind. In his fine English accent, he explained how he worked, told us not to give him any information, and said he couldn't promise which spirits would come forth to speak to us. "I just deliver messages from those who come forward and trust that it's information you need to hear at this time."

We agreed to his ground rules, and he proceeded.

"There is a younger person here, smiling. He has a really good smile. He passed before his time." We could only nod as tears released in unison.

"Everyone was totally unprepared for this. It's like a switch just turned off and his whole operating system shut down. No hospitals or chance to save him. No goodbye. Just poof. Gone. The cause could not have been detected."

"That's right," Doug said, looking down. We still did not know why Tommy had left.

Then Robert let out a short laugh and said, "Others may be wanting to come in and visit with you, but this young man keeps holding up his finger and saying he's first in line and you came to talk to him."

Doug and I laughed and confirmed that he was.

"It was highly unusual for a young man of this age to be telling people he loved them and to believe in themselves. He did that, didn't he?"

"Yes," I said, looking over at Doug who was about to pass out. Only someone who attended Tommy's memorial and heard his close friends speak would know something like this.

"He wanted to try anything. This young man was an open book. You could be out of breath keeping up with him. Older and younger people gravitated toward him. He accomplished a lot in a very short time." *Yes, but he could have accomplished a lot more if he'd stayed!* I wanted to shout.

"He was a teacher, telling people to be themselves," Robert continued. "He also stood up to bullies and helped the underdog, didn't he?"

"Yes," I confirmed, remembering the time Tommy punched another child for making fun of his nanny.

"It's very uncommon for a young male to be that open and not intimated," Robert continued. His message is, "Be who you are."

All we could do at that point was absorb the words that sounded like they were being communicated by our son.

Twenty minutes into the reading, our phone started beeping, signaling that its battery had been drained of power and was about to die. Doug and I looked at each other, confused. The cordless landline phone had been fully charged before our call started and typically lasted a full day on a single charge. Doug ran off to get another fully charged phone from our bedroom and while he was gone Robert said that if we noticed the electrical in our house doing strange things that it was this young man doing it.

"These young male spirits tend to pull a lot of tricks and have some fun at our expense. That's why I always recommend fully charging your phones before a reading. The spirit energy tends to affect electricity and drain batteries very quickly," he said, laughing.

I didn't waste any minutes telling him about the time Doug got up at 3:00 a.m. and saw that Tommy's television had turned on again by itself. Nor about the time I was alone in my bathroom when Tommy's ringtone kept going off without any incoming calls. I continued listening to Robert until ten minutes later, our second cordless phone that had been fully charged started beeping. Doug ran back into the kitchen to get the first one again and we continued to swap phones back and forth every ten minutes until we finally got through the sixty-minute call.

When Robert's reading was over, Doug looked at me and asked, "Did we just speak to Tommy?" I said that I thought we did, but that we should give it some time to see if the reading sticks.

Increasingly convinced that both Pamela and Robert had communicated with Tommy's spirit, or at the very least were talented enough to make me feel like they did, I wondered if Dono might want to try to connect with Tommy through a medium. I thought it might ease his suffering. Give him hope that his brother's spirit was still around. Watching over him. Protecting him. Rooting for him.

"You and Dad have each other," Donovan had said multiple times. "I have no one." That's not how it was, but that's how he felt. No one could make up for Tommy. Not even Ethan, who was considerably older and had been living on his own since Donovan was a toddler. Ethan was close with his youngest brother, but he was also so distraught after losing Tommy that he could barely get out of bed without searching for ways to numb his pain. I never knew when Ethan would be around or what kind of shape he'd be in when he was there. So, that left Donovan, Doug, and me to reconfigure ourselves into some version of a functioning unit.

I didn't know where to start.

Transportation was problematic. Donovan made it very clear that only one of us could take him to his soccer practices and games, because that's how we always did it. One of us took Tommy. The other took him. Dono rarely got both of our attention at the same time, and that's the way he wanted it.

Dining was also an issue. Dono had no interest in attending family dinners at home or anywhere else unless Ethan joined us. A family of three at the dinner table with one empty chair was unbearable for all of us, so without any formal discussion, we all started eating separately, whenever we felt like it.

Even extracurricular activities as a family became infrequent. Dono would not play with us. He could barely talk to us. Tommy was his favorite. Tommy was the one he had always looked for first when he walked through the front door after school. And it was always Tommy from whom he most hated being apart.

"I have no one else to take my anger out on," he bluntly explained to me and Doug. "I can't take it out on my teachers or my friends or my teammates. That would only get me in more trouble. So, I have to take it out on the two of you."

At least we knew where he stood. Still, I had never seen such suffering in a child and thought maybe speaking to a medium would give him some comfort, just as it was giving me.

Dono, whose hair was now buzzed military-style short, flat-out rejected the idea. "I don't need anyone to connect me to my brother. I talk to Tommy directly, and I know it's him because he says things I never would."

As he developed his own relationship with his brother, I increasingly connected with Tommy in my sleep. Sometimes I spoke directly to him. Other times, those from his world spoke to me about him. *"All lines between you and Tommy are clear,"* one woman said to me in a dream after hanging up an ancient-looking cell phone the size of a brick.

As I contemplated her words, she added, *"All healing in the physical and spiritual worlds for both of you has been completed."*

I do not feel healed, I remember thinking during this dream. Then, without another verbal exchange of words, she confirmed that Tommy and I were cleaning up old wounds. Wounds from another lifetime. Wounds that I was not meant to understand in this one.

My dreams had become so vivid and informative that I started keeping a separate dream journal next to my green journal to document them in the middle of the night. It was as if I had one life while I was asleep, and another when awake, and separate journals to compare and contrast the two. When I realized that I couldn't wait to fall asleep every night to dream and wake up every morning to pursue my mission, I knew I was doing something right.

Am I being encouraged to connect with Tommy's spirit directly? I asked myself. *Is that even possible for a regular person to learn how to do?* The notion of it being *impossible* began to light me up. *We have nothing to lose by trying,* my gut told me. *We have the time. The resources. And the purpose,* my mind chimed in. *We also have the love. The will. And the drive,* pumped my heart. It didn't matter how impossible it sounded. It didn't even matter if it would take a lifetime to achieve. I had that long. Feeling fearless, my spirit got sassy and convinced myself that if anyone could learn how to connect this world with the next, it would be me.

PART 3

The Game

CHAPTER 11

EXACTLY ONE YEAR AFTER TOMMY PASSED AWAY, FIELD DESIGNS were completed and gift agreement terms between the City of Los Angeles and our family were agreed upon. Tina continued to be my liaison with the city, and I was so grateful to have someone I trusted teaching me how to speak city language that I didn't think to question her when she said it was time to present Tommy's Field to the community. "Show up with a large group of supporters," she advised. I assured her that I would, even though it seemed silly to make the community show up to present a gift to itself. Regardless, I reached out to close friends, dedicated donors, and nearby soccer clubs, and asked if they would do us yet another favor and show up at the first public meeting to lend support for Tommy's Field.

The week that the first public hearing was scheduled, I had an in-person appointment with a healer named Christopher. I knew before we got started that he was a one-week investment and that each daily appointment would be broken down into two two-hour sessions, separated by a two-hour break. What I could not have predicted, however, was how invaluable Christopher would be for me that week. But, apparently, the universe did, because it was the only week Christopher had open for months.

"I was a Navy SEAL," Christopher told me when we first connected over the phone to evaluate my needs and determine if working together made sense. "I was an elite athlete," he continued. "The epitome of strength and discipline. I pushed limits and went beyond human capacity every day. I was one of the strongest people on the planet, mentally and physically. But while I was the model of peak condition, I was terribly unhealthy. My nervous system was shot. Every part of my body was in pain. I lost my hearing, and my vision was rapidly declining, too. I was such a mess that I couldn't even sleep."

Ah, so he was once a real-world person, too, I thought.

After he explained how he turned his life around and started helping others heal their emotional and physical bodies of pain and trauma, I asked, "What do you specifically do?"

"I take tension, stress, and distortion out of your body and rewire your entire system from the inside out," he responded.

That sounds good, I thought to myself, having no idea what he meant. All I knew was that the experience sounded interesting and would expose me to a new healing technique.

I proceeded to tell him what happened to Tommy. Our family. My life. "Can you help me?" I asked.

"1,000 percent!!!" he said with the same number of exclamation points in his voice.

"Can you help my family, too?"

"Yes, but you are the vehicle through which both of your sons were born. We must help you first and that will automatically benefit your son in the physical world and your son in the spirit world."

By the time I had completed two days' worth of sessions with Christopher and walked into Westwood Recreation Center on May 7, 2018, for the first public hearing on Tommy's Field, I had already repeated hundreds of words after him. He had started attacking the emotional and physical stress of my trauma through strenuous exercises, and I had screamed in pain for hours as he manipulated my organs and intestines, one by one, with his hands. Although every minute felt like a worthy investment in myself, I had no idea how much Christopher was preparing me for what was to come.

The evening of the public hearing, Doug, Dono, and I followed handwritten signs with arrows pointing to a fairly large, nondescript, rectangular classroom located at the back of the building. Approximately seventy-five folding metal chairs were situated in neat rows separated by a center aisle, while shiny aluminum metal benches sat against the side walls of the room for additional seating. Every chair in the room was occupied, dozens of adults were standing shoulder to shoulder in the back of the room and children of all ages, sizes, skin colors, and backgrounds were squeezed in next to each other along the sides. It seemed like everyone we had asked to show up did, and then some, including many of Tommy's friends whose loyalty never failed to lift my spirits and crush my heart at the very same time. Our team looked like the United Nations. Exactly the way Tommy would have wanted it.

Upon entering the meeting room, city officials introduced themselves to Doug and me and then took me aside to explain the agenda for the evening. Soon after, the lead architect from the city's planning department kicked off the meeting. The air was already thick and stuffy, but I breathed easier listening to him describe where Tommy's Field would fit into the park and the many reasons behind its thoughtful design. We had come a long way since he first communicated that my vision for Tommy's Field was impossible, and I felt deep admiration as I watched him try to appease the bureaucracy for which he worked while simultaneously trying to accommodate the needs of our community.

When he finished his presentation, I walked to the front of the room and pressed my black chunky-heeled ankle boots firmly into the ground so I wouldn't tip. They were the same boots Tommy wore when he dressed up as Taylor Swift for Halloween a few years back, and every time I took a step in them, I could feel him strutting around our neighborhood, flipping his blond wig away from his face and roaring with laughter as dads fist-bumped him and girls screamed, "Tommy? Are you Taylor Swift? No way!" The boots grounded me. They gave me strength. And they injected me with Tommy Mark courage.

Surrounded by real-world people on all sides, I spoke less of our tragedy and more of all the love behind Tommy's Field, which filled the room and radiated through me as if I were a skinny antenna receiving and transmitting vibrations. As my heart spoke out loud, my head privately questioned: *Why am I the mother standing up here in front of everyone? Of all the children in the world, why did this have to happen to my child?*

"*Why not your child?*" a spontaneous response shot back at me. "*Would you prefer this happen to someone else's child?*"

It should not happen to any child, my mind reasoned. *But if someone must die, why don't you take someone who prays for death?*

"*Remember, this is part of a plan. Don't judge the plan. Trust it,*" the voice gently reminded me.

When my internal debate ended, I centered myself and made my closing statement: "Tommy's Field is a gift of love to our community, and we thank all of you for your support."

A warm applause followed that was less about what I said and more about the fact that I was up there saying it at all. Fully exposed and nearly crippled by all the love I was transmitting and receiving, I pressed my palms together underneath my chin, nodded, and gave a short bow of thanks to express the gratitude that would have surely broken my fragile voice.

On cue, the park advisory board president, aka my team's designated center back, proceeded to take over the meeting and give a PowerPoint presentation that showed two decades' worth of Google Maps aerial photos of the existing field. It wasn't every day that the park's board meetings attracted such a large audience, and our center back was pumped. Slide after slide, he showed computerized images

of a large brown patch across the entire center of the field that progressively browned and widened depending on the severity of drought
conditions each year. The images from the air looked as awful as the
one I had taken on the ground a year earlier after my meeting with
LAFC and the LA Galaxy. Flanked by board members on both sides of
him, my center back revealed the master plan design for the park that
his board had approved back in 2013, a year before the first incarnation of Tommy's Field was even an idea. Tommy's Field, he announced
to everyone, fit in perfectly with the park's long-term plans.

Clearly in favor of Tommy's Field, he then opened the meeting for
general public comments. This was the moment we had all been waiting for. While I counted approximately a hundred supporters in the
room, I had asked less than a third of them to fill out a white public
comment form that was required to speak. I figured a hundred people
speaking was overkill, especially since these types of public meetings
rarely drew in more than a handful of community members and we
were not expecting much opposition.

As names were called one by one, designated supporters stood
up to make specific points as to why Tommy's Field was important.
The dots in my mind held their positions and moved exactly the way
I predicted they would.

That was until our team got blindsided and the game turned.
A kind-looking blond woman in black-rimmed rectangular glasses
stood up with two elementary school–aged children by her side and
said that she and her family vehemently opposed Tommy's Field.
Her kids didn't play sports, she said in a soft-spoken voice, and her
son felt Tommy's Field would affect his ability to launch water rockets. Her daughter was concerned that the field would disrupt her
picnics. Cheers of rowdy support erupted, indicating that there was
more opposition in the room than I had realized. Surely, I thought,
this woman and her friends simply missed the part of the planning

department's presentation that showed how much natural open space would remain in the park for other one-off activities, like picnicking and launching water rockets.

When the blond woman sat back down, I noticed five other brunettes about her age seated across her row. One of them with distrusting eyes and thin lips glared at Donovan after he gave his own public comment of support and told him he was spoiled. I gave this particular woman the benefit of the doubt and assumed she hadn't heard the part about how a year earlier he had lost his big brother, his best friend, his idol.

One after another, public comments against Tommy's Field were fired at my center back and city officials. They were mean and hostile and the rancor seemed unusually misplaced, given the circumstances. I could feel our supporters fuming in their seats and staring at me in disbelief, but for some reason I still can't explain, all the negativity bounced off me as if my black boots gave me superpowers and I had worn some kind of invisible armor. Christopher's magic was already working.

Sitting next to the door on a hard, cold, aluminum bench, I proceeded to study the neighbors and analyze their arguments as if I were on the sidelines watching one of Tommy's games. We were the stronger team. More polished. More technically skilled. More representative of the entire community. But they were louder. Angrier. And grittier.

One older woman stood up and said that she was a retired elementary school teacher. I assumed she of all people would support creating more safe public spaces where kids could be active. Instead, she exclaimed, "This is a park, not a recreation center!" I smiled to myself, making a conscious effort not to look at close friends who were undoubtedly rolling their eyes. I figured she was like so many others in our own neighborhood who hadn't noticed the wooden signage at both park entrances that clearly read, "Westwood Recreation Center."

Another woman with shaggy dark hair and a manic voice ignored the park's sleepy history and spoke so loudly that her opinion screamed at every one of my nerves. "This is our park! It's our backyard! Many of us live in the apartments right across the street from the park and we don't need more soccer, more whistles, and more noise!" I empathized with what it must feel like to have a public park all to herself and to not want to improve it for the benefit of the entire community it was built to serve. If city rules governing public meetings would have allowed me or the city's head of planning to respond to public comments, one of us would have told her that the open space being considered for Tommy's Field was in the middle of the park, separated from her apartment by two street lanes, nearly 150,000 square feet of green open space, two outdoor basketball courts, and what would be six regulation-size tennis courts.

Building on the opposition's remarkable momentum, a young athletic-looking father, standing next to his two toddlers and wearing a baseball cap, stunned me when he said he loved the field the way it was. "It's beautiful," he said. "Don't replace beautiful grass with plastic synthetic turf." I appreciated his argument, to a point. We had all just seen slides showing the true nature of the dirt field over the previous two decades but in the four months prior to this public meeting, California had received historic levels of rainfall that eliminated more than a decade's worth of severe drought conditions. It was hard to believe that in between the time we started fundraising for Tommy's Field and this first public meeting, a historically wet winter and early spring had turned the field green for the first time anyone could remember and Google Maps could record. During the same period, the city had also fenced off the field, seeded it, and kept the public off it for three months. It was as if the park director at the time, who I would later see huddled with the opposition after the meeting, knew that Tommy's

Field was coming and took very specific measures to prevent its development. Either that, or communication within the park system itself was so poor that one department was spending money to maintain a field that another department was on the verge of tearing up.

It didn't matter, I told myself. We were all well aware that in between the freshly grown bright-green blades of grass, gopher holes and thick, sticky mud awaited those who dared to walk across the center of it. This sporty-looking father who wanted the field to remain the way it was must not have heard both the planning department architect and the park advisory board president say that grass athletic fields were too difficult for the city to maintain and not in alignment with the city's water conservation policies. I sat there wishing I could tell that man that my family would have fully supported Tommy's Field being made of natural turf, but the city could not promise to maintain it, much less water it, and no less than twenty years of history confirmed that it wouldn't.

Sitting on the edge of the bench, just as Tommy used to do watching his older brother's games, I listened to a few dozen passionate public comments against Tommy's Field that echoed in my head like a hundred. Dono sat on the other side of the room eavesdropping on the row of angry brunettes, while Doug planted himself in the middle of the opposition where the fighter in him could catch a closer glimpse of our unexpected enemy. Supporters sat in their chairs, jaws open and eyes tuned in to the reality-television show unfolding in front of them. *If only I had prepared them better*, I thought. Our team came ready to speak to the many reasons why we wanted Tommy's Field, but had not anticipated the need to rebut arguments against it. *If only someone had prepared me better!* I commiserated with myself. Had I known this could happen, I would have asked every supporter in the room to fill out speaker cards and outnumber the opposition with their voices, not just their presence.

The public comment period lasted over an hour, and I was surprised to hear only one older man complain about the loss of two tennis courts. It was the most obvious objection, and the one I truly understood and had expected to hear the most.

Toward the end of the evening when my antenna had almost fully tuned out, a heavyset, balding, white man in a baggy navy-blue suit said, "Why didn't the community hear about this project until now? We should have been told about it when the concept was first proposed so we could provide our input earlier. The process has been flawed." I didn't understand. Who was he? Who did he mean by "we"? Was my family supposed to be thinking of people we didn't know when Tommy passed away and we first developed the concept of Tommy's Field? And, by the way, since when did living next to a park entitle neighbors to consider it theirs and dictate not only how the city designs it, but how the rest of the community wants to use it?

This rather articulate man, who appeared to speak with some authority, said his name was Stan. Stan and his blue suit then announced with sweat pouring down his forehead, that a local neighborhood council in Westwood, with a name I had never heard, was having its regular monthly Wednesday meeting the following evening and that Tommy's Field had been added to the agenda. Blue-Suit Stan invited everyone in the room to attend and discuss the matter further.

When I walked out of the room, dots started flashing. This was all one big miscommunication, I told myself. I would talk to the neighbors, just as Tommy and his teammates were trained to talk to each other on the field during practices and games. I would mend relations. Clarify intentions. Fix the problem, just as I had handled scores of human relations issues throughout my career. It couldn't be that hard. We were all adults, after all. And this was a gift, not a competition. Our community was one team.

As I approached the exit door of the recreation center, I heard someone shout my name. "Nikki!"

I turned and saw a couple of friends walking toward me. They huddled close and one said, "You have to hear what these people just said to us on our way out of the meeting room." Not waiting for my reaction, she told me that two older men she didn't know walked out next to her and one asked which side of the issue she was on. When she said she was a supporter, he said, "It's all those other people that play soccer and they'll be coming here all the time if a field is built. All those Hispanics. We don't need that here." My friend, a fellow soccer mom who managed Dono's soccer team of children consisting of multiple races and backgrounds, then said to me, "I can't believe there are people who think like that in this community." The dots froze. We were just beginning to scratch the surface of what was really going on.

If only that man knew of the history of the land that he was standing on. If he did, he would have known that all those "others" who play soccer and who he and his buddies didn't want in Westwood actually had rights to the land first.

To recover from the evening, I took a scalding-hot bath with generous scoops of pink sea salt and multiple squeezes of organic honey to wash away any negativity that may have invaded my body that evening and tried to settle in. I lit a candle at the edge of the tub and as it flickered, I repeated a dozen sentences that healer Christopher recommended I say. *I am divine love. . . . I am divine light. . . . I am divine truth. . . .* I didn't know if I was any of those things, but focusing on those words kept other thoughts from the evening from further depressing my spirit and making me feel sick.

The next day, I spent another four hours with Christopher and told him all about the public meeting the night before.

"Christopher, there was nothing the neighbors could say to rattle me. Nothing they said penetrated me. I sat there feeling confident about who I was, what I was there to do, and how I was there to serve our community with Tommy's Field. I was surprised and still don't understand my reaction."

"That's right," Christopher nodded. "Because when you start to take stress and distortion out of the body and focus on yourself from the inside out, you operate from love-based states of awareness, like compassion, thoughtfulness, and honesty." My antenna was incapable of tuning in to their frequency.

After my appointment, I drove straight to a breathwork class before stopping home, changing clothes, and driving down the street to the neighborhood council meeting that Blue-Suit Stan had invited us all to attend the evening before. The city's head of planning had emailed me earlier in the day to say that he was unable to attend the meeting on such short notice, so I decided to show up solo for my team.

When I walked into the meeting room located on the bottom floor of a senior citizen center just two blocks from my home, I recognized at least a dozen park neighbors from the night before. I was outnumbered at least twelve to one. *It's fine*, I told myself. I had gotten used to feeling different in every real-world room that I entered.

Without another thought, I sat down in the first empty chair I saw, which happened to be next to a short, thin, older woman with sharp blue eyes and frosted pink lipstick. I named her Pink Lips in my mind and remembered that she was one of the brunettes who had stated the evening before that she vehemently opposed Tommy's Field because she hated synthetic turf. Fair enough. But it was hard to believe that she preferred hard brown dirt with holes and would rather see the field sit empty for another decade rather than have kids, maybe even her grandkids, playing on it. After I sat down next to her, she promptly moved away and made it very clear that I was the bad guy in the room.

I filled out a white public comment sheet and when my name was called, I stood up in front of the governing "board" to present the same story I had told the night before. My son passed away. Our community suggested we build this field to honor him. The community raised the money in very public ways. It won't just be for soccer. It will be for all sports. It will replace an unusable field that has been hard dirt with holes for too many decades. It will have a low fence, no lock, and be open to everyone. It is a gift from our community to our community. I had my spiel down. And the more I said it, the more I felt my suffering begin to separate from my words and my emotions begin to detach.

When I finished my speech, an elderly female board member sitting two chairs right from center combed her fingers through her short, blondish-white hair and leaned back in her seat with her arms folded. As if she were the head honcho of the board, she asked, "Why didn't you bring the project to us before?"

"I didn't know you existed," I responded. "I was a busy working mom before this tragedy hit my family. We have not been active in Westwood politics before."

She stared at me skeptically.

I looked straight into her challenging real-world eyes and added, "This project has never been a secret. We've received thousands of donations and have held several large, public fundraising events. There was nothing to talk about or formally present to anyone until we raised the necessary funding. After we did, the field was designed, and gift terms were agreed upon. The details were finalized just two weeks before this community process began." I still wasn't sure why *they* were considered the community and we weren't, but my ego was the least of my concerns and was more than willing to appease hers.

The president of the council, who appeared to be about my age and sat in the very center of the long row of tables in front of me, then asked questions about my relationship with the city. She flipped her straight bangs, leaned her body forward with her elbows on the table and asked, "When did your discussions with the city start?"

"In 2013 or 2014," I said, struggling to remember the exact year. "I had an idea to build a field for the community," I explained. "It got designed over the next few years and went through a conceptual approval process, but it wasn't until Tommy passed away that our community resurrected the idea and a fundraising strategy was implemented."

An older woman on the board whose short, black hair contrasted with her pale skin asked her fellow board members to explain the layout of the park. She said she couldn't remember it and based on some of her questions, clearly hadn't been in it for many years, if ever. The Head Honcho described the park to her and after a very public exchange, the look in this woman's eyes told me she had no idea what the park looked like or where Tommy's Field would fit into it. Still, she said in a way that sounded rehearsed, "I don't like this plan at all. I'm against it."

The Head Honcho leaned back, crossed her arms, and stared back at me, smelling victory. "It's not your fault," she said. "The city should have guided you better."

Ms. President chimed in with an obligatory, "That's right. We are very sorry for your loss. But . . ."

You don't sound very sorry, I thought to myself.

"The city is trying to steamroll us again," she complained. "This is not how the process should work." They started talking among themselves about how many times the city had ignored them, how sneaky the city was and how long the Head Honcho had been trying to get the city to install new bathrooms at a different park in the neighborhood that she preferred to frequent. They spoke among themselves as if they had forgotten that they were in a public meeting with the rest of us watching and listening. Tommy's Field had become all about them.

Suddenly I heard Tommy talking to me in my mind. We were always talking. Silently, during yoga. Out loud in my car on my way to and from meditation classes. Of course, in my green journal every night before I went to sleep. But when more than one conversation broke out among the board members, the majority of whom were older white females, and I had to sit down to steady myself, an orange angry-face emoji dropped into my mind and I could feel Tommy's presence. He was a big fan of emojis. Everyone in his phone contacts had been given one next to their name. Immediate family members got two hearts. Best friends got one. Teammates got soccer balls. And everyone else was given a personal emoji that represented either a joke between them, a skill or interest for which they were known, or, in the case of those with whom he had beef at the time, an orange angry-face emoji. When the emoji came through in the middle of this meeting, I had to laugh. Tommy was not a fan of these people.

Ms. President gained control of her board and then called on one of the few male board members who was sitting toward the end raising his hand. "I grew up playing football," he said. "You guys don't know what it's like to play sports on a hard dirt surface like the one at this park. It's terrible for the knees and joints, not to mention the lungs when a kid breathes it in. We should be saying thank-you to this woman before she takes this gift to another city. We are the only city in the entire country who would be fighting about a gift like this."

I heard Tommy joke, *"I like this guy."* I started to crack a smile until I saw the president shake her head in disappointment and tell this man that he had spoken out of turn and to "shut up." I later learned that the man wasn't just a board member. He was also her husband. The reality show was getting so good that even I was on the edge of my seat.

Out of nowhere, Blue-Suit Stan came up behind me and whispered in my right ear, "I hope we can work together, Nikki." Something told me he was some sort of ringleader for the opposition and was offering to "work together" for a price. Every hair on my body stood up and waved red flags. Still, I returned home believing everything was fixable. The city couldn't possibly listen to people who didn't base their opinions on fact, but even if they were known to do so in the past, I would find a way to become allies before we ever got to that point.

The very next day, Blue-Suit Stan called me. He told me that he was president of another neighborhood council in Westwood, a second one that had a name that sounded almost exactly like the first one. I couldn't comprehend how one neighborhood not larger than five square miles could have multiple community councils without two second-generation Angelenos knowing about either of them. I was starting to think they were neighborhood secrets for a reason.

I did some homework on Blue-Suit Stan during our call and did not like what I saw. According to local press, he was the man being partially blamed for the demise of Westwood. He was the individual who made operating a business so difficult in Westwood Village that he ran many of the most cherished ones out of town. He was also one of the main activists accused of filing more time-sucking and money-wasting legal appeals against the City of Los Angeles in an effort to prevent development and stall change. To make matters worse, according to my hurried online research, his partner in crime was none other than the Head Honcho. Regardless of his reputation, however, I decided at that moment that I would speak to Stan because, first and foremost, he was willing to speak to me.

Stan spent the first hour of our call telling me about his credentials. He went to UCLA law school. He had been involved in local politics for decades. He was a Westwood guy; he knew the history of Westwood better than anyone; and he told me about nearly every development he had ever supported or fought against. He didn't understand that I wasn't a real-world person who cared about such details. When I felt grief tickle my throat, and realized that he could go on for another hour talking about himself, I cut him off as politely as I could and allowed my gut to speak, "The neighbors' concerns aren't really about Tommy's Field, are they?"

He agreed and took at least another hour to explain why. "You are right. There is a lot of history between this particular neighborhood council and the City of Los Angeles, and Tommy's Field is getting caught up in it."

"Well," I said, "I can't fix old problems. It may seem like city officials have been sneaky about Tommy's Field, but they haven't. City government is just big and disjointed and doesn't know how to communicate internally or externally very well." I didn't have to explain my business experience to him, he made it clear that he already knew everything about me down to my home address and the name of Donovan's school.

Then Blue-Suit Stan grilled me with questions. "How did you raise your money? How much did each organization give? Who exactly are you speaking to at the city? What exactly have they promised you?" The questions went on and on until red flags started waving again and I froze. *"Stop,"* a voice that sounded like my own told me. So, I did.

After nearly three hours on the phone, I told Stan that if Westwood Recreation Center continued to be overly contentious, I might ask the city to reconsider another park for Tommy's Field. The comment nearly sent him into anaphylactic shock. I heard spit hit the phone as his words traveled through it: "I don't give a shit about other parks, Nikki! I care about Westwood. And I want to see Tommy's Field in Westwood's Park." I got off the phone completely confused as to who Blue-Suit Stan was, what his credentials were, and whose side he was on.

CHAPTER 12

As I waited for the next public meeting to be scheduled by the Department of Recreation and Parks, I maintained my sanity by practicing my own game. That's what I used to challenge Tommy to do when a match didn't go his way. "What did he learn? How could he improve?"

I asked myself those same questions and added, "Why couldn't my Westwood neighbors hear me? And, if they could, why weren't they listening?"

"This is not just about them," a message dropped in, holding me accountable.

As I got curious and searched for answers, my body insisted that I prioritize my own well-being. I now had favorite yoga and meditation classes that were fixed daily appointments, and, in between, I opened my laptop for no less than four hours a day to document every detail of Tommy's life and our journey together, ensuring that I'd never forget a thing. By the time Doug and Dono walked through the front door in the late afternoons, I was ready to be the best version of a wife and mother that I could be.

To sustain my energy between healer appointments, I started reviewing recordings and notes from prior healing sessions. I found that this process helped reveal new insights and connections that I hadn't processed when I experienced the sessions live. My yoga instructor, Joan, was the one who suggested early on that the practice of astrology could be very powerful for me. When I told her that

I had never read a horoscope that panned out, she smiled like the wise teacher she was and said the astrology she was talking about was rooted in ancient science and operated on a much deeper level than what I might have come across in newspapers and magazines. Since the discipline had stood the test of time with many cultures outside of the Anglo-Saxon tradition, I decided it was worth investigating. American doctors had not ascertained what had happened to Tommy; perhaps the stars could. Plus, I trusted Joan.

"Tommy was highly activated under the twenty-third frequency the week he departed," the astrologer Joan recommended told me. As he explained why this number was important, I reflected on how much the number twenty-three had been represented in Tommy's life. He had worn it on multiple team jerseys. Inserted it into his email address. Even created a brand slogan around it that he posted in his locker at school. "TM23, it's not a game, issa lifestyle," he wrote on a white piece of paper with an emerald-green, velvet-tipped pen. Maybe it was a coincidence that the number twenty-three was represented in such a substantial way both in his life and his astrological charts, but I no longer believed in coincidences.

"In April 2018, your chart went into a roller coaster," this astrologer proceeded to tell me as his thick foreign accent suggested that he spoke multiple languages and had both studied and practiced his art across multiple continents. "This only happens once every eighty-four years, which is why most people don't experience this. It had to do with your family."

That's when I told him what happened to Tommy that very April.

When this astrologer asked me how my son died, I said that we didn't really know.

"Tommy had a structural issue with his heart called a myocardial bridge," a top pediatric cardiologist had recently explained to Doug and me after a well-respected researcher at UCLA received Tommy's heart from the coroner's department and studied it. "This means instead of a coronary artery lying on top of his heart muscle, a portion of it was buried underneath heart fibers and then came back up through the heart muscle to the surface again." The cardiologist told us that most people don't even know when they have the condition and, if they do, it's rarely fatal. "What is rare," the cardiologist said, "is for a child who is strong and healthy to go to sleep and not wake up because of it. Normally, if a myocardial bridge were to constrict oxygen it would do so during physical activity. There would be signs. Dizziness. Maybe even fainting." He proceeded to construct different scenarios that may have accounted for Tommy's sudden death until Doug interjected and asked, "Do you believe anything you are saying?"

The cardiologist responded, "Not really. In my thirty years of practice, I have never seen anything like this." Then he added, "Even if you had brought Tommy to me instead of his pediatrician that Friday before he played his last game in San Diego, I never would have ordered an angiogram, which is the only way we would have ever known he had this condition. It's too invasive. And too painful for a child who had no signs of needing one."

Then I revealed to this astrologer a part of the conversation Tommy and I had driving down to San Diego:

"We were having a really soulful conversation during our drive, like one we had never had before. Out of nowhere Tommy blurted out, 'It must be hard for a parent to lose a child.' My head whipped around and I said, 'It's unthinkable! Awful! The most horrible thing ever! That is not going to happen here. I go first and then I'll be your angel, that's how it works. We have to come up with a specific sign I can give when I visit so that you know it's me watching over you.'"

"'How about a Grateful Dead song?' Tommy joked with me.

"'That'll be your dad's sign to you,' I said with an exasperated sigh. 'I've already spent way too many years tortured by your dad's

Grateful Dead music. Maybe we can think of some kind of animal, like a butterfly or a specific bird, or even something having to do with soccer, but it has to be distinctive, so you know it's me.'

"'Anyway, T,' I added with a smile, 'we have time.'"

"You ended up giving him the signs, but in reverse," the astrologer assured me. "Now your son will give you those signs." *He already has*, I wanted to tell him, remembering the night the remote control to our audio system turned on by itself at midnight. When a bright blue light suddenly illuminated our entire bedroom and woke me up, I thought I had finally died. Realizing that I was still alive and that my entire room had just turned a bright white blue, I sat up and traced the light's origins to Doug's nightstand where the remote control was shining up at the ceiling. I grabbed it, looked down at its digital screen and nearly fell over when I saw a Grateful Dead song playing. Doug was out of town. No one had used the audio system or touched the remote all day. "Thank you for my sign, T," I said, looking around the room for him. I grabbed my green journal and wrote down every detail before the entire memory had a chance to fade away like a wishful dream.

After my astrological chart reading, I was ready to make a choice. I could choose to believe that the amount of pain I endured was the equivalent of how much I loved my son, and then I could curl up with my pain like an addiction and slowly die with it for the rest of my life. Or I could rise up through my pain, honor Tommy by how I lived, and express my love in a way that served others and potentially honored myself in the process. My commitment to building Tommy's Field had already led me in the latter direction, but for the first time my mind embraced it as a conscious choice.

Whatever was left of my ego told me to keep my alternative healing experiences private, between me and my green journal. Eventually, however, I divulged some of my astrology reading highlights to Doug. In response, he humored me with words of mild interest and support, while his eyes told me what I already suspected . . . he was worried about my mental health. A few days later he confirmed my suspicions when he told me that an old "friend" of his had told him that "Astrology is for psychos." This friend, an accomplished businessman whose arrogance often made my former self feel inadequate, said I was "losing my mind. There's absolutely zero science or truth behind astrology. People who believe in it are mindless and stupid." On the one hand, he was right. I was definitely mindless. On the other hand, I had never felt smarter in my life.

I can only imagine what this friend might have said had I told him about the flickers of light that swirled in my peripheral vision when I wrote in my green journal at night. And what he would have thought had he known about the wisps of air that sometimes brushed across my cheek and tickled my arm like a feather. Or how hard he would have laughed if I had told him about the voice that shouted, *"Mom"* in my ear while I was napping or the one that shouted, *"Nikki!"* in the middle of the night, prompting me to wake up and write down my dreams. But I didn't dare tell any real-world people about any of these experiences because I was no longer one of them and could no longer be impacted by what they thought. My body told me everything I needed to know, and every time it felt the sting of real-world opinions, it warned me to quickly brush them off.

If my mind had been operating on all cylinders at the time, I might have asked Doug to challenge his friend to explain why my weekly healer appointments that tended to the wounds of my heart were less credible than his regular weekly therapy sessions that attempted to fix the persistent wounds in his head. I may have even had the guts to inquire as to whether the drugs this friend used to dull emotional pain throughout his lifetime, prescribed or otherwise, were any smarter and wiser than the astrologers I had seen when it came to addressing heartache. But I didn't have the voice or cognition at the time to think, much less say, any of that. I only had my instincts, which told me that the design of my soul was unique and the opinions of rational real-world minds couldn't fix my problems. Healing had to begin in my heart. My heart's needs were simple. It craved the company of those who spoke the ancient language of the soul and encouraged me to reimagine my life without charging me by the quarter hour or stopping my sessions at precisely the second a clock told them to.

Like the many projects I had brought to fruition in my career, the trajectory of Tommy's Field was becoming more difficult than I ever could have imagined. Sad but hopeful, I sat down with a blank piece of paper and drew a tree trunk using a green velvet–tipped pen that Tommy used to create his TM23 brand slogan. Then I drew a large branch on the right side of the tree for the book I would write. At the very top of the tree, I wrote, TM23 Foundation, the public charity already set up to grow Tommy's legacy and serve our community. On the left side of my tree, I drew a large branch for Tommy's Field and smaller branches for future fields and all the diverse programming they would offer. Then I drew arrows showing that 100 percent of net revenue from all book sales on the right side of my tree would be donated to the TM23 Foundation at the top and be used to fund the growth of the left side of my tree. Day by day, my tree would grow.

The tree took me about a minute to draw. *There*, I said to myself as I stared at the future of my life. *Tommy, this is our plan moving forward. What do you think?* I felt him buzzing with excitement and encouragement. Then, as if he had something to say about it, I wrote in the top right corner in all caps, THINK BIG. ACT BIG. DREAM BIG. Then my inner critic raised her hand and asked, *"What makes you think you can do all this?"* My stomach dropped, and my mind began to buckle until I remembered a woman who visited me with Tommy in my dreams one night. She was wearing a sparkling white dress, had a serene smile on her face and gracefully moved the air between us with her hands. *"Every day we are dying,"* this woman with cropped blond hair told me without moving her lips. *"Tommy is teaching you how to live."*

I had studied this woman so closely in my dream that it was easy to recognize her when later that same day I was cleaning out old boxes in the garage and stumbled upon an old photograph of Doug's parents on their wedding day. His mother was dressed in the same sparkling white gown. Her blond hair was cut the exact same way. Her face was the youthful version of the grandmother I had once known.

I already died once in this lifetime, I told my inner critic, who feared failure and rarely left my side. *I will die again one day, that is all I know for sure. Until then, I have no choice but to live a meaningful life that serves others and helps me find some joy and peace. Tommy showed me how, and I will not disappoint him. We have a plan, and I will uphold my end of it until the day we meet again and design a new one.*

CHAPTER 13

WHEN THE COMMUNITY PROCESS FOR TOMMY'S FIELD FIRST BEGAN, I had the impression that a maximum of three public meetings would be required before Tommy's Field was pushed forward for an official vote. I never questioned who scheduled the meetings, who ran them, or how they were organized. I never even asked who would ultimately be voting to approve Tommy's Field. *Why should I?* remnants of the businesswoman from my first incarnation asked herself. Our council member wanted it. The head of Recreation and Parks wanted it. And the president of the park's advisory board had a master plan that supported it. Who else mattered?

It was only after I had attended a third nasty public meeting in less than two weeks and ended up further away from our goal than when we started, that it finally sank in that when it came to conducting business with the City of Los Angeles, *everyone* else mattered. I had ignorantly assumed that the city operated like a niche start-up—nimble, quick, and decisive. Our opponents knew otherwise and mobilized like an existing public enterprise, taking full advantage of my negligence.

Stalled by the initial backlash but feeling surprisingly confident, I stepped back to check myself. Was Westwood Recreation Center still the right location for Tommy's Field? Google Earth images said that it was. So did my memory. But some park neighbors were so vehemently against it that I questioned my instincts and considered whether all the resistance was a sign that Tommy's legacy was meant to be somewhere else.

In need of some divine guidance, I called Pamela, the medium, for a second reading. I thought she and I would pick up right where my first reading had left off after Tommy's funeral. When Pamela said hello and began describing how she worked, however, it became clear that she did not remember me. I politely reminded her that I had spoken to her once before and she diligently explained that she had very little memory of prior readings. Like every genuine medium with whom I would eventually speak, Pamela said she gave thousands of readings and served only to receive and give messages, not retain them. Her messages were like many of my dreams. If I did not write them down, the details would disintegrate as if they had never existed.

When our call began, I panicked. Maybe Pamela's first reading was pure luck. Maybe I was so desperate to speak to Tommy that I was willing to believe anyone who said they could. Before I got lost in a tedious cycle of maybes, a voice of reason stepped in. This was the perfect moment to test whether or not I had been intentionally seeking information to create my desired outcome or if it was possible that the laws of energy, which I had so brilliantly memorized in high school but had failed to analyze anytime since, might apply to the human spirit.

I contemplated the first law of energy and examined its premise—that energy cannot be created or destroyed; it can only change forms. If that was true, I reflected, maybe Tommy's spirit really did still exist and people like Pamela did have a talent to speak to him. After all, our world is full of people with exceptional talents. *Some people build rockets that land on the moon*, my mind pointed out. *Others talk to spirits*, my heart declared. Both talents were equally incomprehensible to me and, therefore, just as possible. As my imagination pushed me from the inside and reality tugged on me from the outside, I debated within myself until Pamela finished her introductory meditation and began my session. "Did you lose a son?"

"Yes," I said.

After she accurately described him, disclosed the ancestors he was with, and gave me specific details regarding how and why he left, I knew we were back in business.

"Your son wants to talk about you today," Pamela said. "Is that okay?"

My heart skipped a beat. I was yearning for direction.

"Are you writing?" she asked.

"Yes," I responded. I just was not entirely sure what.

"He says you are on the right track and will have to listen internally and really believe in yourself. *'Don't let anything hold you back, Mom.'*"

"Why is he showing me grass and seeds?" Pamela suddenly changed focus.

"We are building an athletic field in his honor," I responded. "It's becoming difficult."

"He says if you get stuck, imagine you got hired to bring this idea to fruition and then you'll get it done. Be the producer of it. This applies to your writing, too, by the way."

Whether this message originated from her or Tommy, the advice was illuminating. If I did not have the confidence to believe in my own start-up, I could default to what I had mastered in my first incarnation, apply it to my second and approach Tommy's Field as if I had been hired to manifest its vision for someone else. Because I had practically convinced myself that Tommy's spirit was communicating with me, it was not much more of a stretch to imagine that I had a boss tracking and guiding me from above.

Pamela's second reading reminded me to approach Tommy's Field like a job. The minute I did, a familiar door leading back to my old self magically opened and welcomed me home. As I walked through it, I remembered that, at my core, I was a worker, one of the hardest I knew, and that my work ethic had rarely failed to cover for my deficiencies. My work ethic taught me discipline. It stretched my will. And, like a drug, it made me high.

Just prior to the *fourth* scheduled community meeting for Tommy's Field, I paused to consider my next move. While I felt inspired to build Tommy's legacy from above, my goal was to create meaningful change below, and I had yet to find a way to bridge the two. *I have to start thinking like a real-world person*, I told myself. *I need to convince real-world minds that Tommy's Field is not only meaningful to this neighborhood, but that it is also important to the future of our city.* That's when my head started tingling and a familiar voice dropped in while I was driving across town. It suggested, *"Collect data."*

This particular voice was not mine, or Tommy's. I became increasingly able to distinguish between the voices in my head and had become well-acquainted with this one. Its messages resembled thoughts, but they were clearer, sterner, and, frankly, wiser. The voice used simple words, no more than a few in a row and it presented them when I least expected to hear them, like when I was on a neighborhood walk, in the middle of yoga, or driving. This voice was the one that drove with me and Tommy to San Diego and fed me one-liners. It was the one that guided me the day Tommy departed and encouraged me to surrender. It was also the one that spoke to me a couple of months after Tommy passed away and whispered, *"Do art."*

When I first heard this voice instruct me to *"Do art,"* I was driving and thought it was a silly idea. A few weeks later, however, I heard the same voice yell at me, *"Do art!"* The voice was no longer asking for my opinion. I stopped my car. Researched the closest art school on my phone and scheduled my first art lesson the very next day.

"An oil painting is created in layers," the instructor informed me. "After the first layer of paint is applied, it will need time to dry. You can return next week to add a second layer, adjusting colors, adding details, and continuing to shape your painting until, many weeks and layers from now, it is where you want it. Paintings are rarely completed in a day." The top of my head started tingling and time stopped.

"This is how to write a book," the *"Do art"* voice dropped in.

I got the message. The book I would write would have many drafts, and, layer by layer, my story would take shape. Just like me. *"Do art"* did not mean that I should become a painter. It meant, *"Do art"* and the process would help me find my way.

By the time this voice suggested that I *"collect data,"* I trusted it implicitly. The mandate came in fast, purposefully, and entirely out of left field, which helped differentiate it from the other thoughts fighting for space in my head. I drove to Westwood Recreation Center, planted my blue canopy soccer chair under a young oak tree, and opened my laptop to a rudimentary excel spreadsheet that I quickly designed to document my research. I essentially created an outdoor virtual office where, for hours at a time, I sat and monitored how and when the open space was used relative to the rest of the park. My spreadsheet documented every detail, and when I got bored, which was nearly every minute of the day, I read books, took calls, walked around the park and even made quick visits home before returning at the top of every hour when I figured large groups of visitors were more likely to arrive for scheduled activities. It wasn't a perfect science, but it was good enough, I told myself, aware that my inner critic felt differently.

Recognizing that real-world people would question the validity of my research, I snapped pictures and recorded videos of every data point and texted them to myself so the dates and times of each observation were saved in multiple locations and could not be manipulated. From thick, slippery mud and round pools of water to toe-tripping gopher holes and nubby little roots that burrowed themselves under the field and popped back up like innocent ingrown hairs, I documented it all.

I spent the rest of my time scouring the park for neighbors and eagerly awaiting all the picnics, kite flying, rocket launching, and other free-play activities that the neighbors were insisting Tommy's Field would displace. As weeks rolled by, however, I never saw any of them. The only activity I saw was the one they did not want. Soccer.

When I first bumped into the young Hispanic coach whose team arrived in the late afternoon, he planted himself and all his gear under a tree next to mine. He reminded me that we knew each other from back in the day when I was president of Tommy's youth soccer club down the street at the VA, and he promptly gave his condolences. After we reminisced about Tommy, which I was learning was the most effective way for me to connect with real-world people before opening myself up to other real-world topics, I asked why he was holding practices at Westwood Recreation Center. He said he was coaching for a soccer club based thirty minutes away but that his teams were practicing at this park because the field we were standing on was literally the only available area on LA's Westside that he could find.

He inquired about our progress on Tommy's Field and, after I gave him an update on our struggle, he revealed that he, like Tommy, had grown up at the park.

"I've never seen green grass on this field before now," he said.

"I know," I said shrugging my shoulders. "Neither have I. The record rainfall this year has been great for our city, but it is not helping us get Tommy's Field approved."

"The field is still terrible. I spray white paint around the gopher holes so my players don't turn their ankles in them."

Our discussion confirmed what Tommy's Field opponents were trying to make me forget, that the existing field was a liability waiting to happen.

Then he told me something I had not considered and believed real-world decision-makers needed to hear. The open space wasn't exactly as "open" as the neighbors thought. "I got a permit for my teams to use the entire field on weekday late afternoons. We tried to get access to the smaller artificial turf field over there, but it's impossible. It's always full."

So, while the neighbors were insisting that the park did not need more soccer and that it would increase noise, make parking problematic, and prevent individual community members from having access to the space, what they didn't seem to understand was that more soccer and the "others" who played it had already arrived.

After sundown, when the soccer teams cleared out, I watched the field sit dark. Around it, the tennis courts remained open and lit for business while the outdoor basketball courts and small synthetic soccer field bustled with activity under bright white lights until the park closed. *If I were this piece of land*, I reflected, *I'd be sad watching all this activity going on around me. No wonder this field has looked depressed for so many decades. It must be painful sitting here every day not serving its purpose and watching the rest of the park thrive.*

Weekend activity on the field was even less eventful and more disturbing. Except for a one-off surprise event like a men's flag football game at the northern end or a toddler soccer clinic in the southern corner, the field sat empty for multiple hours at a time with no more than a lone leashless dog or a sleepy homeless person nestled on top of it. Even squirrels and birds appeared to ignore the field and spent the majority of their time in and under the trees that surrounded it.

"Where are all the neighbors?" I asked one particular squirrel who started visiting me every day.

Curious, I drove to Cheviot Park, a few miles southeast of Westwood, and then to another park a few miles west to gauge the level of activity on those fields at the same hour. I was not at all surprised to see kids frolicking across them playing multiple sports while Westwood Recreation Center's controversial piece of barren land remained hidden, desolate, and utterly forgotten.

One morning, I walked across the field and found myself heading straight into Pink Lips, the skinny neighbor with the frosted pink lipstick. Her small white chihuahua walked beside her in a pink canvas coat and thin black collar, which was free of any leash. Pink Lips looked at me and said, "Aren't you are the mom who wants to build the soccer field here?"

"Yes, I am," I responded with a tone of kindness that felt undeserved but was actually genuine. "I'm Nikki. And it's a multipurpose field, not just a soccer field."

"You don't really want to replace this beautiful green grass with plastic, do you?" she asked in a far less strident tone than she displayed in public meetings.

"It's not beautiful grass," I clarified. "Besides, this field has had grass on it for about a minute—we all know that. And it has been sitting empty and unusable for decades. We want to see children playing on it."

"But why not build a soccer field and keep it natural grass?"

"I would love for the multipurpose field to be made of natural grass, but the city has made it clear to all of us that it doesn't have the financial resources or manpower to maintain a natural-grass field this size and we have seen enough proof to know it doesn't."

"What if you put all the money you would be using for the plastic turf and instead gave it to the city to properly maintain the field?" she asked, which was a legitimate question.

"It would be money wasted. Given our history of drought and the city's stringent water-conservation policies, the field won't get the water it needs. Even if it did, grass field can't accommodate high usage. Also, fertilizers and all the chemicals that go into maintaining grass fields these days aren't exactly great for the environment." It was hard to believe that the two of us had both walked out of the same three public meetings and were still having this debate.

Unmoved by my explanations, she startled me by asking, "How did your son pass away?"

Many real-world people who heard our story, whether they knew us or not, seemed increasingly uncomfortable talking about our loss because they either did not know what to say, did not want to upset us, or were too fearful to relate. It was a rare breed who understood that talking about Tommy, sharing stories, and offering words of support were essential ways to help our family heal and move forward.

"One night he went to sleep a happy, healthy child and the next morning he just didn't wake up," I responded, my lips quivering and all-too-familiar tears escaping the outer corners of my eyes before the last word had a chance to leave my mouth. I still could not believe my own story.

"I am a mother. I can't imagine your loss. I am so sorry." Her tears mirrored mine and then she squeezed my arm.

"Thank you," I said, no longer interested in the cost-benefit analysis between synthetic and natural turf.

She proceeded to explain that she lived in a condo across from the park and, like me, she was a mother, but her two children were older and out of the house. When she asked about my background, we discovered that we had some mutual relationships in common and proceeded to talk about them for the next thirty minutes while we stood on top of the contentious open space, forgetting about what divided us and bonding over what united us.

I glanced at the sparkling leash hanging out of her purse, looked down at her chihuahua and asked why she did not take her dog to the brand-new dog park at the east end of the park, where dogs were allowed to run off leash.

"I don't like the dog park," she said, scrunching her face. "I prefer this area."

I imagined how thrilled Ginger would be to have an adult-sized athletic field all to herself, too.

By the time Pink Lips and I parted ways with a hug, her frosted pink lipstick was more subtle and was arguably a nice complement to her sharp blue eyes. And while she was skinny, I was skinnier and had no business judging her weight, given how frail I had become.

I walked back to my blue chair feeling indescribably lighter. Several weeks of park data had not made me feel the way this particular human interaction had. It didn't matter if Pink Lips continued to oppose Tommy's Field. What I had just learned mattered more to me—that we could express our opinions without escalating them into a personal feud about who was right and who was wrong. I still wish that the mother in Pink Lips had identified more strongly with the mother in me, but her loyalty to her immediate neighbors and her overriding discomfort with change were too strong for any one of my rational arguments to overcome.

Just when it seemed like my research project was paying off dividends that I hadn't anticipated, I walked around the park and noticed a flyer taped to the tennis court fence closest to the field. I leaned in to read it.

"WHAT ARE WE UNITING AGAINST?" it asked.

"The City of Los Angeles and privatized youth soccer interests," it falsely responded.

"WHO IS BEHIND THIS SECRET PROJECT?" it continued.

"The Executive Director of LAFC," it incorrectly answered.

"WHO DOES THIS SERVE?" it questioned.

"Lucrative private clubs including LAFC and its youth academy," it posited. The idea that LAFC, which had a full training facility in East Los Angeles forty minutes away, was planning to use Tommy's Field for its own needs was ludicrous.

"HOW WILL THIS IMPACT YOU?" the sign went on.

"You will lose the last precious open space not only in the park but in the entire district . . . and . . . it will be a private fenced space in a public park to be used by private interest groups," it lied.

When I was done reading, I looked up at the block of seventies-style apartment buildings and condominiums that lined the east end of the park and wound their way around the south end of the park. I calculated that no less than hundreds of residents lived in each one. Standing there, it dawned on me that while my team had multiple thousands of donors and supporters spread across the city, the opposition pretended to represent as many or more living in a single-block radius of the park. Their proximity to each other and the park already made their collective energy appear much bigger, louder, and more threatening than it really was, and I sensed that our council member, who preferred to stay behind the scenes, would eventually be swayed by all of their noise. My stomach began to ache.

I whipped back around toward the field and saw the man who had posted this nonsense. It was the same one whose photo I had taken earlier in the week as backup for one of my data points. I scrolled through the pictures on my phone and found the one that showed him standing on top of the field dressed in a white shirt and black shorts and talking to three other Tommy's Field protestors, including Pink Lips, while each of their respective dogs wandered around the field off leash. Now I stood there watching this man hold a stack of flyers in his left hand while he handed one out to an innocent park visitor with his right. Anger slammed my system. Pure rage. The kind I rarely let myself feel in my first incarnation and had yet to race through my veins in this one. Triggered by this man, my anger challenged me to rip down his flyer, confront him at that moment, and ask how he could be so dishonest. So heartless. So cruel. But anger was not my specialty and given the fragility of my mental and emotional state, I did not want to risk melting down in public and damaging the credibility of Tommy's Field forever. Dots formed in front of me, but I was in too much distress to address them. So, I snapped another photo, this time of the flyer, and drove home to figure out how to play the game on my own terms.

When I walked through our front door less than two miles and five minutes later, I showed the flyer on my phone to Doug. He was sitting on the couch with his tablet in his hands and one-upped me by flashing an online petition that already had one thousand signatures opposing Tommy's Field.

"What the fuck?" I asked.

Without a word Doug responded by showing me a website that protestors of Tommy's Field had launched. When I looked at it closely, I saw that the same information from the flyer had been copied and pasted to the site.

My stomach fell. "Are you kidding me?"

"I'm not done yet," Doug said, pulling up an online site which marketed itself as, "A place where communities come together." He proceeded to read a slew of nasty comments posted about Tommy's Field and revealed who had written each one.

"How do they know how to do all this?" I asked.

Blue-Suit Stan and the Head Honcho had to be behind them, we agreed. Given how many times that duo had sued the city, they were the ones most likely to know how to work the system and launch an effective public relations campaign so quickly.

Without another word, Doug typed a response online that called out each one of their lies:

> My name is Doug Mark, father of Tommy Mark, whose legacy will be honored with Tommy's Field and whose mother is Nikki Mark. At our visit to Westwood Park today, I noticed your flyer, which contained a few significant misrepresentations, which I believe are an intentional effort to deceive the public in your efforts to prevent the development of our gift of a large, beautiful turf field to replace the unused, mud and dirt space that has been the "field" for thirty years.
>
> The falsehoods are as follows:
>
> 1. You claim my wife Nikki is the Executive Director of the LAFC Academy. Although she was for three years, her tenure ended in 2017. Tommy died in 2018 and we commenced fundraising in mid-2018. So your claim is untrue.
> 2. In relation to the above, you claim that the field will serve "lucrative private clubs." Nikki and I are the largest contributors and this is a public gift, funded by this community. You have zero basis to claim that LAFC is involved in any training or private use of this field. They are not. It is a public gift.
> 3. Your flyer claims this will be a "caged" and "fee-based field," even though you know that is false. You know from the last meeting that the "fence" will be four feet high (to keep out dogs and to prevent balls from leaving the area) and there is no locked gate.
> 4. Your flyer claims that the field will be a "soccer field," when you know it is a multipurpose play area.

5. Your flyer claims "no meaningful time for local children to use this space," even though you know that claim is 100 percent false. You know from the last meeting that there will be substantial free playtime for local youth. Yet you persist.

You are afraid to conduct a legitimate debate, with legitimate opposing reasons, namely that the neighbors don't want this unused, unplayable space of thirty years to finally see substantial activity. You must immediately remove all flyers you have posted, with the lies constituting a substantial portion, and replace them (if you'd like) with truthful arguments.

I am copying our council member's office on this email because if a substantial opposition arises because of your patently false claims, I would like the council office to be aware of it.

Sincerely,
Doug Mark

The park neighbor with the manic voice who shouted that the park was "their park" and "their backyard" in the very first public meeting, lashed back out at him with her impulsive fingertips:

"Women don't fret," she wrote. "Doug Mark lies, lies, and keeps on lying as there is no compelling reason for a second field in the park. Worse, he's a cyber bully. He'll threaten to tell the councilman on you, so beware. No buddy-buddy connection there! (The councilman needs to disclose how much money he's been given from the soccer elite.) Mark has conned the city to believe this park is a disaster when it's used daily by citizens, hundreds of them, all ages, for many purposes from all over the city. He has no evidence, so he lies."

These were not just park neighbors we were up against, Doug explained to me. They were NIMBYs.

"What's that mean?" I asked.

"A NIMBY is an acronym for "not in my backyard." It's a movement by people across our country who fight local development in their neighborhoods and make change difficult. It doesn't matter if they are renters or property owners. They believe they have a right to dictate what happens to and on the land next or near to where they live."

The neighbors proceeded to attack Doug online like a swarm of bees, and then turned around and charged at our supporters, our neighborhood, our tax bracket, and our purpose.

"This process has not been fair to us!" they repeatedly charged, accusing city officials of being negligent and suggesting that my family had been given special privileges.

But no matter what tactics they pulled or how loudly they shouted, I sadly realized that they would never be the underdogs in this game.

We were the underdogs.

The more closely I examined their selection of words, the intonation of their voices, and the subtleties of their body language, the more I understood what these neighbors never would. No matter how hard they tried to manipulate the situation and no matter how much I wished it were not true, my family was the underdog in this game, and every nightmare, every chest pain, and every wave of grief that brought me to my knees would never let me forget it.

Doug and I were dumbfounded. It was the same dozen neighbors, the Dynamic Dozen, as I started privately calling them, who rallied field opponents living in the apartments next to the park and convinced dozens of them to attend public hearings and write letters of opposition to our council member.

Doug and I stared at each other in disbelief and wondered, "How are we getting outplayed by a dozen core park neighbors?" Doug was a successful lawyer. I had an MBA. We were businesspeople. Respected community members. And we were supported by the entire Westside soccer community. And still, the Dynamic Dozen was kicking our ass.

CHAPTER 14

Desperate for direction and a sliver of hope, I scheduled my third medium reading with Pamela.

"Why do I keep hearing, 'Don't give up'?'" she asked. "Your son is telling his little brother to believe in himself and 'not to give up.' He keeps saying, 'Don't let him quit. He can't give up!'" Her choice of words was alarming and seemed beyond mere intuition.

"His little brother wants to quit everything, including soccer," I said.

"Don't let him quit. Don't let him give up soccer," Pamela said emphatically. "He can't stop playing because it reminds him of his brother. That's all the more reason to play. It honors him."

"Your son says he's the big brother and knows what's good for his little brother. He's playing the big brother card and does not want you to let his little brother be average. He keeps saying, 'Do not let him quit.'"

I downloaded that message and applied it to my entire life. Maybe I would quit on myself, but I would never quit on Tommy or Donovan.

Doug wouldn't, either. He immediately engaged with neighbors online and pushed back on every one of their nasty accusations. At the same time, I outlined a community engagement strategy and began implementing it by asking Ethan to create our own online petition and disseminate it throughout the community. He was the most technically savvy member of our family and could do in minutes what would take me hours. Plus, I wanted to give Ethan a reason to get out of bed. To make him an active member of our team. To help him step outside of his own tortured head and find some relief by engaging with us and our community. So, I gave him one.

"We need to get ten thousand signatures, Ethan, or else we shouldn't do this at all," I implored, knowing the petition would backfire if we didn't show overwhelming strength in numbers.

While Ethan wrestled with Tommy's death in ways I did not understand, like watching *South Park* reruns all night and sleeping all day, rising up to help build his brother's legacy was one thing we could get behind together.

Tommy's Field had become a full-time job, and, just when I thought things couldn't get any more dramatic within a single twenty-four-hour period, a reporter from KTLA-TV called. She actually called our council member, but his office directed her to me and suggested she may want to hear both sides of the story. Despite the short notice, I agreed to meet her at the park that afternoon.

I arrived a few minutes early and from my outdoor virtual office I watched her interview the Dynamic Dozen, who had clearly pulled a favor and were hoping for a smear piece. I did not mind. By that point, I knew every one of their arguments, and was fully prepared to respond to each of them.

When the blond reporter asked her first question, I was ready for it. I knew why she was there and that the best outcome I could hope for was that she heard the truth, saw through their tactics, and produced a balanced piece.

The camera started rolling and I gave her my spiel. When I finished, I noticed that her bright blue eyes looked watery. *Even she can feel my pain*, I thought, reminded that reporters were also human beings.

"The neighbors say Tommy's Field will be a fortress or a stadium and the community will never be able to use it," she said, swallowing her emotions and challenging me exactly as I expected she would.

"Well, I don't know why they would say that," I responded, before providing her with specific details about the low fence and open community hours.

"Oh," she said, sounding surprised, "They don't know that."

"Yes, they do," I responded with unwavering confidence filling my voice. "I have attended every public meeting that they've attended. They just aren't listening."

"The field does look beautiful, why would you want to replace it with synthetic turf?" she asked.

I looked down at the pointy heels on her feet and then responded, "Because if you don't just stare at it but walk across it you will see how dangerous it really is." I proceeded to show her the photo of the field that I had taken a year earlier when Doug and I first met with the two MLS teams. Never did it cross my mind when I took that photo that I would need it to convince anyone, much less my own neighbors down the street, that Tommy's Field was a far better alternative than the crispy dead one that we had all been standing on at the time.

"I took this photo less than a year ago to remind myself of how meaningful this gift will be for the community." Then I urged her to look at the last twenty-plus years of Google Maps images. "This city has had an unusual season of historic rainfall. The field has never looked this green before and it likely never will again."

"So why are they so upset?" she asked.

"We don't know why," I answered. "Our intentions are to improve our community and honor our son. That is all."

When the interview ended five minutes later, the reporter shut off her microphone, told her cameraman they were done, and said to me, "What is this? Some kind of 'not in my backyard' issue?"

"Exactly," I said, my tone devoid of attitude. These neighbors had seen our supporters and recognized that Tommy was part of a larger community that included soccer players and coaches who looked to them like a team of "outsiders." They did not want these people in "their park."

"Some of the neighbors you interviewed say they like the idea of Tommy's Field but just not in 'their park,'" I added. "They want us to take it to 'another park.'"

She rolled her eyes and said, "I report the news based on facts, I am not going to make up a story to support NIMBY arguments or any kind of arguments that aren't based in reality or on fact."

She ran her news story later that evening and I was pleased to see that the opposition did not get the boost for which they had been hoping. While the piece was fairly balanced and included many of the points I had made, it did not move the needle one way or another. Given how poorly things were going for my team, it practically felt like a win.

On the morning of the fourth public meeting, I woke up feeling restless. A frenetic energy was dancing through me and was making me uncomfortable. I called Tina to address it.

"How does a large bureaucratic organization like the city work?"

It was such a loaded question that I knew I had to break it down.

"I mean, I have only ever worked for start-up organizations. Each one had a visionary at the top and every layer of the organization existed to serve a specific mission. If everyone at the top wants Tommy's Field, isn't that all that matters?"

Tina gave a hopeless sigh before cutting to the chase. "Los Angeles operates from the bottom up, not the top down. Council members in this city are accountable to those who elect them," she added. "Each of Los Angeles' fifteen council members run their districts differently and have their own unique styles and quirks."

From what I gathered, the council member in our particular district had a reputation of being an honest and decent man who usually followed through on what he said he would. Yet, when it came to Tommy's Field, he preferred to stay behind the scenes and let residents hash matters out until it was absolutely necessary for him to publicly voice his support for one side or the other.

Maybe it was the complicated history of Westwood Village that prompted his low profile. After all, the posh college town and once-popular tourist destination that lived up to its intended name of Hollywood of the West, had crashed. No longer were its charming narrow streets packed. No longer did the Village offer the hottest movie premieres, restaurants, and late-night entertainment that had made the Village feel like spring break every weekend. That party ended one random evening in 1988 when gangs encroached on the neighborhood and fatally shot a twenty-seven-year-old innocent bystander. Although security was beefed up and the Village resurrected itself for the next couple of years, riots broke out across Los Angeles in 1991 after a Black motorist, Rodney King, was brutally beaten by four white police officers. Racial tension escalated across the city, and a week later, angry youth shut out of a Westwood movie premiere vandalized cars and looted stores. Westwood Village never recovered. Government officials, local activists, and community members spent the next three decades arguing over various stopgap solutions that inevitably failed to make the Village what it once was.

What no one understood was that when the soul of a person or a place is decimated at its core, neither can simply be repaired and made to function the way they once did. They must be rebuilt. Renewed. Re-created. Just like I had to be. And just like the Los Angeles Police Department and City of Los Angeles have been trying to do ever since.

Dono articulated this point to me only months after Tommy left. "I don't know who I am, Mom," he said, staring at himself in his bedroom mirror. "I died the day Tommy died. Friends want me to be the same kid I was before, but that kid died when Tommy died. I don't know who I am, but I'll never be that person again. It's impossible."

That's what happened to Westwood. It died. So, while the Head Honcho and other local community leaders tried to protect and retain what made Westwood Village special back in its day, the aftermath of their various solutions was brutal. Residents stopped visiting, cherished businesses permanently shut down, and tourists went elsewhere.

By the time Tommy's Field entered the drama thirty years later, college students looking for places to play and affluent neighbors searching for appealing dining and shopping options were butting heads with old-school community leaders, much like the Head Honcho. These territorial leaders were still reacting to old wounds by banning certain activities, like dancing, and keeping the Village empty and insulated, just like the open space at Westwood Recreation Center where we wanted to build Tommy's Field.

After Tina and I discussed Los Angeles politics, she dropped an unexpected bombshell. The president of the park's advisory board, my chosen center back, had been temporarily taken out of the game and was not allowed to lead the next public meeting to be held by the city. Park neighbors had slammed our council member and the GM of Recreation and Parks with letters and calls, accusing him of having a conflict of interest, being dishonest, and ramming through the proposal for Tommy's Field in a way that avoided a proper community process. The neighbors attacked him personally and professionally, even publicly threatening a lawsuit against him. Although their complaints were unaccompanied by proof and they were entirely baseless, city officials avoided the battle by benching him for this next meeting and appointing its head of planning to lead it instead.

"Bring lots of supporters," Tina advised in a tone that was less than reassuring. "The meeting has been moved to the large indoor gymnasium in the park's recreation center to accommodate the hundreds of park neighbors who are expected to show up."

Unlike the very first public meeting, also held in the recreation center, attendance had tripled in size for this fourth meeting, and the atmosphere was much louder and more frenetic. The city's head of planning did a solid job presenting the design and addressing questions raised in the three prior public meetings, but he did not know how to play the game the way our center back did and he lacked the strength to control the opposition. I'm not sure why anyone expected him to. He was a thoughtful and gentle landscape architect and civil engineer, who designed city parks and neighborhoods. He was not a moderator and did not look thrilled playing the role of one.

After he spoke to the design of Tommy's Field and was berated by nasty comments, I was given yet another opportunity to present my spiel. I peered out at nearly two hundred supporters who represented local soccer, football, and lacrosse teams, as well as parents, coaches, friends, and local business owners, and did my thing before a sea of black TM knit beanies cheering me on. When I glanced over at the hundred or so anti–Tommy's Field protestors that the Dynamic Dozen had convinced to join them on the other side of the room, I saw their arms crossed, eyes glaring, and handmade signs threatening. Ignoring their scowls, I pointed to the photograph of the field that I had taken a year earlier and had blown up to poster size specifically for this meeting. My hope was that if they didn't believe in computerized Google Earth images, they might find truth in an old-fashioned photograph taken with multiple witnesses by my side. Instead, when I referenced the photograph an older man in the front row shouted at me. Not knowing what he said, I stopped mid-sentence, stared at him, and blurted out the only word that came to mind: "Really?"

Before I could contemplate my reaction, my eyes were drawn to the back of the room where a man and a woman in their thirties traded off holding their baby and heckling me as they aggressively chewed on candy that I had left in a bowl for our supporters. The tone of the meeting was set, and the evening progressively worsened from that point.

Fortunately, this time, my team was prepared, and we came with multiple responses to every one of their now-repetitive arguments.

Toward the end of the meeting, the opposition was left with only one legitimate rallying cry around which they could all unite: "Save our open space!" In response, Tommy's friends approached the microphone and expressed in their own words what they knew their friend would want them to say, "Don't let this land continue to sit dark and empty. We want to play."

Throughout the evening, there were boos, hisses, and cynical laughter from both sides, and the chaotic energy in the room made me sway. When I glanced periodically at our moderator, my heart ached, watching him endure personal attacks on his integrity, his design skills, and his inability to control the meeting. The neighbors were turning our gift of love into an endowment of hate and there was nothing I could do about it except change the frequency of my thoughts and tune them out.

After Dono stood up and voiced his own words of public support, a twenty-something-year-old woman, with excellent vibrant purple hair and pretty tattoos that Tommy would have admired, glared at Dono and flipped him off. With Tommy's friends backing him up like sturdy bookends, Dono released a nugget of his own anger and told her to "fuck off." That was the moment his voice started changing.

When his edges sharpened. When his respect for boundaries vanished. Even though it felt like our team had won the match that night, it was clear that our entire community had hit a new low.

More than two-and-a-half hours of public comments later, the meeting ended, and, without any resolution or feedback from city officials, the room emptied. I glanced at the exit and watched our supporters shuffle out with their heads down and shoulders slumped. The Dynamic Dozen and their unscrupulous tactics were running circles around us and masterfully controlling the game.

Doug looked at me from across the gym and the anger in his eyes lashed out at me, *"Why didn't you get out in front of these people earlier before we started holding community meetings?"*

My eyes shot back, *"You should have done it yourself if you were such an expert on all this. I thought our thousands of donors were the community!"*

In that moment we both knew I was no longer the same woman he had married fifteen years earlier. My ego no longer had an interest in competing against lost tempers, flexed egos, and pointed fingers. My heart no longer had the will to crush another's even if that other's was trying to crush mine. I was dying and awakening at the very same time, layer by layer. So, when I looked at Doug from across the room and reacted to his accusatory stare, my eyes screamed back, *"You are either working with me or get off my team."*

Startled by the distorted expression in my eyes, Doug grabbed my hand. He knew I was falling, which was unfathomable since fate had already completely flattened me in one fell swoop to the bottom of human existence. What he didn't know, however, was something I had failed to recognize myself. I hadn't fallen in years. Maybe decades. In fact, unlike Tommy, who begged to train with a skills coach at five years old and reported after his first lesson, "That coach taught me how to fall, Mom. Now I'll never be scared. I want to learn more from him," I never learned how to properly fall or what to do when I did.

Fortunately for Tommy, his dad was an expert at falling. There were the bottoms he hit early in life when he turned to alcohol and drugs to numb his childhood resentments. The hard landings that resulted from his precipitously falling grades in high school and the day he was labeled a certifiable underachiever. The low point he reached the day his first marriage unraveled, and he became a single dad with a toddler named Ethan. Each new bottom eventually led him to sobriety and ultimately reshaped his lenses to the point where he found an Ingalls-type girl like me. By the time both of his parents had passed away, Doug understood loss and pain during multiple stages of life and had persevered through the depths of bottoms that often destroy lives. That was partly what attracted me to him. What I admired about him. Why I married him. Anyone who knew how to fall and get back up was someone I wanted on my team.

But the day Tommy left made all of Doug's former struggles seem like minor speed bumps on a country road. The pain of losing him was bottomless, and I could hear it in his cries. Although Doug had touched multiple bottoms in his first fifty-nine years of life, the pain of all of them combined did not come close to how he felt losing Tommy. The fighter in Doug was far too experienced to get out-played, but the strains of grief were worsening for both of us and watching me free-fall was pushing him to yet another edge.

Having fallen too far for Doug or any rational mind to save me, I woke up the morning after that brutal fourth public meeting and did yoga with Joan. She could feel my emotions lingering from the evening before.

"Address the anger, Nikki. When your energy spikes down because of anger, Tommy's spirit can feel it."

"Okay," I said, rationalizing that if I could feel Tommy, it made just as much sense that he could feel me.

"Remember, there is a reason you and Tommy are mother and son and having this experience," Joan reminded me in between poses. "It is not just about mother and son in this lifetime. It's also about the relationship you had together in your last lifetime, too."

That's what I told Tommy on the way to San Diego.

During that Friday afternoon drive, I looked over at him and said, "You know T, I know we were meant to be together. And I believe you chose me as your mom because I keep you grounded and teach you some of the character traits you need to successfully manage your gifts and talents."

"You balance me," Tommy responded, looking over at me with genuine gratitude.

"And I believe in you," I responded, staring directly through his eyes.

As Tommy went on to explain why he chose me as his mom, divine instructions began pouring into me. *Stare at his face and burn every detail into your memory. You're never going to want to forget what he looks like at this age or how much love you feel for him at this very moment.* I looked over at him, studied his profile, and then turned my attention back to the road.

I did not understand what was happening to me. I had never had these kinds of thoughts before and figured . . . *I must be feeling sentimental because he's becoming a teenager.*

When I shared this experience with Joan, she tried to lift my spirits. "Tommy may be out of his body, but his soul is who he still is. He is around you, Nikki, and has this supercharged energy. Make it work for you. Use it for your betterment and the things that you want to manifest."

I swallowed Joan's advice like sacred medicine, and my body, mind, and spirit all reacted at once. I was done. Done falling. Done wallowing in my circumstances. Falling hurt like hell, but if Tommy could learn how to do it well during his short lifetime, then so could I in my long one. I had fallen harder and faster than my human mind could comprehend, but I wasn't helping myself or my team by looking down like a victim. *"Look up!"* my bossy inner voice shouted as if it were one of Tommy's coaches screaming from the sidelines. *"You're in the middle of a game! Get back into position, find your center, and keep pushing forward!"*

CHAPTER 15

NOT KNOWING HOW TO GET TOMMY'S FIELD BACK ON TRACK BUT
trusting that there was a way, I was relieved, but not surprised, when
a friend informed me that Westwood had yet another neighborhood
advisory council in town. A brand-new one. A third group that had
recently been formed to represent UCLA students, Westwood Village business owners, and certain residential districts surrounding
the campus. The name of this new council sounded awfully similar
to the name of the other two councils in Westwood, but its board
was full of a diverse group of community members who were fed
up with seeing the students and residents of Westwood bullied by
Blue-Suit Stan, the Head Honcho, and their respective old-school
councils. If anyone doubted the shit show that Westwood had
become, all they had to hear was that the neighborhood had three
local neighborhood councils, along with three surrounding homeowners' associations, all pushing and pulling on Westwood as if it
had no center.

"Nikki," my friend said hopefully, "Tommy's Field may just be
the issue that finally brings Westwood's problems to the surface and
unites this community around positive change."

While the idea was too much for me to digest, something told
me that it was not too much for Tommy Mark.

I promptly emailed the president of Westwood's newest neighborhood council and asked if I could present Tommy's Field to his
board at their next regularly scheduled meeting. When he agreed to

add Tommy's Field to the next agenda, I looked up and whispered to my Boss a sincere *"Thank you."* We were not out of options yet.

With two weeks to prepare for my presentation, I continued to pursue a resolution. I reached out to a young father whom I noticed had attended every public hearing wearing khakis, a button-down shirt, and fashionable eyewear. When he used his sixty-second public comment period to recommend that both sides come together to find a solution, I asked for his contact information and scheduled a meeting with him the following week in the park.

Sitting at a picnic table located between bustling basketball courts and the empty field, I strained to hear this soft-spoken man tell me he was married, had two young children, and worked as a civil engineer in a building located catty-corner from the park. He said he had lived in Westwood for three years, or maybe it was five, and was quick to acknowledge that the open field had been "rubbish" ever since he arrived in town. In fact, where we wanted to build Tommy's Field, he said, was the area of the park he intentionally jogged around the fastest after work because it was "dark" and "sketchy." Appreciating his honesty, I fed him my spiel and added some personal details in hopes that he would feel the genuine nature of our gift in every one of my words.

Then I got curious and asked if he could help me understand the root of the neighbors' opposition. He offered that the problem for his family and many of his fellow neighbors was the fence. The park had a number of fences. There was a fence around the dog park. Multiple high fences around the tennis courts. And a fifteen-foot fence around the smaller soccer field to the south. No matter how low and unlocked the fence would be around Tommy's Field, it was still another fence. To him, fences represented divisions between people.

Seeing his point and eager to compromise, I asked, "What if we don't have a fence at all?"

"That would be very interesting," he said.

"But if the neighbors don't respect the NO DOGS OFF LEASH signs," I warned, "we will have to put a low fence up at that time."

"That sounds very reasonable," he replied, cautioning that the solution may not appease all of the neighbors but that it would at the very least appease him and his thin brunette wife whom Doug and I referred to as Slim. When we parted, Slim's husband was no longer just an unreasonable opponent of Tommy's Field. He was also a normal man who loved his family, was dedicated to his career, and cared about his local park. It was hard to believe that we weren't on the same team, and I grew hopeful that after our conversation we could be.

On the evening of this fifth public meeting hosted by the new advisory council, however, I was reminded of how dangerous *normal* can be. Sitting next to Doug and surrounded by a healthy number of loyal supporters, I listened as the city's head of planning presented an updated design of Tommy's Field. Not only was it now fenceless, but bleachers that the Dynamic Dozen believed made the field look like a stadium had been removed. In addition, the head of planning announced preliminary after-school and weekend "open play" hours for the field, which I believed would put to rest any notion that the field would be privatized.

Bursting with optimism, I waited for my new friend and his wife, Slim, to turn around and give me some sort of signal. A smile, maybe. Or perhaps a whisper of "Thank you." Maybe even a discreet thumbs-up. Instead, they looked at each other, scowled, and lined themselves up with the rest of the Dynamic Dozen to voice new public objections. It was as if he and I had never spoken. As if no design change or concession on our behalf would ever make a difference.

One by one the Dynamic Dozen, along with approximately twenty other park neighbors they had recruited for the evening, stood up and argued against Tommy's Field. It did not matter what the field looked like or how it served. They simply did not want it.

It finally sank in that there was no effort I could make to address neighbor concerns and build consensus. They were parking all of their players in front of my team's goal to ensure that no matter how creative we got, no matter what moves we made, and no matter how collaboratively we worked, we would not get through their defense and reach our goal.

After board members listened to formal presentations both for and against Tommy's Field, our council member strolled in to officially ordain the new council. Had he chosen to stay and listen to the next ninety minutes of public arguments for and against Tommy's Field, he might have prevented the moment when one of my best friends was physically bumped out of the public comment line by the brunette who had called Dono spoiled in the first public meeting. Had he stayed, these two women might not have erupted and openly challenged each other in the middle of the room. Had he stayed, my blond feisty friend who was a lawyer dedicated to social justice and free speech might not have called the brunette out for pushing her and the brunette wouldn't have innocently shrugged her shoulders and practically winked when she said she didn't. But our council member did not stay. Instead, he walked to the front of the room, interrupted our discussion, had his picture taken, said a few congratulatory words to the new council, and walked out. If he could have run, I'm sure he would have. After five public meetings, Tommy's Field was a giant mess, and it was clear that our council member was not in the mood for messy.

I did not blame him. From what I had already seen and heard from others in the community, the NIMBYs in Westwood and the community activists supporting them, like Blue-Suit Stan and the Head Honcho, were not only out to block change, but to destroy people and their reputations. Since our council member had one of the largest districts in the city and over 260,000 residents to appease, I sympathized that it was likely better for all the residents he served if he diligently put out hundreds of smaller fires before expending all of his time, resources, and energy on one massive one like Westwood Village, which comprised nearly fifty-five acres and was only burning itself.

After our council member left, over an hour of public comments ensued until the new neighborhood council's president, looking exhausted, apologetically announced that the council had to move on to other agenda topics and table our discussion for another time. By that point, it was after 10:00 p.m. Not only had I survived the real world for three straight hours, but I was no longer thinking about Tommy's Field. My butt was sore. My throat was dry. And the start-up girl in me was mesmerized by Blue-Suit Stan. I couldn't take my eyes off him. I marveled at the way he worked the room. The way he knew everyone by name and made sure everyone knew him. The way he paced back and forth across the back aisle of the room, periodically finding a seat among Tommy's Field opponents and whispering in their ears before jumping up like a mad scientist and pacing back and forth some more. I gaped at the way he interrupted the council on multiple agenda items to show off his knowledge of useless city codes and procedures, and made sure everyone in the room knew what he knew, even though no one cared to know any of it. Blue-Suit Stan had made himself the star of the show.

I had two days to recover from that meeting and prepare for the Head Honcho's next regularly scheduled council meeting, our *sixth* public meeting in less than five weeks. For Tommy, recovery between games meant rest, fluids, ice, body adjustments, and stretching. For me it meant breathing, writing, and meditating, while simultaneously securing dozens of additional supporters to show up by our side. Fortunately, the more public meetings Tommy's Field supporters attended, the more passionate they became and the more our stamina improved. With Doug and dozens of teammates by my side, including some of Tommy and Dono's close friends, we walked into the boardroom feeling determined but apprehensive.

One hour later, the Head Honcho and the advisory board she served were very self-satisfied when they officially voted against Tommy's Field. The Head Honcho had masterfully staged the entire show. She led a very well-rehearsed motion against Tommy's Field through which she beautifully stammered and pulled off an Academy Award–winning performance. "I motion that our council vote against Tommy's Field unless it is made of natural grass . . . unless it's made of natural grass and has no fence. . . . I mean, unless it's moved to another park. . . . Okay, what I mean is I motion that our council vote against Tommy's Field unless it's made of natural grass AND has no fence OR is moved to another park." When she finally spit out the words that had been so obviously prepared, the women on the board were the first to back her up and enough of a majority to push through her motion. She wasn't technically the president of the council, but she sure acted like she was.

"Forget about it!" a familiar voice shouted at me as I stood up to leave.

I agreed. The fall didn't matter. I saw it coming. It was how I reacted to it that my Boss was tracking.

"Recover!" the voice insisted, just as every single one of Tommy's coaches had.

That's what they shouted when he fell. When he made a mistake. When he lost the ball and the other team scored.

"Recover!"

That's what they demanded when referees made egregious calls. When they forgot the rules. When they missed obvious fouls and failed to count legitimate goals.

"Recover! Recover! Recover!"

Did he cry? Argue? Talk back? Throw in a few sneaky jabs of his own to his opponent when a referee was not looking?

Or did he play his game? Rely on his skills, instead of his sharp tongue? Maybe even exaggerate a flop or two to earn an extra penalty shot for his team?

Every opportunity to recover turned out to be a critical moment to learn who he was, who he could be, and why it mattered.

Like Tommy, I would recover from this neighborhood council's vote because I wanted to. I had to. I was being told to.

As I exited the room, Blue-Suit Stan gave me a nod that said, "Good night." He may have been sweating, but he wasn't gloating. He was just being the faithful disrupter that the Head Honcho had groomed him to be. But he was the only Tommy's Field opponent who said Hello and Goodbye to me before and after each meeting. He was the only one who made a point of regularly acknowledging my family and our circumstances, and who complimented Donovan after every one of his public comments. And he was also the only one to call me in between meetings and attempt to broker solutions, even though he kept me on the phone for multiple hours at a time and failed to require any compromise by the other side.

When I gathered Dono and Tommy's friends to take them home, Dono broke down before we even got to the car. Not only did he think that the council's vote was final, and that Tommy's Field had been officially voted down, but the entire process of building his brother's legacy was breaking him. Dono was losing faith in a world where adults lied, name-called, and showed no compassion for one another. He was losing trust in a world where children went to sleep and did not wake up. I had underestimated the toll that this match was having on him and vowed to better protect him and explain each step of the process moving forward.

As for my team, Doug was fuming. Every falsehood on which these neighborhood council members based their decision violated his moral codes of conduct and insulted every fiber of his legal mind. Close friends were shaking their heads, wishing they could do more.

I did not know why I was incapable of disparaging the opposition and was developing a mild form of compassion for them instead. I did not understand how I left the toxicity of those meetings behind. And I could not articulate why the pressure of the game had not made me fold, considering that I had a growing list of valid reasons to shut down and quit. Maybe it was all so minor compared to our loss. Maybe it was all part of some larger plan, like Tommy's exit.

There's something bigger going on, I convinced myself. That's when Tommy, the trickster, started shaking things up.

What am I supposed to be learning from this? I pondered in my green journal.

Watching both teams argue like modern Jets and Sharks fighting over turf in *West Side Story*, it wasn't long before an answer came to me, *"They feel unheard."*

The neighbors confronted me over and over again in my mind. *"They are challenging you,"* a familiar inner voice said to me.

To do what? I wondered.

As I began to unravel that question and seek the many lessons that Tommy's Field had in store for me, the city went back to the drawing board and I stuck to my personal survival regimen by seeing the next healer on my list.

I arrived at Kelly's home wearing black sweats and a plain white T-shirt and had an overnight bag with a brand-new metallic gold–colored journal in it that I had purchased just for that occasion. I was a note-taker, and this occasion felt worthy of its own notebook.

After Kelly's assistant greeted me, I sat down on large mattress-size cushions that covered her entire living-room floor, and scanned a wall of bookshelves decorated with sparkling healing stones, colorful spiritual artwork, and dozens of lit candles in all shapes and sizes. Although Kelly and I had talked for an hour on the phone prior to my arrival, I didn't understand what she actually did. I didn't care. My mind would not retain the details of it anyway. She came highly recommended by a friend.

Sensing my confusion when she sat down in front of me, Kelly asked me, "Do you know what you are doing here?"

"No," I said, pulling a blanket over my legs and remembering her saying something about using natural, plant-based medicine to help me heal.

"We will do a healing session that involves natural plant medicine. It will open your heart, expand your mind, and make it easier for you to connect with Spirit."

Whose Spirit? My Spirit? Tommy's Spirit?

"Ultimately, you have all the tools to heal yourself," Kelly said. "The medicine will help you receive what you need to heal, and I am here to support and guide you through it."

"Okay," I said, trusting her expertise. I was not a drug person, and this was not a party. Kelly was a shaman who had been initiated into the healing traditions of her family's Peruvian lineage and successfully helped countless patients all over the world overcome depression, PTSD, and grief. While some of her clients worked with a hallucinatory-plant and vine-tea mixture called ayahuasca, which I learned was a ceremonial medicine originally used by indigenous people of the Amazon basin, she recommended that I start with a light dose of hallucinogenic mushrooms called psilocybin. "It can be milder than ayahuasca," she said, "but still very powerful. It has been used in both healing and religious rituals throughout our world for over a thousand years. The ancient Egyptians considered it 'food of the gods.'"

Without a single question or hint of fear, I took her magic mushrooms and for six hours straight, dumped the darkest corners of my loss on her.

"Start at the beginning," Kelly said, as shamanic-type music and ritual-sounding chants gently played in the background.

"The weekend before Tommy passed away," I began, "I drove him to San Diego for a soccer game. We made a weekend out of it and had the only spiritual conversation we had ever had together."

I recounted the entire conversation for her.

Kelly, who vowed to maintain a safe space for me, listened attentively as I shared my story and dumped multiple layers of my grief on her.

As memory poured out of me, time stepped aside and it was just me, my pain, and Kelly.

"In the middle of our conversation," I continued to explain, "my voice cracked, and I got really hot. Deeper thoughts seeped into my mind that sounded too preachy and sentimental to say to a twelve-year-old boy, but they were relentless and kept badgering me. So, I turned to Tommy and said, 'You know, T, you love so many things. You love soccer and basketball . . . football and snowboarding . . . horseback riding and Krav Maga—you even love golf—and you love reading and music . . . history and politics . . . being with your friends and family. It's incredible that you make time for all of these activities and you're passionate about so many of them. I really admire you because most people don't find one thing in their life that they love, and you've found so many and make time for all of them.'

"Tommy looked over at me with gratitude in his warm eyes and said, 'I know. That's so true.'"

Kelly's smile encouraged me to continue.

"I thought to myself at that point, *I wonder if it's sustainable. So many activities squeezed into such a short time.*"

Now Kelly was holding my hand. She was a mother herself, and I was living her worst nightmare. Not only was she speechless, but she no longer looked like Kelly. She had morphed into an old grandma, like a friendly witch. Not mean or ugly, just old, gray, and magical. The medicine was doing its job and encouraged me to purge.

"Kelly, I reviewed my son's entire life with him. I told him how proud I was of him. How much I admired him. And I made sure he knew that whether he became a professional soccer player or not, he was loved. What if I hadn't? As horrible as I feel today, I would feel so much worse had we not had that conversation. I told him everything a mother would ever want their child to know. I'm so grateful for that."

When I paused, Kelly got to work. She grabbed a round decorative pillow off her couch and said, "Nikki, right now you have a wound that is the size of your entire heart. There is no bigger wound that a human being can endure on this earth. Imagine this pillow is your heart. It is one big nasty wound. Your heart and the wound are one and you can't feel anything beyond it. But, in time, eventually, parts of your heart will heal, and your wound will get smaller relative to the rest of the heart muscle around it. One day, the wound will become a scar that lives in your heart and you will carry it with you every single day. The scar will never go away, but a beautiful healthy heart will grow around it and help you live."

I still did not want to live that long but was beginning to accept that I would.

Around midnight, six hours after my private ceremony had begun, Kelly told me to close my eyes, lie back, and take the rest of the evening to connect with myself and receive any messages that Spirit wanted me to receive. The medicine would take care of me, she said, and my gold journal and blue ballpoint pen were by my side to write down any messages I received or thoughts I wanted to remember.

Like the adept listener my first incarnation had taught me to be, I did as she said and found myself sitting up straight when the first message dropped in.

"Mom and Tommy forever. We will be together again. We are together now." A warm energy that felt like Tommy's danced inside me and the message repeated itself a couple of times without making any sound.

"Write it down," another energy advised, as if I had a team of them guiding me that night. I opened my journal, drew a big heart, and wrote inside of it, "Mom and Tommy forever. We will be together again. We are together now." The words were crystal clear. So was the love behind them.

I shut my eyes again, surrendered deeper to the medicine, and walked straight toward my pain. The closer I got to it, the less angry it sounded and the more loving it became. It wanted to help me, and hearing what it had to say was the fastest way to make it go away. I inched forward, weeping.

As I got closer to the center of my pain, the music changed, the room brightened, and a new message was gently delivered.

"This is a gift."

"What?" I asked telepathically, stunned by those words.

"There is a gift in this tragedy for you. I promise."

I grabbed my journal, struggling to believe what I had just heard, and wrote down the incomprehensible. *This is a gift.*

When the medicine started wearing off, Tommy left me with one final message, short and sweet. *"Be who you are, Mom."* That was his motto. Now it was my personal mission.

Following that first session with Kelly, the nature of my dreams began to shift. While Tommy still regularly darted in and out of them wearing his gray practice jersey and black shorts, I spent hours cleaning and purging in my sleep. Dream after dream, I vacuumed, cleaned toilets, and swept floors, as if I were scrubbing my own soul.

I also spent a great portion of my dream time in classrooms. Listening to lectures. Reading digital screens full of information. And presenting myself to the class. My presentations were usually titled, "All about Me," and my story never failed to end the day Tommy left.

Morning after morning, I woke up exhausted, as if I had literally been up studying, learning, and transforming all night long. After several months, my teachers became replaced by warm, clear energies that waved gently in the air and spoke to me telepathically without a sound.

"You are helping the world by living through this experience," one translucent energy advised. *"Around the second-year mark, you will feel a shift."* I woke up hopeful that as my love for Tommy and the rest of my family continued to grow, my suffering would diminish just as this energy assured me it would.

When Father's Day rolled around the weekend following the first official neighborhood council vote against Tommy's Field, Doug asked us to pretend it was just any other regular day. Those were hard enough. No presents, he said. No grand speeches. No celebrations. Father's Day, which had once been so meaningful to our family, was now a day that selfishly ignored men who didn't have children, fathers who had lost children, and children who had lost fathers. Only on Mother's Day did I feel even worse. Still, Ethan and I took Doug out for dinner, while Dono tried to enjoy a week away at summer camp, and we all did our best to enter the real world and pretend that the way it functioned did not hurt.

After nibbling on a meal that I could not even taste, the time came when we would have normally ordered Tommy's favorite course.

Feeling like frayed strands of a shoelace that had lost its glue, we tried to distract ourselves. We glanced over at a family of three whose table had moved closer to ours and was now less than a foot away.

Together we watched the father next to me accept a present from his two grown children. We were such zombies that we did not even try to look inconspicuous. When the man smiled upon receiving his gift, I wondered if material items would ever mean anything to me ever again. Dono once said it best: "The only present I ever want is Tommy on Amazon."

My mind drifted as the man ripped open his present and rolled the wrapping paper into a tight ball. That's when I heard Doug exclaim, "Are you kidding me?"

Startled, I clicked out of my inner world and saw the man flipping a flat square item between his hands. My eyes zoomed in and focused more clearly on the object he was holding. Slowly it registered that he had received a vinyl record. Not just any vinyl record, but an acclaimed rock opera. The first one ever, about a boy with a title track we sang to Tommy when he was a toddler. This record was the one that made him beam with joy because it was titled *TOMMY*. When I saw those five capital letters sprawled large and proud across the top of the album cover, I knew instantly that the gift was not meant for that man at all. It was meant for Doug.

I let out a deep chuckle of air. Doug and Ethan started singing a key song from the album, "Tommy Can You Hear Me?," while memories of Tommy singing it filled the air between all of us:

> Tommy, can you hear me?
> Can you feel me near you?
> Tommy, can you see me?
> Can I help to cheer you?
> Ooh, Tommy . . .

Doug turned pale, like he had seen a ghost.

"Nothing is an accident," I said, smiling back at him, sharing my sacred belief system. Of all the restaurants we could have chosen. Of all the families who could have sat next to us. Of all the gifts this particular father could have received. The moment was orchestrated to perfection.

"This is a sign that Tommy is here in spirit wishing you a Happy Father's Day," I said, sitting back in my chair and feeling the top of my head tingle.

Doug smiled as if to humor me, while I carried on the conversation in my mind:

Yes! Tommy can hear me.

Yes! Tommy can feel me.

Yes! Tommy can even see me.

And yes! I can help to cheer him.

How could I cheer Tommy?

I could recover by having some dessert and enjoying the sweetness of life. I could recover by looking up, seeing the big picture, and playing the way he showed me how: With a smile on my face, enthusiasm in my step and the spirit of competition in my soul.

For the first time all night, I ventured outside of my own miserable mind and genuinely smiled at my husband, who wanted nothing more than to see me and our entire family recover.

"I will always be in recovery," Doug told me, revealing the ancient wisdom of his own soul. "It's like AA. Every day I will think of Tommy and work on my recovery. I will never get over his death, but I will work on recovering from it every single day."

Our water glasses clinked as the three of us further surrendered to our circumstances. Each in our own way. On our own time. And according to the fine print of our own souls.

CHAPTER 16

AFTER THE HEAD HONCHO'S NEIGHBORHOOD COUNCIL VOTED against Tommy's Field, Dono pleaded, "Please can we move?" He didn't want to leave Los Angeles. He didn't even want to leave his neighborhood. He just wanted to leave the only home he had ever known.

Resisting the idea, I told him that moving wouldn't take way our pain. That the loss would follow us wherever we went. That leaving a home full of so many wonderful memories might make us feel even emptier. He said he knew all that but explained, "At least if we move, every room in our house won't remind me every second of the day of something I would normally be doing with Tommy."

It took a two-week trip to Peru for me to get his point. I had planned the trip for Doug and me, knowing that the three-and-a-half week period between the first anniversary of Tommy's passing and what would have been his fourteenth birthday would be excruciatingly difficult for all of us. Peru was for everyone. My soul craved spirituality. Doug's wanted adventure. And Dono's needed time away from us and our broken home and wanted to stay with friends whose families were intact. The trip was also an effort to celebrate our birthdays. My fiftieth and Doug's sixty-first. We could not ignore them forever and if anyone would have wanted us to celebrate, it was Tommy. Plus, a trip to Peru had been near the top of Doug's bucket list for years, and it felt like the right time to cross it off.

For ten days, Doug and I trekked across the Andes mountains. Step after step, my boots sank into Mother Earth until the soles of my feet slowly regained feeling and my lost spirit finally found my body and gently settled back down into parts of it. Meditation had taught me how to breathe. The trek showed me how to walk. Putting one foot in front of the other for over eight hours day, I listened to nothing but the sound of my breath, the stomping of my feet, and the ancient wisdom emanating from the sacred mountains that surrounded me. Day after day, the relentless pressure between my ringing ears eased and at some point along the muddy trail a message dropped in that I conveyed to Doug, "Dono is right. We need to move."

The decision was reinforced the minute we arrived back in Los Angeles. I walked through our front door and was greeted by a cluster of emotions that had been left to fester in our house by themselves for two weeks. They immediately surrounded me, slapped me in the face, and tried to break me down. But my feet were sturdier now, as if they had grown roots in Peru. I held my ground and turned to Doug with tears welling up in my eyes, "We definitely need to move." Tommy's spirit and all of our favorite memories would come with us wherever we went, Peru taught me. The tragic ones were ready to be left behind.

Organizing the mail that had stacked up in our absence, I opened an Amazon package with my name on it. Inside was a book that an American woman in our trek group had encouraged me to order while we were on the trail. She was an author and a teacher, and said the book was full of exercises that tested the ways of the universe and completely changed the way she viewed the world and her place in it. I opened the book a few nights after we returned to Los Angeles, skipped to the first exercise that resonated with me and read it out loud exactly as the book told me to do, modifying a few minor words to sound more like myself.

"Universe, if you are real. I need a gift. And I need this gift delivered to me within forty-eight hours. This gift has to be unique and meaningful so that it can't be misconstrued with any other kind of normal gift or everyday occurrence." To make sure the universe heard me, I repeated the challenge multiple times, in a variety of ways, never modifying the forty-eight-hour deadline specified in the book's instructions. Then, feeling silly, I closed the book and went to sleep.

Thirty-six hours later, having forgotten all about my silly challenge, Doug and I went on an impromptu stroll around our neighborhood. "Let's walk to a house that's for sale up the street," he said on our way out our door. "I drove by it earlier and saw that it's having an open house today."

I agreed and we headed that way.

When we approached the white 1930's colonial house with gray shutters and a bright-red glossy door, I had no expectations. When I walked through the front door, however, I took one look at Doug and knew the house had our name written all over it. The front lawn was ideal for soccer. The second floor had only two bedrooms.

Doug started chitchatting with the seller's agent and I walked away before she got around to asking the one question I was dreading: "Why are you looking for a new home?" Doug broke the news and minutes later, the agent was hugging me, crying, and telling me how sorry she was. She knew all about us. Her husband happened to be a colleague of Doug's and the two of them had already donated to Tommy's Field. Wiping streams of mascara away from her kind eyes while laughing at herself for crying on the job, she said that the original buyer of the house dropped out of escrow the previous week and that since the seller had a one-way ticket to Bulgaria and was departing in a couple of weeks, she was extremely motivated to unload the house quickly.

She and Doug began talking financials, while I ventured into the backyard and tried to envision what life would be like there for a family of three, plus Ginger, and Ethan coming and going. I pondered whether Tommy's spirit would follow us here. Would our lights still flicker? Would our televisions still turn on? Suddenly, I came face-to-face with a severely sun-faded yellow birdhouse that was as tall as I was and looked as old as the house itself. It was wooden, like an old-fashioned Swiss cuckoo clock but had a hole for a nest where the face of the clock should have been. The bird-house transported me back to a dream I had had in Peru. "Nikki," the mother of one of Tommy's friends said to me in this dream. "You must get the birdbox app. Do not forget the word *birdbox*. Okay? Remember, *birdbox*." She repeated the word three times while pointing her finger at me and looking directly into my eyes until her energy woke me up and prompted me to write the word down. *Birdbox*. I could not recall ever learning that precise word before. But a week later, I found myself standing directly in front of one and knew exactly what it meant. *This is my birdbox.* Chills shot through me and confirmed it.

I left it to Doug to determine whether or not purchasing the home made economic sense for our family. In the meantime, I said nothing about the birdbox to him. I was only beginning to experience connections between my dreams and my future, and did not expect him or anyone else to understand what was happening to me when I barely did myself.

The following day, I resumed my daily routine and went to one of my regular meditation classes that incorporated healing crystals and essential oils. I sat on my mat in the far corner of the room, as I always did, and waited for the instructor to begin.

"I have a special announcement before we get started," she said.

The room settled down and I listened.

"I have pure lavender oil from Bulgaria for all of you to try. It's very special and I encourage you all to pass it around and put some on the inside of your wrists to enjoy during class."

Oil from Bulgaria? Really? I practically choked on my own laughter. *I don't recall hearing anyone in Los Angeles talk about Bulgaria in my entire life, and now I've heard the word twice in a span of two days?*

That's when I knew the house was ours and the universe had delivered my gift.

Two weeks later, escrow closed, and I prepared to put our old home up for sale. When real-world friends asked if I was excited about our move, I said, No, I wasn't excited. This was a forced transition, nothing more. Our circumstances had initiated this change and, although I could see flashes of peace and happiness in the future, excitement was not part of my vocabulary.

To prepare, I cleaned our old home from top to bottom, just as my dreams had taught me to do, and then I vigorously purged the rest of my life. Unless something had been given to me by a family member or a close friend, it had to go. Ninety percent of my clothes and shoes, regardless of their price tags and labels, got relegated to trash bags and donated to homeless shelters. Knickknacks that once cluttered closets and shelves were trashed and carried away by junk-removal companies, never to be thought of again. When it came to Tommy's things, I kept what was special to both him and our family and gave the rest away to those I knew would cherish it all. I was learning to play simple in more ways than one.

As I shed parts of the past that no longer served my future, my Boss from above stayed busy and sent a living, breathing angel our way, one we immediately signed to our team. His name was Michael. He was the father of an elementary school classmate of Tommy's. He had been following the progress on Tommy's Field and heard that we needed some help. When we spoke, he suggested that Doug and I meet a political consultant with whom he had personally worked and who not only had experience going up against the Head Honcho and Blue-Suit Stan but had also helped several of his clients prevail.

"Aaron knows all the players. He knows how Westwood works. At the very least, I think he can help you figure out what it's going to take to push this project through." Then our new teammate offered to make a generous donation to help pay for a portion of Aaron's fees so our foundation would not incur any costs until we were sure Aaron's services were worth the investment. It was an offer we could not refuse.

After engaging Aaron's services, I immediately took some pressure off Tina. She was more than thrilled to give her blessing and stood by to help in any way she could. Two weeks later, to our delight, Aaron scheduled our first face-to-face meeting with our council member and his staff. The head of the Department of Recreation and Parks and the president of Westwood Park's advisory board, our center back, were also in attendance. It was ironic that park neighbors had accused me and Doug of paying off our council member for favors when up until that very day, neither of us had ever even had a direct conversation with him about Tommy's Field.

When our council member walked into his conference room where we were all already seated, he looked over at me, gave me a hug, and said, "I'm so sorry for your loss. I can't imagine losing a child. Thank you for honoring Tommy in this way." Suddenly, he was no longer just a politician who didn't like messy. He was a human being who cared about me and my family.

"I've sat with many of the neighbors and heard their concerns," he said to everyone seated around the table.

You have? I thought to myself. *I didn't know that. We had to hire a political consultant in order to get our first meeting with you. They just had to be loud, mean, and threatening?*

"Can't we find a solution that works for everyone?" he asked, sounding exasperated.

"I thought you supported this project?" I said, concerned that he was backtracking on the support that his team had given me and the Department of Recreation and Parks when we started fundraising.

"I do . . . I did . . . But I didn't know this project would be so contentious."

"It's not contentious," Doug interrupted. "It's the same dozen park neighbors and neighborhood council who have been fighting change in Westwood for decades. We all know this field needs to be improved and no design change will satisfy them."

"Listen, I know this field is terrible. It has been an eyesore the entire time I have served as council member of this district," he responded, which my memory gauged was at least a decade. "That's why I figured Tommy's Field would be a no-brainer. I drive around this city every day and see synthetic turf fields all over the place that are full of adults and children playing all day and night, rain or shine. I envision Tommy's Field being a place where people come together to play the way they do in other parts of the city. But I have to tell you, Westwood is the most challenging neighborhood in my district. The residents in Westwood can be very difficult to work with. Tommy's Field would not be a problem in any one of my other neighborhoods."

His staff commiserated with him and as if that were his cue, the head of Recreation and Parks proceeded to lay out a new design for Tommy's Field that he said he and his entire department fully stood behind. No longer would Tommy's Field replace the existing open space that I had spent days and weeks tracking in my Excel spreadsheet. Instead, it would replace six of the existing eight tennis courts that sat vacant right next to it.

"The tennis courts are already flat. They have lights. And they are mostly empty all day. We will demolish six courts, upgrade the remaining two courts and build two new ones on the east side of the park so that the result is four brand-new courts total. Since we have heard very few complaints out of the tennis community and our research shows the courts are extremely underutilized, this is a solution that should appease everyone. Tommy's Field will make better use of public space than the tennis courts. It will accommodate more community members per square foot and help fulfill the demand our city has for more soccer."

"As long as the park has four tennis courts minimum, I'm okay with it," our council member said.

The head of Rec and Parks continued. "We will also have to move the outdoor basketball courts to another corner of the park, but the current courts are due for new hoops and need to be resurfaced anyway so moving them won't be that much more expensive. We already have the money for this, too."

Dots started assembling in front of me.

Lastly, he confirmed, "This means the open space where we originally designed Tommy's Field will remain untouched. The community will get Tommy's Field *and* the open space."

Dots started flashing and bumping into each other like a stuck pinball machine, while my gut start jabbing me from the inside out. I did not like this plan at all.

"You know that these people will find new reasons to fight against this design, right?" Doug said. "They don't want anything. It doesn't matter what it is."

One of the council member's staff chimed in at that point and said, "I don't think so. I have already put feelers out there among the opposition and the reaction so far is positive."

The businesswoman in me silently evaluated the plan and determined it was too big. Too destructive. And ultimately, way too wasteful. Not only did the new design inflate the budget by another $4.8 million, which the Department of Recreation and Parks had sitting in an account specifically for capital improvements to the park, but tennis courts that were otherwise in fine condition would be destroyed. The idea of it pained me. Our goal was to enhance our community and honor our son. Not to take away anything or sacrifice common sense in order to accommodate lies and appease unreasonable demands.

Still, every decision-maker at the table believed this new design would significantly improve the overall park and also resolve any opposition to Tommy's Field. So, Doug and I surrendered. "Whatever you think is best."

Half of me walked away from the meeting feeling disheartened by the ways of local politics. The other half walked away feeling inspired to get loud. Being grieving parents, raising $1.2 million, and playing nice wasn't enough to get the job done. Tommy's Field needed more from me, and the neighbors were pushing me to deliver it.

I opened my laptop and began to outline a strategy to turn this game around. Then I started writing letters, hundreds of them, and sending them to Tommy's Field supporters for their input and signatures. I followed up with emails, made phone calls, and walked around the neighborhood asking everyone we knew to start bombarding our council member and the entire Department of Recreation and Parks with their support for Tommy's Field. I even walked up to UCLA's sorority houses with a friend and stalked athletes on campus, telling them our story, flashing my photo of the existing field, and convincing them to sign letters defending the need to improve our public park for the benefit of the entire community.

My team was all-in. While I continued facilitating city government–related conversations, Doug defended our goal while simultaneously pushing our agenda forward between business calls and artist negotiations. Dono fired off updates across the city via his and Tommy's network of friends, teachers, and parents. Ethan drove our public relations campaign and pushed our online petition, which already had five times the number of signatures that the opposition had but was still half of where we needed it to be. Tommy's friends walked around Westwood Village like a formidable TM23 street marketing team and got stacks of letters signed by Westwood residents and frequent shoppers. And our extended tribe of loyal supporters cheered us on like dedicated fans, checking in regularly for updates, lending advice, and motivating us to perform.

By the time I showed up to the *seventh* public meeting, nearly one thousand individual calls and letters supporting Tommy's Field had already bombarded City Hall. Our team had become a legitimate nuisance. It all felt so wasteful and over the top. And, yet, it was the only way I could think of for the bottom to be heard. No matter how Tommy's Field opponents viewed me and my team, there was no denying that we were at the very bottom.

This particular public meeting was designed by our council member's office to be a roundtable discussion. Our council member handpicked seven individuals to debate the new design of Tommy's Field and answer the community's questions about it. Among the individuals selected to serve on the board were Slim, now a spokesperson for the neighbors; our center back, who the city had vetted and invited back to represent the park's advisory board; and a former regional park supervisor who had spent the last twenty years overseeing Westwood Recreation Center, as well as every other park in our region. Doug and I were not asked to participate and since no general public comments were being entertained or tallied, we gave our community a break and showed up to the roundtable meeting with only a few close friends and our political consultant, Aaron, who had yet to experience one of these spectacles live. To our surprise, a small group of dedicated supporters who had received a mass email from the city notifying them of the roundtable discussion, were already there when we arrived. "We wouldn't miss it for the world," they whispered when we sat down. The reality show was just too addictive.

A few hours before the meeting, Blue-Suit Stan called me. The new design to be presented to the community that evening had been leaked to him. "Nikki," he said sounding enthusiastic, "I like this new design a lot."

Since I did not like it at all, the fact that both he and the city did, made me feel like I might never understand the real world again.

"It solves a lot of problems, Nikki," Stan shouted at me, his spit hitting the other end of the phone. "I don't know what the tennis community will think of it but, hopefully, the rest of the neighbors respond well to it tonight."

I was growing tired of Blue-Suit Stan saying one thing over the phone and supporting another in person, but his enthusiastic out-reach made me cautiously optimistic that this would be our seventh and last public meeting on Tommy's Field.

When I walked into the park's gymnasium that evening, Pink Lips gave me a hug before sitting on the opposite side of the room. The rest of the Dynamic Dozen were also there perusing the new designs of the field that sat on multiple easels positioned around the gym. The Head Honcho was slouched in her metal chair with her arms crossed. The young dad with the baby who heckled me with his wife was pacing back and forth with his child in his hands. And the row of brunettes who began this mess in the first place all sat next to one another whispering and plotting. Approximately three dozen addi-tional park neighbors sat among them, while the council member's chief of staff positioned herself in the front row prepared to record the entire meeting on her phone while homemade signs questioning her integrity, as well as that of our council member's, were being waved high in the air behind her back.

Feeling confident about how the next hour would unfold, our center back opened the meeting by acknowledging the neighbors' commendable win.

"Congratulations. The open space had been saved."

While those words didn't land quite right with me, I noticed that one opponent stood up, gave Doug a hug of thanks, and walked out. The rest stayed. They did not care about the field itself. They cared about the fight.

Everyone listened as the new design was explained by certain members of the roundtable. With every new detail, the energy in the room darkened.

Slim raised her hand and said, "I am speaking on behalf of the neighbors and opponents of Tommy's Field so please bear with me and don't shoot the messenger." *Fair enough*, I thought.

"We want to know why Tommy's Field can't be built in another park," Slim questioned. "I personally went to two other parks in the neighborhood and my measurements show it will fit in both."

The former supervisor of the region with a southern drawl from Texas responded with the same answer that his colleague, Valerie, had given me when I first asked which neighborhood park was the best fit for Tommy's Field. "That's a good question, ma'am," he began. "We have measured both of those parks multiple times and determined that Tommy's Field won't fit in either one of them. Plus, these parks are highly programmed with other popular activities that we do not want to disrupt. Tommy's Field at Westwood Recreation Center will enable us to add important programming, not take any away."

Dissatisfied with his answer, she persisted.

"We demand that the city provide written documentation of the research it has done on these other parks and tell us exactly why Tommy's Field can't be built in one of them."

He said he had no problem providing such a report and that not only would he get it done quickly but he would deliver it to the head of his department and the council member's office. By this point, I had started calling him Texas in my mind. His calm demeanor and friendly sounding voice were backed by his genuine knowledge of all the parks in our neighborhood and I found him to be so informative and professional that I wondered why the city hadn't put him in the game sooner during earlier public meetings. I also sat there wondering why this report hadn't been generated weeks ago. The neighbors had been asking for it since the second public meeting and the fact that the city hadn't yet provided it gave them yet another reason to question the process.

Dozens of questions were posed to the roundtable until Slim took over and began to dominate.

"We are concerned that Tommy's Field even in its new location will affect picnics and kite flying on the open space and be dangerous for small kids playing on the existing open space next to it."

"With all due respect, ma'am," Texas responded, "I have walked every inch of this park for over twenty-five years. No one picnics or flies kites on this field. It is mainly used by dogs running off leash and people walking from one end of the park to the other."

"That is not our experience," she said before firing off her next demand.

"We want to know who will use Tommy's Field. When it will be open. And which sports will be played on it. We also want to approve the community's free-play hours."

"Excuse me, ma'am," the director said, with his polite tongue getting a little chippy. "You got your open space and now you want to dictate how we run the rest of the park, too?"

"I am just expressing the concerns of our community," she responded sheepishly. Her innocent sweet act was getting tiresome.

"We want to make sure there aren't any logos or signs on Tommy's Field," Slim boldly continued. "We don't want a donor wall, either. The baseball diamonds across the street have signs and logos plastered all over and around them. We don't want that here."

That's when anger crashed my system and I turned to my Boss for answers. *"What the hell is happening now? Who does this woman think she is? Why am I in the middle of a complete circus!"*

Hearing no good answer, I looked around and saw Blue-Suit Stan pacing. He was sweating and grunting.

Then Slim, nearly out of arguments, saved her best for last. No longer able to resort to her favorite rallying cry, "Save the Open Space," she threatened, "How will the tennis community feel about this new design? It has just been sprung on all of us. The tennis community isn't represented here and has not had a chance to weigh in on this. This process has not been fair."

She was right. While the roundtable was informative and provided a forum for the city to finally respond to the community's questions about Tommy's Field, the rollout of the evening made the city look as underhanded and disingenuous as the neighbors already thought it was.

Part of me agreed with Slim's concerns about the tennis community, even though I was well aware that she didn't care at all about tennis or those who played it. But another part of me, the one that was committed to the larger vision, wondered, *What tennis community is she so concerned about? The one that doesn't use the courts? The one that hasn't shown up to any of the previous seven public meetings in the past seven weeks? The one by which the city apparently already ran this grand idea?*

Had I been on the roundtable, I would have told Slim that every other recreation center in the neighborhood had public tennis courts. Lots of them. So many, in fact, the supply clearly exceeded the demand. My excel spreadsheet, which I had expanded to include the other parks in the area, proved it. After clarifying that reality, I would have pointed out that there was not a single full-size public athletic field with lights anywhere in the same district. That although the rest of our country averaged nearly seventeen athletic fields for every hundred thousand residents, Los Angeles averaged *four*. In fact, youth soccer was the number-one youth sport in the city, played by more than 27 percent of children under the age of eighteen. Tennis was played by only 9 percent of youth and barely made the top ten, along with gymnastics and martial arts. It didn't seem like that huge of an ask for tennis to give up four courts in order to accommodate a much larger and much more diverse community of children who had nowhere else to play.

A brand-new dot jumped in front of my screen and warned me that I would meet this tennis community soon.

The meeting ended with a city representative announcing that the public meeting process for Tommy's Field was officially over. The next step in the process, he said, was to present Tommy's Field to two of five Recreation and Park commissioners who would serve as a "task force" evaluating all aspects of the project before allowing it to be put forth before the full commission for a formal vote. Blue-Suit Stan was apoplectic.

He raced over to me. "Nikki, this meeting was a sham! The city can't get away with this. The neighbors have legitimate concerns that are not fairly being addressed."

"I'm not running this show," I responded, having noted every obvious blunder in my mind and feeling helpless that I wasn't in a position to fix any of them. This was not my operation, and it was not my way.

"I also can't believe who they asked to sit on the roundtable," Stan said with his angry brown eyes bulging a few inches from my face. Even though he had clearly advised and prepared Slim for her round-table performance, he considered it an insult that the Head Honcho wasn't asked to be part of it. "Given all of her years representing the community, she should have been included," he rambled on, making me further question the nature of their relationship and his true motives.

I pressed my black boots firmly into the ground, looked him dead in the eye, and challenged him as if I were a real-world person and no longer only a grieving mom stepping out of her dimension. "You called me two hours before this meeting and said that you supported this design. You said you liked it, 'A lot.'"

"Not like this," he said, walking away shaking his head and running his beefy fingers through his sweaty hair.

The room was in utter chaos. Park neighbors were yelling in the faces of city representatives while the council member's very tall chief of staff stood among them and calmly concluded, "Now I see. . . . If it's not one thing, it's another. You all just don't want anything."

For the first time, after seven highly contentious public meetings, our council member and all other city representatives involved in the project could no longer ignore that the opposition was not about Tommy's Field. It was not even about their love of the open space that none of them used. It was about fear. Fear of change. Fear of losing. Fear that their dreaded "outsiders" might win.

CHAPTER 17

THE DRAMA THAT HAD UNFOLDED AND THE DIVISIVENESS THAT had ensued over Tommy's Field began to feel like a microcosm of our country. The neighbors spun Tommy's Field into a class issue. "Go back to your fancy golf course park and leave our park alone!" They made it a race issue. "We don't want those other people in our park!" And they made it an identity issue. "This is ours. Not yours!" Like the many leaders who have shaped our country at the top, Tommy's Field brought to the surface decades of anger and divisiveness that had been quietly festering at the bottom. Tommy's Field did not create Westwood's problems, but it exposed them until they erupted with such heat and destructive force that they could no longer be ignored. The top of America and the bottom, where I found myself fighting, were like mirrors of one another, directly reflecting the hostility and distrust that permeates every level of our country in between.

"Why do adults always fight battles for their kids?" Tommy used to ask me. He was annoyed by parents who made a serial habit of calling school principals to complain about other kids in school without first attempting to speak to the parents of those children or taking the time to teach their own children how to resolve certain conflicts themselves. School principals appeared so threatened by these parents that they attempted to handle matters that every other generation of children across the planet had worked out on the playground themselves. "I take care of myself," Tommy announced in reaction to his own question. "I don't snitch or lie to get kids in trouble. If I have an issue, I tell them myself and that's that. We work it out, or we don't, but then we move on with our lives."

I admired Tommy's ability to stand up for himself and defend others, but there were some issues he couldn't resolve on his own. Although his lungs and sinuses were finally clear, his allergies were under control, his body was injury-free, and he was sleeping peacefully every night for at least nine hours, he wasn't in the clear yet. Tommy's middle school principal called me just a few months before Tommy's departure to tell me something was wrong with Tommy's head. The #MeToo movement had just exploded a few weeks earlier and a girl in his homeroom class complained that Tommy put his hand on her leg during class. The middle school director was concerned.

"Are you kidding me?" Tommy said when the middle school director and school therapist called for a special meeting to talk about it. "We were having a debate and I put my hands on her leg, just above her knee when I was trying to stress my point. She was wearing black leggings like all the girls wear these days. It wasn't sexual at all!"

Tommy hated playing defense, especially when he was not mentally prepared for it.

"Well," said the school therapist, "we're also getting complaints from other girls, some of whom are your friends, who say that you make inappropriate sexual comments to them."

"What friends?" Tommy asked. "Friends that don't have the guts to say something to my face aren't friends."

"We can't say who."

"What comments?"

"We can't tell you."

Nothing fired Tommy up like a good debate. "Well, I'm innocent until proven guilty and I can't be proven guilty without any facts!"

I could not disagree with him. Since the time he could talk in complete sentences, Doug and I encouraged Tommy to stand up for himself. To seek his own solutions. To help others who were unable to defend themselves. But none of that was relevant this time. It was important that he understood what he was doing or saying to upset the girls around him. After only one warning, the school wanted him to see a therapist, and so he did.

Tommy was livid.

I thought back to all the boys who had chased me in school. The ones who stretched the sleeves on my shirts when they almost caught me. The ones who almost got close enough to kiss me. Tommy's offense seemed so minor, relatively speaking, but still, times had changed, and therapy was the modern consequence.

"No chance," Tommy said. "I'm not going to therapy."

"Well, yes, there's a big chance," I responded. "Like a 100 percent chance. Or else your phone, soccer, and your entire social life go away."

"Fine. You can take me to therapy, but you are just wasting your money. There's nothing wrong with me."

"It's not about something being wrong with you. We just want you to be comfortable with who you are, Tommy. Life gets more complicated as we get older and knowing who we are can be confusing at different stages of life. Your dad and I will be working with the therapist to reevaluate our house rules to make sure they best support you. It's not like parenting comes with a manual. We could use the help, too."

Tommy said he had no idea what I was talking about. "I could be doing something a lot more productive with this hour," he pouted. "So could you!"

The truth was, Tommy knew he had a big mouth and took Krav Maga to protect himself from it. But the other truth was that Tommy respected girls. He championed them. And more than we ever knew, he cared about making them feel better about themselves.

Still, off to therapy Tommy went.

"His name is Jason," I told him, "and you will see him at least four times before we will reevaluate the situation further."

"He's a surfer," I added, before he could complain.

"Oh, great," Tommy said, rolling his eyes.

While Jason, his tan skin and long, curly, sun-kissed surfer hair spent an hour every week assessing my son, Tommy made his own judgments. "He's an intense guy," he told me, which sounded like an immediate breakthrough. Jason evaluated Tommy as a kid who was "all-in in this lifetime," curious and enthusiastic. "At the same time," Jason added, "he's a lightning rod. Everyone knows him. Some love him. Some hate him. Some want to be him. There's pressure all around him to conform and he's struggling to be himself."

Jason said we only had a short window to help Tommy know and trust his authentic self because in another year or so it would become harder to find. Middle school years are all about defining the self, Jason said. High school is about fitting the self into the world. That's when kids start getting into serious trouble and it's much tougher to reach them.

It took Tommy only a few therapy sessions to figure out that Jason knew pretty much everything going on in every middle school across LA's Westside. As large as Tommy's middle school community was, Jason's was bigger, and it became painfully clear that the middle school years aren't very kind to anyone. Jason helped Tommy navigate the world of middle school temptations. From girls and hickeys, to music, technology, books, and sports, they debated and connected over all of it as Tommy ate his way through Jason's snack drawer. Remnants of Tricky Tommy began to disappear as the deepest layers of Tommy's authentic self became exposed. Like every soccer training he ever had,

Tommy engaged, processed, and quickly advanced, never looking back or wondering why. His relationship with the female gender of our species appeared to only get stronger.

By the time Tommy and I drove down to San Diego for his last match, he had been seeing Jason for two months. Not only was their time together coming to an end, but Tommy was a month away from heading to Europe to train and attend eighth grade.

One night, a compassionate energy visited me in my dreams and asked how I was feeling. I said, *"Better."* Then I retracted that answer. *"I'm not feeling better,"* I said, pausing. *"That wasn't the right word. I am feeling stronger."*

"Stronger is a good word to use," the energy responded before waking me up so I could write it down.

While I may have been feeling stronger, the future of Tommy's Field was not. The emotional toll of losing Tommy, combined with the struggle to build his legacy, had creased the skin around my eyes, sunken Doug's, and rounded both of our shoulders. This time, however, it was Doug who called on some outside spiritual support. He set up another phone appointment to talk to Robert, the British medium whose first call had drained the battery life of both our cordless landline phones. Doug wanted to talk to Tommy by himself, even though he still didn't really believe anyone could.

"There's a younger male here who in his short time here did a lot," Robert said in his finest British accent. "He knew he wouldn't be here long and tried to do everything at least once."

Doug's metallic silver pen wrote every word down and started bleeding between letters.

Robert went on to describe Doug's father, the nature of their complicated relationship, and the impact that Tommy's life was having on Doug in this world and Doug's father in the sacred world.

"This young male says, 'My mom talks to me every day,'" Robert disclosed.

Doug didn't really know what that meant. He didn't know that I talked to Tommy out loud while I drove around the city in my car. Or that I spoke to him energetically during meditation and in my dreams at night. Or that every daily input in my green journal was written in the form of a letter and always started with, "Hi T." *I knew he could hear me*, I thought to myself when Doug shared Robert's reading with me, not wanting him to think I was more delusional than he likely already thought I was.

As if he were trying to assemble a complex jigsaw puzzle, Robert jumped around and presented different pieces of our son's personality and life.

"Are you having a problem with one of your vehicles? He says you have an old car in the shop, and it's been left there for too long."

"Yes," Doug said. It was true. He owned a green 1964 Buick that Tommy loved. Doug promised to give it to him when he signed his first professional soccer contract. A few months after Tommy passed away, Doug dropped the car off at the mechanic. It leaked oil, needed new brakes, and had other old and discontinued parts to be addressed. Overwhelmed by grief, the ongoing controversy over Tommy's Field, and his efforts to keep both our family and his practice functioning, he never followed up on it. The car had been sitting there for nearly a year and didn't matter much to Doug anymore. Tommy was the one who loved to ride with him in it.

"He says that even if that old car causes you a lot of trouble, you must go and get it. There will never be another one like it. Whoever is working on it, chase them down to get it done. Snap at someone's heels. He says it's not replaceable, just like he's not."

Maybe Robert's choice of words was his own, but when Doug repeated them to me and I saw them written down, I knew at least one of them was Tommy's. He was the only person I had ever met who actually admitted that he was not replaceable. In fact, he had written a song about it. When he sat at his keyboard one evening and first played it for me, I asked, "What's it called?"

"Irreplaceable," he said.

After hearing it twice, I told him the truth. "I love it." And then came my motherly, "But . . ."

"But what?" Tommy asked.

"I think you should change the title."

"Are you insane?"

"Tommy, you aren't the most humble kid. All of your swagger already rubs some people the wrong way. Do you really have to write a song about how irreplaceable you are?"

"It's called poetic license, Mom," Tommy replied. "I can say whatever I want. Besides, my music teacher likes it, and Dad says it's good."

He wrote the song the day after his coach told him he wasn't selected to travel with his team to a fairly prestigious youth soccer tournament. Tommy was not only an emotional wreck about it, but he was also sick, literally. He had been going through one of his seasonal bronchial flare-ups, showing up for practices loaded with cough medication and mucus clogging his lungs, draining his energy, and tightening his muscles. "My coach told me I'm not in form to go," Tommy reported to me and his dad. "But he knows I've been sick," he complained. "He knows I'll be well by the tournament. It's three weeks away!"

Like his father, Tommy was a fighter with his words, and he sat down at his keyboard and wrote "Irreplaceable."

It was only a few months after Tommy passed away that I stumbled on a quote by a Spanish philosopher named Miguel de Unamuno. He said, "Our greatest endeavor must be to make ourselves *irreplaceable*," so that when we die, others are aware that something meaningful is gone and cannot be replaced. Soccer had challenged Tommy to believe in himself and tested to see whether or not he had the courage to live up to the title of his own song.

Doug was sobbing when he got off the phone with Robert. His practical mind didn't believe anything Robert said, but a deeper place of knowing received it all.

Maybe it was the roundtable meeting that shifted something inside me. Maybe it was Robert's reading. Or maybe, it was just time. But the start-up girl in me finally got a reality check.

When we received word that the park commission's "task force" would be evaluating the latest design of Tommy's Field—the one that involved destroying six tennis courts, building two new ones, and leaving the decrepit open space as it was—Doug and I felt as demoralized as Tommy did when he wrote his song. I grew increasingly confused when we learned that all five commissioners who would eventually vote on Tommy's Field did not even report to the council member or the Department of Recreation and Parks, and, therefore, did not always vote in their favor. They reported to the mayor, who, in practice, gave them full autonomy to make their own decisions and rarely held them accountable to any particular vision set by him at the top.

"I don't know how the commission is going to vote on this one," the GM of the department said to us after being downloaded on highlights of the roundtable meeting. "This particular group of commissioners can be difficult," he added. "They don't always listen to me." *Just our luck.*

Suddenly, a new disconnect clogging the governance of Los Angeles blew up like a giant dot that blocked every possible route to our goal. While I had been following the ways of our opponents and instructing our team to bombard the GM and our council member with support for Tommy's Field, the Dynamic Dozen, guided by Blue-Suit Stan and the Head Honcho, had been showing up to public Rec and Park commissioner meetings across the city and getting way out in front of us by holding private conversations with the commissioners behind the scenes. While I was playing the right way and forcing my team to follow strict protocols and chains of command, the neighbors were playing by their own rules and making brilliant connections with the only five people who mattered in the end. The start-up girl in me had met her match and was being beaten at her own game.

"Enough defense!" a message dropped in fast and hard. Tommy did not like playing defense. Sure, he had to learn it. To defend his position and protect the middle of the field. But, ultimately, he was a midfielder who was designed to press forward. To get the ball closer to the goal. To even smash it in himself. If his team was on defense the entire game, he was not doing his job.

"No more defense," I agreed. My head was tingling. I had to start playing Tommy-style. Otherwise, this match was over.

I was ready. By this point, I had the discipline and self-care routine of an elite athlete.

Nearly every waking hour of the day, I was in training. Reading. Writing. Painting. Breathing. Talking to friends. Exercising. Visiting healers. And avoiding substances that agitated my nervous system, including sugar, alcohol, and caffeine. That's what it took for me to visit the real world for more than sixty minutes at a time. That's what it took for me to perform at my best when I got there. That's what it still takes for me to recuperate when I get home.

Heading into the final rounds of public meetings for Tommy's Field, it was time to go hard. Time to credit the strength of my opponents, despite their hostile and devious ways, and appreciate that every great game is contingent upon a great fight. And it was time to absorb what my Boss had likely been trying to teach me all along. That the best games in life are never easy. If this one were easy, it would not be as meaningful and in the end I might never advance.

CHAPTER 18

BLUE-SUIT STAN CALLED ME THE DAY AFTER THE ROUNDTABLE meeting to rant about the corruptness of our center back and the park's advisory board that he served. He also complained about the weaknesses of our city government and broke down every city code that the meeting had apparently violated. The gap between us was only widening.

That same afternoon, our political consultant, Aaron, informed me that it would be at least another month, if not two, before Tommy's Field would be presented to the Recreation and Park commissioners. The department's staff needed time to prepare its formal report and the commissioners needed a summer break. As for the rest of us, the fun would not stop.

Aaron promptly scheduled a meeting with the GM of Recreation and Parks. I had a number of questions, like: Would any changes be made to the design being presented to commissioners? What role would our family have in commission meetings? When would the report on other park locations be finalized and how would it be presented to the public? The commissioners may have been due for a summer vacation, but I was using every minute of mine to prepare.

When Doug, Aaron, and I reconvened with the GM, however, he arrived with his own agenda. He told us that the unsigned gift agreement that had been drafted and verbally agreed upon before the community meetings had started already needed to be revised.

The twenty-one-page document had thoughtfully addressed every facet of the project, including the amount of our gift, what the city was obligated to build with it and who had what rights and for how long. It was all surprisingly straightforward, until now.

"If you want to improve the chances of getting this field approved, we have to take the donor wall out of the agreement," the GM said. "The commissioners don't like donor walls."

I looked up at Aaron whose eyes urged me to *"Say nothing."* I looked back at him as if to say, *"Oh, so you mean, 'Don't say that it would have been nice to know this before we promised large contributors that we would have a donor wall at the field acknowledging their contributions?' You mean, 'Don't say, we fulfilled our end of this deal why can't you?' You mean, 'Don't remind him that the commissioners' job descriptions clearly state that their roles are to support the vision as set by him, the general manager of the department?' You mean, 'I can't say any of that?!'"*

That's what I would have said in my first incarnation. That's how direct I liked to play. That's the level of transparency I expected from the top.

My heart intervened and convinced me that was not the right shot to take. The angle was all wrong. I was being too volatile. And my focus was ineffectively scattered. Reason agreed and reminded me that I was not there to compete or to make any kind of short-sighted move that could get me thrown out of this game entirely. I was there to collaborate and reach our goal. Together. That's how Tommy would have played.

With the self-control of a dedicated athlete, I shut out the noises in my head and allowed my heart to speak its mind.

"Before we started fundraising," I responded, feeling a new strain of conviction rising up through my voice, "I was told by your team that a donor wall would not be a problem. We will not go back to our donors and renege on this point. They trusted us." My spine straightened and my body language added, *Do not fuck with me on this.*

I was well aware that the GM did not need the headache of Tommy's Field and that he probably wished he could dump the entire idea on some other adjacent city by that point. But I was also aware that he was too invested in it to turn back. This was not just another athletic field anymore. Tommy's Field was an opportunity to reclaim his authority. To strengthen his department. To address all the senseless layers of bureaucracy that had plagued our park system for too long and made his job absurdly difficult. No longer was Tommy's Field only a gift to our city, our community, and our local park. It was a gift to him.

My stare softened, but my intentions behind it never wavered. It was time to make a choice.

"Which team are you on?" my stare asked. *"The one that talks big but plays scared, or the one that has already lost everything and is fearless?"*

After studying my reaction, the GM rephrased his suggestion. "I recommend we take the donor wall out of the agreement for now and reintroduce the idea for approval after we get the field itself approved. I agree a donor wall makes sense, but if it's going to affect the way commissioners vote, let's leave it out for now and work together to get it approved later. Most important is that we get the field approved and move it forward."

His choice was made. We were his team.

"Fine," Doug blurted out, not wanting to waste another precious moment on the topic.

Aaron nodded and the GM continued. "The commissioners also don't like logos. We need to take the two Major League Soccer team logos off the field."

I looked up at Aaron again. His eyebrows raised and baby blue eyes pleaded, *"Just say YES."*

Are you kidding me? My thoughts roared. *What's the logic? Why would anyone be against both of our city's MLS teams uniting for the benefit of youth sports? What better message would a city want to send to its youth? And, by the way, who are these commissioners and why is everyone bowing down to them? There are Clippers and Dodgers logos on parks all over town!*

Anger raged through my system for a split second before transmuting into an icy-cool fierceness that I remembered feeling in my former incarnation but never dared reveal. On the outside, I took great care in my first incarnation to act right, just as the Ingalls daughters did on my television screen every weekday after school. On the inside, however, I spent considerable time honing a strong competitive spirit that simmered beneath my skin and became my secret weapon. It was always prepared. Always lurking. Always watching for the exact right opportunity to strike.

When the GM of Recreation and Parks disclosed that the MLS logos had to go, he activated my competitive spirit and motivated me to approach my role in a new way: Calm but explosive. Creative but practical. Collaborative but fierce. Just like a center midfielder. The kind that gets scouted. The kind that earns college scholarships. The kind that goes pro.

I admitted to myself that I did not know how to design a park. But there was one thing I knew how to do better than anyone else in the game, and I was ready to acknowledge it. No matter how much I tried to be a grieving mom contributing from behind the scenes, it was time for me to step up and deliver Tommy's Field from start to finish. I no longer cared who held what title or how many years of public service anyone in the game flaunted. I had an expertise that would no longer be denied. If in my former incarnation I was determined. In this one, I had become relentless.

"You can take the logos off the field and out of the agreement to appease the commissioners," I told the GM, fully embracing my elevated role, "But after this field is officially approved and before it is built, I will get in front of whoever it takes to overturn that decision." I suddenly grew taller in my seat. *I will connect with everyone I know. I will attack from every angle. And I will find a way to reach this goal.*

The GM sighed. "I agree that we need a more thoughtful approach to this. You can talk to whomever you want to get this changed. Do your thing and I will not stand in your way. In fact, I will personally lobby whomever I need to convince decision-makers to reevaluate the city attorney's position on this. My department needs the sponsorship money to upgrade our parks and meet the current needs of today's society."

"Great," said Doug, his "time anxiety" kicking in and prompting the discussion to move along. "TA" was one of the first nicknames I had ever given him. When I was first informed by a licensed psychologist that time anxiety was an actual modern syndrome, I immediately diagnosed Doug with it. His anxiety about time revealed itself early in our relationship in ways that I found both baffling and concerning. Like when he jaywalked across insanely busy streets at rush hour just to save a minute. Like when he honked and weaved through the crowded streets of Los Angeles as if he were a New York City cabdriver. It didn't matter where we were going, how much time we had, or how nauseated and flustered we were when we arrived, what mattered to Doug was that he got us there as fast as he could.

While Tommy regularly complained about his dad's driving and other TA ways, he too exhibited similar traits. He shoved so many activities into a single day as though each could be his last, and his dad ironically supported so many of them that Tommy ultimately took up most of the precious time that his dad was so anxious about.

Tommy and Doug manifested their time anxiety in different ways that challenged each other and others, but, on the flip side, it also made them the first out of bed, the first to arrive to work and school every morning and the first to help someone in need. Regardless of where this chromosome mutation originated, Tommy's spirit was pressed for time and he and his dad were destined to be racing together.

Sensing Doug's urgency to move the discussion along, the GM addressed his next point.

"As for signage . . ." he began, his eyes darting back and forth between me and Doug.

He will not dare renege on the name, Tommy's Field, my eyes warned, thankful that Doug was sitting next to me if he tried.

"Instead of the MLS team logos in the middle of the field, I suggest we write 'Tommy's Field' in the center circle and at the very least, honor the two MLS teams with some sort of plaque or well-positioned sign."

Now we're talking.

"Really?" I smiled. "I love that."

"It belongs there," he said, triggering a lonesome tear that escaped from the far corner of my right eye and reminded me that he remembered what the spirit of this field was about in the first place. Suddenly, I was filled with appreciation for how much this man had already endured for Tommy's Field. He was on the front lines every day. Slammed with phone calls. Bombarded with letters. Badgered by the opposition for meetings. Beyond all that, he also had to deal with *me*.

When our meeting with the GM ended and Doug, Aaron, and I reconvened outside, Doug looked at me and said, "Just sign the agreement, Nikki. Don't even read it again. The contract doesn't matter at this point. If everything goes well, no one will ever look at it again."

"But what if the city changes more language and I sign the contract without reading it? What if they don't maintain the field to our standards? What if they take out our option rights?"

"Just sign the fucking agreement, Nikki!" Doug pleaded with me. "They aren't going to start messing around with other terms without telling us what they are. Let's get this field approved and worry about the finer details later. It's in everyone's best interest to make this field successful."

"Fine," I said. No more letters. No more online petition signatures. No more phone calls. My brain was no longer wired for such details anyway, and none of that would make a difference at this point. To push this game forward, it was time to be a CEO, like the ones for whom I had always worked.

By the time we got home, the crown of my head opened and a clear message dropped in. *"It's time to attack!"*

As if he received a similar message at the exact same time, Doug turned to me not a minute later and said, "We have been on defense the entire time, Nikki. We need to attack!"

Then Doug asked me, "What do you think Tommy's thinking about all this?" Do you think he's thinking, *"These people are assholes. Take my field somewhere it will be appreciated?"*

I wasn't sure. Would Tommy want us to take his field east where the soccer community had welcomed him with open arms? Or would he want to fight to improve a field in his own neighborhood, which desperately needed one?

What would Tommy do? I pondered over and over until my memory finally produced some invaluable advice that I had once bestowed on him.

At the time, Tommy's coach was coming down harder on him.

"Work harder!" his coach would shout. "Be more consistent!" he would yell. "Defend better!" he would grumble, without stopping to teach him how.

One day after practice Tommy said to me, "My coach told me today to stop smiling while I play." That's when I knew that this particular coach did not understand Tommy and was struggling to develop him.

"Don't ever stop smiling, T," I responded, "Or I will take you out of soccer." I thought back to when I first started controlling my smile to look serious and smart, and vowed to never let him make the same mistake. Besides, the more he smiled the better he played.

A few weeks later, Tommy announced, "Mom, I may want to be a rock star instead of a soccer player."

The relationship with his coach was worsening and starting to affect his game.

"Why do you have to decide what you want to do at this age?" I responded. "You can pursue both soccer and music until the universe forces you to choose."

As he processed my words, I gave him the out he wanted. "T, you can quit soccer if you want, but then you'd be letting one coach dictate your life instead of recognizing that difficult experiences can teach you a lot about yourself. The last one even motivated you to write a great song."

As I watched his bare feet fiddle with a soccer ball, I elaborated.

"You will encounter similar challenges and people whichever route you choose. That's how life works. Whether you choose to pursue soccer or music or any other path in life, similar obstacles will present themselves, and the same amount of work will be required to overcome them. So, pursue what you love because you will be challenged either way."

Tommy never mentioned quitting again. Instead, he added morning workouts to his routine before school and called Ethan, a college soccer defender, and his former coach, Julio, to work with him on defense. As his confidence recovered, so did his game. Still, Tommy and his coach were barely speaking.

Recognizing that the relationship was unhealthy and counterproductive, I walked into Tommy's bedroom one evening, sat on the edge of his bed, and peered over his microphone and keyboard where he was FaceTiming with friends on the laptop in front of him. Headphones covered his ears, a ball spun between his feet, Cristiano Ronaldo graced the wall to my left, and hundreds of books were stacked up neatly on the navy-blue bookshelf behind the desk in front of him.

To Kill a Mockingbird caught my eye. It was his favorite. He read it for the first time during the summer before fifth grade and by the beginning of middle school he had read it three times. "Mom," he asked me more than once, "Can you help me find more books at that level?"

"What level is that, T?"

"The Pulitzer Prize–winning level," he responded, pointing to the round sticker on the front cover that he could barely pronounce. Tommy liked to surround himself with winners. But it wasn't only the sticker that resonated with him. It was Jem, the narrator's older brother who loved, tortured, and defended his younger sibling the same way Tommy did. By the third time Tommy read the story, he and Jem were the same age. They were both football crazy: Jem about the American kind and Tommy the European. They were both adventurous spirits who both impressed and exhausted others with their curious tongues. And both had fathers who were attorneys.

But there was nothing in *To Kill a Mockingbird* or on his walls that could improve his relationship with his coach.

"T," I said, forcing him to hang up with his friends and look up from his screen.

"What is your plan A? Do you want to stay on the team or find another one?"

"I want to stay on the team and feel like my coach believes in me," he responded emphatically.

"Okay, then," I said. "That is your plan A. Never focus on a plan B when you are trying to achieve plan A. If, for any reason, you don't achieve plan A, that's when you come up with a plan B. At that point, your plan B will become your new plan A. It might even turn out to be better for you than your original plan A. You just can't have a plan A and B at the same time because then your intentions become spread out and you may not achieve either one. So, commit to what you really want. Believe in it. And go all-out for it. You never need to worry. There will always be a plan B."

The advice sank in. His stress dissolved. And Tommy's coach started giving him the positive reinforcement for which he yearned.

Less than two months later, however, plan A unraveled.

"I'm too young for this game to feel like a job," he explained.

"What do you want to do, T?" I asked, already sensing his answer.

"I want to keep playing soccer, but find a new team."

A few days later, I watched from the sideline of the field as Tommy extended his hand and told his coach, "Thank you for the opportunity, but I don't think this is the right team for me this season. I need to leave."

Then I watched the coach shout at him and leave Tommy's hand frozen in midair with nothing to shake.

Seconds later, the coach's boss walked over and shook Tommy's hand. "Good luck," he added, expressing in two heartbreaking words everything Tommy already knew to be true. He believed in himself more than they did.

Tommy turned around, walked back toward me on the other end of the field and started crying. He had achieved his plan A, but the time had come to pursue a plan B. By the time we returned home less than ninety minutes later, there were two already waiting for him.

A week later, Tommy secured his plan B, and would soon have a hard time remembering why it hadn't been his plan A all along.

My own advice came back to me when Doug and I contemplated whether Tommy would want us to move his field east or continue to push for its development in Westwood. Westwood Recreation Center was our plan A. It was not time to be contemplating a plan B.

So, all I could do was ask myself: *Why is building a field in a park for kids to play on so hard?*

A simple response shot back at me, fast and clear. *"Change is hard."*

That's when I realized, *If I can't change my opponents, I must change myself.*

Overdue for a healing session, I called Kelly and made another appointment with her and her plant-based medicine. I invited three close friends to join me who were all healing from their own traumas. When our ceremony began, I disclosed that my intention was to "Connect with Tommy and receive whatever knowledge I needed to build Tommy's Field."

Candles flickered, gentle music played, and colorful paintings on her walls started swirling as I surrendered to the medicine and crawled into a corner.

"Why did you have to leave, T?" I asked telepathically, a question I will likely ask every day for the rest of my life. *"You should have stayed. I should have left. Whatever our plan was, we could have changed it."*

As if he couldn't bear to hear me wallow, his response was instantaneous.

"Mom, we are more powerful this way. With me here and you there, we can do a lot more."

I surrendered deeper to the medicine. He sounded so certain. So thoughtful. So final.

Then I heard Tommy say, *"Mom, don't forget about Dad and Dono. Take care of them. Don't miss out on life to be connecting here."*

At that point, I tapped into Doug's energy and was overwhelmed by how much he loved me. How proud he felt as the father of his three boys. How heartbroken he was over losing Tommy, and how strong he was trying to be for me, Dono, and Ethan. While I was on a wild journey of survival, he was at home holding down the fort and loving me from across our crowded city.

Then Dono's energy tumbled in. Pure. Bright. Reeling with pain. He had lost his best friend. His mentor. His idol. And he had no one who could begin to understand what suffering was like from his perspective. His relationship with Tommy was like the one described by Jem's younger sister in *To Kill a Mockingbird.* "He antagonized me sometimes until I could kill him," she said. "But when it came down to it, he was all I had."

I tapped into Dono's energy and acknowledged his emotions. I wrapped my arms around him energetically and promised to give him what neither of us knew he needed.

As the medicine peeled away layers of my being, another energy unexpectedly dropped in. It was female. It was wise. And it was not alone. She had a team of energies surrounding her. I could feel them.

She pointed the conversation in a new direction and advised, *"Set up a meeting with the two of them. Ask them to help unite everyone. To help you fix this together. This field is about community."*

I understood that she was talking about Tommy's Field and that *those two* meant the Head Honcho and Blue-Suit Stan. A surge of energy rushed through me. *"You must go straight to the most negative one,"* she continued. I understood that *one* meant "her." It was hard to believe that I hadn't thought of that before. I was a midfielder who had yet to go 1v1 against the starting midfielder on the opposing team.

"*Allow her to be the hero we need her to be,*" the energy suggested. "*Remind her of all the good she used to do for the neighborhood. Honor all she has done and ask her to teach. To mentor. To share her wisdom. It's time for her to pass it all down, starting now.*"

Okay, I responded telepathically. The advice was so beautiful. So logical. The Head Honcho was nearly eighty years old. Suddenly, I was filled with compassion. She felt threatened by the very community she had spent half her life championing, for better or worse.

"*Get to her through him. Speak to them together,*" the energy advised.

"*Okay,*" I agreed. "*I will ask Blue-Suit Stan to facilitate this meeting. He's a critical part of this and it's important for him to feel like it.*"

For hours this energy and I forged a strategy, and every so often I was reminded to take notes before the finer details of our discussion disappeared forever.

When the entire message was delivered and our conversation ended, I sat up and saw Kelly sitting with my friends across the room. I called her name.

"Coming," she said, promptly kneeling down in front of me. My friends surrounded me. "Now I know what I need to do." Then a rush of energy flowed through my system so hard and fast that I started vomiting. For hours. With Kelly by my side, I purged every ounce of medicine that remained in my body and along with it deeper layers of grief.

When I woke up the next morning at Kelly's and drove home, I immediately dialed Blue-Suit Stan's number. I would not give my rational mind a minute of real-world time to doubt myself or my messengers.

"I would really appreciate a meeting with the two of you," I told Stan when he answered my call. "It's time to bridge this community.

I can't do this without you. Can you set this meeting up as soon as possible? I will accommodate both of your schedules."

Blue-Suit Stan was more than receptive. He was surprised to hear from me and sounded reinvigorated to be playing a pivotal role moving forward.

I never told anyone besides Kelly and my three friends who were physically there with me that night what prompted me to call Stan and the Head Honcho. All anyone else needed to know was that I did.

"They'll just lie, twist your words, and hold whatever you say against you," a few close friends and supporters warned when I told them that a meeting had been scheduled.

"You are wasting your time," Doug insisted, succumbing to his time anxiety.

"Don't bother talking to those two," a council member's staff member said when she spotted me talking to Blue-Suit Stan at a coffee shop in Westwood to prep for the meeting. "You do not need either one of them to get Tommy's Field approved."

She was wrong. They were all wrong. I did need them. The energy that had visited me said I did, and a knowingness buried within my own self confirmed it. This was my attack and I needed to do it my way.

A week later, I entered the Head Honcho's stark white penthouse condominium that overlooked a giant private golf course. I walked across her white marble floors, sat at her glass dining-room table, and looked at Blue-Suit Stan on my right when he handed me a bullet list of discussion points.

I was aware that on the outside, I looked like the grieving mom I would forever be. But on the inside, I was now the lead actress in a serious drama and the CEO of my own start-up.

"I want you to hear my story," I heard myself say, ignoring the sheet of paper in front of me. "You can ask me any questions you want. My story has been consistent from the start. It will never change."

As the Head Honcho analyzed my every word, truth radiated through me inside and out. "I am here to ask you to help bridge this community. Westwood is too divided. Neighbors should not be fighting with one another about improving a field in a public park. You both have the authority to bring people together. You have done a lot for this neighborhood, probably a lot more than I even know, and I'm asking you to help. It's not as if my family is the only one fighting for this project. There are thousands of residents, students, and business owners across Westwood and this entire city who are behind Tommy's Field. Given the positions you have on two separate neighborhood councils in Westwood, you have an obligation to represent and accurately communicate our interests, too."

The Head Honcho leaned in as Blue-Suit Stan sat back. In that moment, the dynamics between them became clearer. This was her show. This was between her and me. Our "1v1" had begun.

"No one is against Tommy's Field or you trying to honor Tommy. If the city has legitimate reasons as to why Westwood Rec Center is the only park in the area that works for Tommy's Field, then the neighbors will just have to accept the city's expertise and I will get them to back down. The city has given too much misinformation to our community about this park in the past, and that's what a lot of this is about. It's not all about Tommy's Field."

Her tone was calm. Smooth. Experienced.

"Frankly, I haven't even been in that park for decades," she added, which would have insulted me to my core had my secret weapon not taken such delight in it.

Blue-Suit Stan fiddled in his chair and added, "We need that report, Nikki. The neighbors have been asking for it for two months now. If Tommy's Field can't fit at Cheviot or another nearby park, they need to tell us why."

I looked at Stan, who appeared rather hyper, compared to his elder teammate. "You told me the first time you ever called me that you were a Westwood guy. That you wanted Tommy's Field in Westwood, not any other park." I didn't even have to look at the Head Honcho to feel the hairs on her neck rising with surprise.

His brown eyes shifted between the two of us and then fired back. "That was before I saw how many neighbors were against this."

You mean like the Dynamic Dozen who continue to be bolstered by all the false information you both send out to neighborhood council and homeowners' association databases that you control and continue to confuse with your propaganda?

Fully prepared to go one-on-one with him, I again explained that I had personally visited the other parks in the area and watched the city measure them. That I had been given the same answers that everyone else has. That both Doug and I were more than open to putting Tommy's Field at another neighborhood park, but that we had no intention of picking a fight with a different group of park neighbors. Every park on the Westside was surrounded by NIMBYs who strongly believed they had the right to determine how "their" park was designed and operated. If he wanted to get the necessary approvals and city permits to build Tommy's Field at another local park, we would gladly accept them, but we had no intention of deviating from our plan A and starting over.

Still, wanting to sound supportive, I turned to the Head Honcho and said, "I will urge the city to provide its report on why Tommy's Field will not fit in any of the other local parks." I wholeheartedly agreed that this should have already been done and expressed my genuine frustration that it wasn't.

Suddenly, Blue-Suit Stan shoved his checklist in front of me again.

"We do not like your political consultant, Aaron. He is a very bad guy. We will not work with you unless you get rid of him."

I see, you want me to get rid of the only guy who knows how to defeat you. I listened to Stan rant, knowing he would soon get lost on a tangent and forget his point.

For the next three hours, I watched my opponents as closely as they watched me. When they went right, I went left. While I played direct, they swerved. When they pressed, I defended. My attack was subtle, but it was beginning.

At one point it dawned on me that Blue-Suit Stan had checked his phone at least a dozen times. *Is he recording me?* I wondered.

Doesn't matter, I reasoned. *It won't change my performance one bit. I already live my life as though someone is watching.*

By now, I was long overdue for a serious cry. I had suppressed innumerable waves of grief and could not withstand the energy and ways of the real world much longer. Mentally. Physically. Emotionally. I was stretched far too thin and had to begin my exit.

I looked at Stan and thanked him for not only scheduling this meeting but also for his previous attempts to find solutions. Although none were successful, I appreciated his efforts.

"It has been a lot of work," he admitted, "And it's not as if you are paying me, Nikki."

A giant red flag started flapping in front of me. *This is the second time he's mentioned that I'm not paying him. If only I was. If only I had listened to the person who told me to hire him as a consultant when all this started. If only I wasn't such a straight shooter, maybe this would have all been over months ago.*

Nearly four hours after our meeting started, the Head Honcho finally cracked a thin smile and said, "We will make Tommy's Field happen one way or another, Nikki. Now you are no longer an outsider, you are an insider. Together we will get this done."

Her words echoed in my ringing ears. *Now I'm an insider? No longer an outsider? Doug and I are second-generation Angelenos. Tommy was third, and so is Dono. Doug was also born in Westwood. What makes her an insider and us outsiders?*

By the time I walked out of her condominium, my lungs were wheezing, my throat was practically closed, and my heart was very much aware that the Head Honcho, a mother and grandmother, had still not given me a single word of condolence.

CHAPTER 19

WHEN I WALKED THROUGH MY FRONT DOOR AFTER MEETING WITH the Head Honcho and Blue-Suit Stan, Doug was waiting for me. I collapsed next to him on our navy-blue couch. Ginger jumped on me, like the lapdog she thought she was, and laid her belly flat on top of mine.

"Well?" Doug asked.

"She said I'm no longer an outsider. Now I'm an insider."

"She's so full of shit!" Doug said, ready to defend and attack all at once.

Not my problem. I've done my job. I took her on. My efforts were genuine. How she reacts moving forward is up to her.

I spent the next two days recovering and building my attack for the *eighth* public meeting on Tommy's Field to be hosted by the third advisory council in Westwood, the newest one, which had heard arguments both for and against the project but still had not voted on it.

When Doug, Dono, and I walked into this council's boardroom, I was relieved to see it filled with kids, parents, and coaches—all there to support us.

The Dynamic Dozen, on the other hand, had shrunk. Their voices were quieter. Their hisses were less aggressive. Their energy was weaker. I couldn't help but wonder if the news camera set up in the corner of the room had anything to do with that.

I proceeded to summarize the trajectory of Tommy's Field in a ten-minute presentation that was based on data, loaded with visuals, and packed with heart. Slide after slide, I attacked every argument that the opponents had ever created, changed, modified, and twisted. I addressed the timeline of Tommy's Field. The number of public meetings to date. The actual visuals of the field for the prior twenty years and the data behind our city's needs for more fields. I did not say anything that hadn't already been said in the seven prior public meetings, but I organized it. Simplified it. Defended it.

Then I attacked. First, gently.

I turned to the nineteen board members in the room and shot low. "If you do not vote in favor of Tommy's Field, you will be voting to keep an open space that has been unused for at least twenty years. You will be supporting underutilized tennis courts. You will be missing out on an opportunity to reinvigorate Westwood Village and attract new visitors. You will be failing to support the city's efforts to create affordable athletic programming for youth in this community."

Empowered by truth, I turned to everyone in the room and shot harder. "The city has modified the design multiple ways and times to appease the concerns of immediate park neighbors. My family has agreed to every single change."

Then I looked straight into the Heckler's eyes and took a direct shot.

"First, you did not want to lose the open space. Now the open space has been saved. So, what in the world are we still fighting about?"

Not waiting for a response, I turned to the board and shot high. "I hope you will accept our gift. The city wants it. The park wants it. The broader community wants it. This is a gift that comes with no strings attached and we hope you vote to accept it."

When I finished my presentation and thanked the board for giving me the opportunity to speak, my left foot stayed glued to the sole of the chunky heeled boot that protected it, while the heel of my right foot lifted and reached for the eternal. My heart was calm. My mind was clear. My body was burning up. The room erupted with applause as if I had just scored my first goal in a professional match. Even some of the Dynamic Dozen were on their feet. One was clapping. Another was crying. The Heckler stayed seated and just stared at me. He looked tired. Ambushed. Defeated.

I sat down next to Doug, shaking from adrenaline.

"That was your best speech yet," he whispered.

My ears were bombarded by high-frequency tones. My back was sticky.

"You are finding your voice," my Boss commended.

Slim stood up and proceeded to explain the opposition's side of the story, although it was clear that I had cut off most of her angles. She panicked. Retreated. Resorted to her underdog act. "We don't have a presentation prepared tonight. . . . We clearly don't have the right backing or know the right people. . . . I just don't feel this process has been fair." She sounded flustered. Unprepared. As if she were the victim that my family and I actually were.

Less than an hour later, the board voted almost unanimously in favor of Tommy's Field. Energy was shifting. Our momentum was building. Our attack was working. Now we had one official neighborhood council in favor of Tommy's Field and one against it. At some point along the way, I had learned that Blue-Suit Stan's council was not officially recognized by the city and would not vote at all. So, soon it would be up to the Recreation and Park commissioners to determine which of the remaining two councils' opinion mattered most and make their own decision.

A few days later, the Heckler emailed me. "Nikki, would you send me a copy of the gift agreement with the city? That would go a long way toward building trust."

"I will gladly give you a copy of the gift agreement in person," I replied before taking a direct shot at him. "When we meet, however, I would like to know what you are willing to do now to help. My family has done so much work to collaborate and find solutions. Now we need your end to be willing to work with us and make some effort to bring this community together."

He went silent on me for days and eventually wrote back saying he no longer needed to see the gift agreement. I could feel the Head Honcho and Blue-Suit Stan's fingerprints behind every one of his typed letters.

As my attack gained momentum, Doug got creative and made some new moves. He contacted a *Los Angeles Times* reporter whose longstanding column he had always admired and pitched the story of Tommy's Field. He had every right to attack from his position and when he did, the reporter picked up the story, interviewed everyone who would speak to him, and released his article both digitally and in print. Fortunately for us, the article elevated the awareness of Tommy's Field across the city, urged the city's leadership to find solutions, and spotlighted the park neighbor who went on record disclosing that he preferred hunting for gophers on the field than improving it for the entire community to play on.

Before I even saw the article or knew it had been released, the Head Honcho emailed me. "Did you get this article written, Nikki?"

Without waiting for my reply, she added, "I can't collaborate with you anymore."

I emailed her back. "Why? I did not personally ask the article to be written but I was interviewed for it. I believe the reporter reached out to you as well for your comments. I told him to." *We are "insiders" working together right?*

I would not apologize for my teammate's tactics and skills. Doug was doing his job and I was learning that mine included respecting his position and getting out of his way.

"Well," she responded, with disgust piercing through every syllable, "this article may help you, but it will not help us. Please do not tell anyone I was talking to you. My side does not know of our conversations."

At that point, I abandoned every well-intentioned effort to collaborate with the Head Honcho. She had drained me and offered nothing in return. Besides, I had more serious problems to address.

Tommy had been gone a year and four months by that point and Dono's sadness had turned into a nasty anger that corrupted his sweet smile and was poisoning his pure heart. Soccer was his only motivation. It connected him with his brother. Allowed him to hit an opposing player shoulder to shoulder at maximum speed and pretend they were going at each other 1v1. It provided a safe environment where he could run from his problems and toward a defined goal.

"I play for Tommy," he announced, revealing his chosen path forward. It wasn't long before he was wearing number twenty-three on his back, pointing at a TM patch stitched on the heart of his jersey when he scored and playing the attacking center-midfield position for two. No coach had to tell him to work harder. To defend tougher. To be more consistent. They only had to remind him to smile.

No matter how hard his lips tried, nothing made his eyes smile. Not friends. Not goals. Not even Ginger.

"Remember, Dono," I delicately said, trying to avoid being verbally attacked by his aggression. "Tommy smiled more than anyone. To smile is to honor him."

His mood darkened. "What if the world just went dark?" he asked one day as we sat in my car in the driveway. "No humans. No animals. No plants. No nothing. I daydream about that sometimes."

I responded with silence.

"Life is too hard here," he continued, giving me a peek inside his mind. "There are too many problems. Everyone's got problems. Even Cristiano Ronaldo has problems. It doesn't matter how many goals he scores. How hard he works. How many games he wins. If he does one thing wrong, people threaten him, attack his reputation, and try to bring him down."

He had a point. Real-world people could be vicious when they forget they were of the same species and were meant to advance together.

I became deeply concerned that his thoughts were depressing his spirit and his spirit was depressing his thoughts. So, I turned to Kelly and her medicine for advice.

"You must heal yourself in order to help him," Kelly gently advised.

"I understand. I've been working on that."

Her silence indicated that I still had a long way to go.

"I'm sure you believe that you and your husband are prioritizing Donovan," Kelly said, "but his soul needs more." More of what, she did not say.

So, I asked the medicine and my divine teachers how to give Dono "more."

Should I tell him "more" about my dreams?

Like the time I dreamt that I was reading a newspaper article and a sentence jumped out at me as if I had suddenly put on magnifying glasses. "I'm always watching over him!" the enlarged text flashed multiple times until I believed Tommy was sending a message to his little brother and I needed to wake up to write it down.

But I did not think Dono would believe my dreams. After all, I was the only one in them.

Should I give him "more" advice? Maybe share some words of wisdom. Teach him how to create new thoughts and reinvent his future.

But if that was beyond difficult for an adult brain to comprehend, it had to be nearly impossible for a grieving child to grasp.

When Kelly's medicine kicked in, an energy advised, *"Mother him out of love, not fear."*

Before I could digest that advice, my eyes sprang open and I saw a silhouette of Tommy's profile on the ceiling. I clenched my eyes shut, believing the medicine was playing tricks on me, but when I reopened them, his silhouette was still there . . . for hours. From the jawline and shape of the nose to his unmistakable haircut, it was undeniably Tommy.

When Kelly's assistant checked on me, I stood up to examine Tommy's profile more closely. Suddenly, a coffee thermos that had been resting on a table underneath Tommy's silhouette flew off by itself and crashed to the floor.

"Whoa!" Kelly's assistant exclaimed. "Did you see that?"

"Don't worry," I said, sitting back down and closing my eyes. "That's just my son."

When I returned home the following day and looked into Dono's distant eyes, all I could see reflecting back at me in his shiny windows was a thick nasty scar holding my heart together.

My memory searched for guidance.

"Will we have sad eyes forever?" I had asked Doug after Tommy's memorial.

"Not forever . . . but for a very long time," he responded with such certainty.

Reason informed me that there was nothing more I could say or do to help Dono if my eyes looked sad and all he saw when he looked through them was a giant scar.

I had a choice to make and directed it at my heart.

It's time for my scar to shrink and allow new heart tissue to grow, just as Kelly once assured me it would.

Then I spoke to Tommy.

"I thought I was sharing my heart equally with you and Donovan, T, but now I understand that he can't see or feel any of it. This scar has woven the fragments of my heart back together and enabled me to survive, but now it must shrink and give me more space to live. Dono must start feeling the love I have for him and not just continue hearing about it."

I received Tommy's blessing.

I closed my eyes and began shrinking my scar with my mind. No matter what size it was, it would forever adorn my heart, inside and out, and never let me forget. My imagination proceeded to reshape it into the TM logo that Tommy had designed with his green velvet–tipped pen and that both Doug and Ethan had permanently inked under their left arms in black. A lifetime of love was being sewn into each initial as I vowed to always wear it like a badge of honor.

"I am honored that you are my son, T. Honored to have had almost thirteen full years with you. Honored that you and Donovan will forever share my heart."

Later that day, when Donovan and I got in the car to leave for soccer practice, I directed energy from my heart directly at Dono's, which was shut tight and did not want to open. It was terrified of all the grief it had already suppressed and was unwilling to expose itself to more.

Recognizing the near-impossible task in front of me, my secret weapon surfaced and offered some advice.

One way to give Dono "more" was for my soul to speak to his.

A fierce love crashed through the crown of my head. My body heated up and thoughts scurried out of the way when my soul began to speak through me.

"Keep playing, Dono," I heard myself say.

Dono looked away. His hearing was perfectly fine, but he couldn't digest my words.

Undeterred, my soul silently connected to Dono's through an invisible cord that bound us together.

"You have swallowed your brother's spirit, Dono, and have the power to play for two. So, attack, Donovan. Attack this beautiful game with all the love that you have for your brother, and with every shot you take, share that love. Honor it. Shine for it. Tommy wants you to shine, Donovan. The brighter you shine, the easier it is for him see you. To connect with you. To advance with you. So, play your heart out, Donovan, the way your brother showed you how."

With a sigh, my soul retreated and the divine wisdom that I had received during my last session with Kelly dropped in.

"Mother him from a place of love. Not worry or fear."

A surge of energy shot through me as if I had found the key that unlocked a hidden treasure chest full of golden wisdom.

The technique was simple. It was also universal and applied to every thought, choice, and decision I made. *Am I doing this or saying that out of love or fear?* The answer to that question rarely failed to present an obvious step forward that minimized my own confusion and maximized results. I could immediately feel the difference, and so could Dono.

I applied the same question to Tommy's Field and allowed the answers to guide my next move. Only love would drive my attack, I decided. I would attack *harder* out of love for my son. *Faster* out of love for my family. *Stronger* out of love for my community. While anger confronted me, it would not fuel me. While resentments challenged me, they would not penetrate me. My intentions were so motivated by love that when darkness approached, I switched on like a light and made it disappear.

CHAPTER 20

EVERY STEP FORWARD ON TOMMY'S FIELD RESULTED IN AT LEAST three steps backward. The two-commissioner task-force meetings that soon followed all the various local neighborhood council meetings were no exception.

During a four-week period, two of the five commissioners showed up at two separate parks in two separate parts of the city for two separate task-force meetings. During both meetings, the same two commissioners listened as Department of Recreation and Park employees presented Tommy's Field and both supporters and opponents voiced their sixty-second opinions.

"Why do I still not have a report explaining why this field can't go in another local park?" one commissioner fumed at a city employee in the middle of her presentation. I wondered the same thing, but found it strange that her tone had forgotten that they all worked for the same city, were supporting the same department, and technically, were on the same team.

Then this particular commissioner pushed harder. "Why do I see a donor wall? I don't like donor walls. This language must come out of the design and the gift agreement. I thought I already made that clear." The only thing that was clear to me was how unaware she was of the number of donor walls, monuments, and memorial benches were already installed across our city's parks.

I studied the GM, who was seated next to this commissioner and was forced to watch members of his own department flail.

Finally, this commissioner nodded her head as if to indicate that the department for which she worked had finally done something right. "I see that all logos have been taken out of the gift agreement and off the field itself."

The Dynamic Dozen smirked as the Head Honcho and Blue-Suit Stan looked on.

I found her comment rather hypocritical, since the very park she was sitting in had logos on multiple fields and scoreboards right outside the recreation center doors where we were congregating.

When the public comment period began, I looked around for the first time and noticed that dozens of new faces had filled the room. Although I didn't know their names, their bright white polo shirts, squeaky clean sneakers, and black sleek sweat outfits told me everything I needed to know.

Tennis is finally getting in the game, it hit me.

When Tennis took their positions and began to speak, they came out swinging. Their legs were strong. Their shots were hard, and because they had missed eight prior public meetings, their follow-through was spinning with passion.

Tennis and the Dynamic Dozen outnumbered Tommy's Field supporters at least three to one by the time the second task-force meeting commenced. I had once again scaled back the number of supporters in attendance because Doug and I agreed it was more important to preserve our team's energy for the final match when all five commissioners would be in attendance and vote. Despite being outmanned in both task-force meetings, I did not regret our decision. The meetings were far from Westwood. They were early on a weekday morning. And they were more of the same. There was only so much madness a human being could take and whatever the outcomes of these two meetings, our team already had a guaranteed spot in the final round.

Still, I listened closely. Tennis did not understand why the city thought the courts were underutilized. Tennis did not see why anyone would be tearing down tennis courts when there was an empty field sitting there next to them. Tennis did not want to be assholes, but they were highly organized and had already convinced hundreds of families in their database to write passionate letters against Tommy's Field, producing a groundswell of new opposition.

Tennis was also spoiled. Tennis had thirty-two public courts across three neighborhood parks all less than two miles from Westwood Recreation Center. It had multiple private tennis clubs in the neighborhood, of which many of the main tennis advocates were also members. And for the most part, Tennis lived in the hills north of the park where beautiful estates with private tennis courts were plentiful.

What Tennis may not have contemplated was the degree to which soccer reflected the changing demographics of our city. We weren't living in the 1970s anymore, when Westwood Recreation Center was designed. At that time, our state was 80 percent non-Hispanic white, and tennis was our country's favorite sport to play. When we came along with Tommy's Field, nearly fifty years later, our city's population had grown by over three million people and Hispanics comprised more than 47 percent, compared to the 29 percent of the population that remained non-Hispanic white. Furthermore, soccer was not only the fastest-growing sport in our country but had far eclipsed tennis and become the fourth most popular sport behind American football, basketball, and baseball.

We had no desire to confront Tennis. I understood how hard it could be to lose something you loved and believed would last forever. Plus, the tennis advocates were not unreasonable people. For the most part, they were respectful, empathetic, and so impressively united by their sport that they were willing to drive forty-five minutes in early LA morning traffic to stand up for it.

Despite my team's weak showing in numbers, we were prepared to teach Tennis how far we had come and how much they had missed along the way.

First, a representative showed up on behalf of our council member to give his formal public vote of support for Tommy's Field. His position was finally on the record.

Then, the executive director of the homeless shelter and preschool located across the street from the park gave her unwavering support for Tommy's Field. "This field has been empty and dangerous for years. My families will not play on it. Tommy's Field will be a beautiful addition and will greatly benefit our families and children living across the street." I watched members of the Dynamic Dozen roll their eyes at the thought of kids from a transitional living center playing in "their" park.

Finally, a mother whose family had donated the children's play area in the park twenty years earlier announced her formal support.

"The neighbors did not want our gift, either," she had explained to me when we initially met and she described that the vision of the play area was to serve children of all circumstances and abilities. "This was before online community chats were set up. Neighbors sent me handwritten death threats. They showed up at the neighborhood meetings claiming that busloads of handicapped children would be taking over 'their' park." After her son passed away, the playground was eventually approved and became the most visited attraction in the park, even by those who had once threatened it.

When it was my turn to speak, I took the opportunity to give Tennis and the two commissioners a reality check from the bottom. "Virtually every person and organization who deals with children in our neighborhood and across this city wants to upgrade Westwood Recreation Center with Tommy's Field." I proceeded to rattle off the names of dozens of public and private schools, local businesses, and venerable national and local nonprofit organizations, along with our city's two MLS teams. The red light flashed, and I dared it to cut me off.

"Tommy's spirit of play connected all kinds of people," I finished. "That is what this field will do for Westwood."

The strength of my own voice surprised me and carried my words farther than they had ever reached before. Tommy's Field was not anti-tennis. Anti-neighbors. Anti-environment. Or anti–anything else. Rather, it was pro-children. Pro-community. Pro-diversity. And proactive in making the best use of our public space to accommodate the changing needs of our diverse city.

The female commissioner's small brown eyes stared vacantly at me before she and her colleague swiftly moved on to the next public comment, and the one after that.

After listening to over an hour of comments and watching the red light cut off tennis players who were not used to the city's procedure, the second commissioner finally spoke.

"All I know is we certainly need more athletic fields in this city, not less. Soccer is what the majority of youth want to play in this city and our parks have not been able to accommodate the demand."

Finally, my head assured me, *there is still hope.*

Maybe, my gut responded, *but not much.*

Dots started forming. They were shaking like little icons on a cell phone about to be deleted and I couldn't get any of them to find their positions and connect.

I returned home and immediately grabbed my green journal to make sense of it all.

I found myself back at the beginning.

"Tommy," I wrote, *"How do we go back to our original design? The one I explained to you on the way down to San Diego. The one that*

faces north to south and upgrades the existing field the way it sits now.
The one that doesn't impact tennis or any other aspect of the park." It
was the only design I had ever truly envisioned.

I released the question and let it float between our worlds. Then
I got open to receive.

"We need to get to the mayor," a message dropped in. Everyone in
the know had told me and Doug that our city's mayor would NEVER
get involved in land-use disputes but that was just another way of
asking me and my secret weapon to defy the impossible.

"Let's get to the mayor, T," I said, first aloud and then again in my
green journal. *"I will try to get to him from here. You try to get to him*
from there, and together let's find a way."

"Tommy's spirit never sleeps," healer Christopher informed me
when I scheduled an hourly tune-up appointment and updated him
on the status of Tommy's Field. "Call him in," Christopher advised.
"Ask him to work with you. You have to invite him in when you want
his help. He has the time. He has the perspective. And he most definitely has the desire. He will help you get this done."

So, I did. Then I emailed a letter to our mayor hoping I could
get his attention and my letter would not get lost in his daily pile of
complaints:

> My husband and I are trying to gift the city $1.2 million to
> build an athletic field in a park for kids to play on, and sixteen
> months and eleven public meetings later, I am increasingly
> dismayed to see no end in sight. I realize you have far more
> pressing matters to address for our city but, then again, if the
> city can't accept over a million dollars to build a community
> soccer field in a public park that conserves millions of gallons
> of water a year and supports the most popular youth sport in
> our city, then what can it do?

Three days letter, the mayor's chief of staff emailed me to say that my letter was received, and she would get back to me on a date and time for a meeting.

The impossible had just become possible.

Still, I knew better than to rely on one long shot.

"Finish!" Tommy's coaches would shout from the sidelines when he approached the goal and discerned which shot to take.

"Go to the park and talk to the birds," healer Christopher further suggested.

I started laughing.

"I am serious," he said, calmly and firmly while the colorful beads that divided his long black dreadlocks clapped in support. "Talk to the trees, the grass, and the birds. Connect with the spirit of the park. Ask if they would like children playing on the land. Ask if they would like to see it be better taken care of. Ask if it's okay to put synthetic turf over it. Talk to them. Listen to them. Explain what the field will look like. Share what it will feel like. Describe the grand opening event and how much joy and laughter this field will provide for children. Then listen."

Intrigued, I grabbed my blue chair the very next morning and sat at the north end of the field under the oak trees where my excel spreadsheet and I had spent considerable time together conducting our field research. I acknowledged the birds chirping in the branches above me and told them they had pretty voices. Then I took the opportunity to explain who I was and what I was trying to do. I figured they had all seen me many times before and hoped they trusted my intentions by now. Whatever they decided, I said, I would still love and appreciate them.

Accepting that my imagination had already outdone itself and reached a point of no return, I got up, walked across the field and boldly asked the grass and its knobby weeds if they were happy or if they were ready for something new. "Would you like to serve more people?" I inquired. "Would you like to look and feel beautiful? Would you like to have fun?" Then I promised never to abandon it or allow it to sit dead with holes ever again. Whatever nature in the park decided, I said I would understand.

Then I walked through the park and spoke to the trees. I asked if they would welcome more families sitting under their shade. If they wanted to watch children playing sports in front of them. If they would like to feel Tommy's spirit of play blowing in between them. I encouraged them to talk to the birds and the grass and even the squirrels, and collectively decide if they wanted Tommy's Field or not. If they did, I asked them to find a way to support it. The final commission meeting was being scheduled, a vote would take place and we were running out of time to turn this game around.

As I walked across the field and back toward my car, parked just the north of it, a hummingbird fluttered beside me.

"Hi, pretty hummingbird," I said, using a higher octave voice that I usually saved for Ginger.

The hummingbird reminded me of the one that had brought Doug to tears a few months earlier. That particular hummingbird had greeted Doug in our front yard one morning, led him up the brick stairs to our front door and danced forward and backward as he sang in Doug's right ear. By the time Doug walked through our front door, he was on the ground.

"Tommy just visited me," he said. "It's the only way I can explain it."

It was the only way I could understand it.

I had learned during our trek through a hummingbird forest in Peru that hummingbirds were historically symbolic to the native cultures where they exist. To the North American Indians, they symbolized eternity. To the Mayans, there were thought to be magical beings given their speed and how quickly they appeared and disappeared. And to the Incas, whose culture surrounded me in Peru, they were considered messengers between worlds.

"Hummingbirds break all rules when it comes to birds," our tour guide informed us. "They are tiny but fast. Playful but fearless. Friendly but tough."

I took mental notes and jotted them down in my green journal when I returned later that day to our lodge.

"Hummingbirds are remarkable athletes," I wrote down as our trek group watched a video on them later than evening. "Their wings flap up to 200 times per second and rotate 360 degrees in an infinity pattern. This is why they are able to perform such complex aerial maneuvers. This is why they are able to hover in the air with such stamina and grace. This is why they are uniquely agile and able to dart at sixty miles per hour in every possible direction, including backward."

I voraciously took notes.

"Hummingbirds are extremely talented and like to show off," the video proceeded to explain as it zoomed in closer on these tiny creatures in their natural habitat. "They are skilled communicators who get in your face. They are promiscuous performers who sing and dance to woo their mates. They are glowing fashionistas whose feathers change color and sparkle in the sunlight to make heads turn. They are also exceptional learners with quick processing speeds and fantastic memories."

The natural world had been transformed into a classroom, where nature and culture connected, and life lessons played out right in front of me.

"But don't underestimate these fearless little birds," the video warned. "They are impulsive little fighters with the courage of a lion who will defend their territory at all costs. Try to steal their nectar and they'll stab with their long, sharp beaks and trap with their forked tongues."

My hand was aching. My heart was pumping. My mind was racing.

"Hummingbirds have the largest hearts of all animals relative to their size and weight," the video pointed out at the very end. "Unfortunately, they live such fast lives that these speeded-up creatures constantly live on the edge and only live up to a maximum of twelve years."

My heart skipped a beat. My lungs missed a breath. *Twelve years, huh?*

The hummingbird that approached me that day in the park after I had spoken to the birds, the trees, and the field itself, also reminded me of the one that had visited me the very next morning after Doug had been visited by his. Mine had a ruby-colored throat; hovered at eye level in front of my dashboard window; flew around to the passenger side window, as if it were my right ear; and also started performing for me. And just like the one that was flying next to me as I crossed the field at the park and headed to my car, it reminded me of someone I knew.

"Hi, T-bone. Thank you for my sign," I said, feeling tears well up.

Then like magic, the bird disappeared.

When I returned home from the park and reported back to Healer Christopher, he advised, "Now, go back to the field and offer it something."

"What do you mean?" I asked.

"Go purchase five clear crystal quartz rocks and cover them in a bowl filled with warm water and pink Himalayan salt. Place them under the moon overnight and then under the sun for a full day, and then grab a small shovel and take them with you to the park. When you get there, dig a twelve-inch hole in each of the four corners where you want the field to be situated. Bury one crystal in each corner. Each rock represents a different aspect of our world—the spiritual, emotional, mental, and physical. Then dig a hole in the

center of the field and bury the fifth crystal, which represents whatever higher power you believe in. As you bury each, pray and have
the conversation."

I accepted my assignment and returned to the park the next evening. While the rest of the park was active and illuminated around
me, the field and I were in darkness. With a black hoodie covering my
head, I dug a hole in the northwest corner of the field, which was wet
and slippery with stinky mud, and I buried the first sparkling clear
quartz rock sitting in my pocket. "May you accept this gift of love," I
whispered to the land.

Then I walked to the southwest corner of the field, which was
dusty and dry, and nearly broke my small shovel as I searched for a
section of dirt that would allow me to dig a hole and bury a second
raw, jagged stone in it. "May you accept this gift of love," I repeated,
treating all four corners as equals.

After completing the first part of my sacred test and glancing
up at the tennis courts that were in fact full, I stood in the middle of
the field, dug a fifth hole, and spoke to my Boss as I buried the last
quartz stone. "I hope you accept this gift from Tommy, our family,
and this community. In return, I promise this field will bring new
energy to this park. I promise it will bring joy to more children and
adults. I promise it will bring positive change to Westwood."

When I returned home from burying stones at the park that
night, I was relieved to see Sheila and her massage table waiting for
me with candles and incense burning.

Sheila was an acupuncturist and intuitive healer, not to mention
a new-dimension friend, who had been coming to my house every
Tuesday evening to help move energy though my body with needles
and teach me how to connect with Tommy in my dreams. She was
young, enthusiastic, and wicked smart. She also spoke fast and talked
about spirits, energy, and the divine ways of our universe as if she

were an elder passing down centuries of divine magic. I often had to remind myself that she was only thirty.

"Let's go one step further," she responded enthusiastically after I divulged the details of my ceremony at the park earlier that evening. "Let's do a flower offering, too."

Why not? I asked myself.

"I will meet you there tomorrow morning at 7:00 a.m. before anyone shows up at the park," Sheila insisted. "Then I can also see what's going on there energetically."

When I arrived at the park the following morning with my hands full of brightly colored bouquets of roses, Sheila was already there waiting for me with her bag full of tricks. The park had not yet awakened and about a dozen tents for homeless people on the east side of the park remained tightly zipped shut.

We strolled through the park, and I explained the many twists and turns of Tommy's Field. All the public hearings. The misrepresentations. The distortions. The deceit. The letters. The egos. The wasteful redesigns. The burgeoning budget. I once again heard how absurd it all sounded.

"What's made this entire process even harder," I continued, "is that since the drama around Tommy's Field has escalated, more people know about the park, the community has started using the field, the neighbors suddenly care about it and board members on old-school local councils who haven't used the park in decades suddenly are taking ownership of it. It's as if nature is fighting against us."

"It's more like nature is preparing itself for you," she said.

"What do you mean?" I asked.

She proceeded to explain that every project has a gestation period, just like a pregnancy. "Before a baby is born, the body spends nine months developing it. The body nourishes the baby. Provides a proper environment for its growth. Creates the necessary energy for it to thrive. You can't just make a baby and deliver it the same day. It takes time for the universe to prepare for it."

"It's the same process for this field or any type of new development or growth," she continued to explain seeing my confusion. "The land was left dead and abandoned. Then your family comes along and wants to give it life. The gestation period begins. It rains. Someone seeds it and starts mowing it. The grass starts growing. People start talking about the field. More people start paying attention to the park and visiting it. It's all part of a standard gestation period that is bringing energy to the field and preparing it for life. The problem is that everyone has gotten overly excited about the possibilities and now the new design no longer fits the energy of the park. The project is stuck."

Being stuck was like watching a soccer match end in a nil-nil draw. Two teams play their hearts out. Loyal fans cheer them on to the bitter end. Neither team finishes. The clock runs out. The final score flashes 0–0, and everyone walks away disappointed.

The thought of it made my stomach groan.

"Energy is not all woo-woo," Sheila assured me, giving me encouragement. "It's very mathematical and a lot like geometry. Energy works according to very specific grids. Just as the truth has very distinct lines and edges that never shift, the park has an energy grid within which this field is meant to fit. This field *must* be designed in the north-south direction. It's the only layout that works energetically in this park." No wonder it was the only design I had ever truly believed in.

We proceeded to dig one small hole in each of the four corners of the field and bury fresh red rose petals in them. With each offering, we asked the land to help the community make the right decision about Tommy's Field.

Then we dug a hole in the center of the field and buried a mixture of red, pink, and yellow rose petals, along with a tobacco and cedar mixture that, unbeknownst to me, Sheila had concocted and burned for our ceremony the evening before.

"This is for the Tongva native American tribe who originally settled on this land and had it taken from them," Sheila said. "Their spirit is in this park, too, and it's important to recognize them, to honor them, and to help heal them. Someone took this land from them at some point, without fair compensation, and it's time to give something back. We can never take without giving in return. The universe will always find a way to correct any imbalances."

After our field ceremony, Sheila encouraged me to walk around the park and ask the neighbors' ancestors for compassion.

"Really?" I asked, wondering if there was any kind of spiritual limit one could reach.

"Totally!" she said, her piercing blue eyes shining back at me as if they were divinely possessed. "We all have ancestors and family lines in need of healing, and it is through those of us living on this physical plane that this can be achieved. What most of the neighbors are so angry about has nothing to do with this field. Have compassion for them. For their ancestors. For their situations. Ask their family members in the sacred world to get involved and start healing their family members in this one for the benefit of each other, this park, and our city."

Since facts and knowledge weren't getting Tommy's Field done, I was willing to bet on my imagination.

Sheila and I parted ways and wandered separately around the park, each of us having discreet conversations with other people's ancestors.

First, I addressed our mayor's ancestors. *"If you could please talk to our mayor and convince him to meet with us and hear our story, I would really appreciate it. Our mayor is the only real-world person left who can save Tommy's Field in Westwood. He's the only authority who can hold his commissioners accountable for implementing his vision for our parks. If you could nudge the mayor to set up our meeting and hear me out, I'd really appreciate it. Whatever he ultimately decides about Tommy's Field we will accept."*

Next, I addressed my own ancestors. *"We have a lot of healing to do."*

"It's time to finish," I whispered aloud, imagining my great-great grandparents, and the son they lost at Tommy's age, smiling down on me. I didn't just mean finish Tommy's Field. I also meant finish succumbing to the curse that had viciously been woven through our family line and had made its way to me. I meant finish learning whatever life lessons our loss was designed to teach and start ensuring that no one in our family ever endured a tragedy like mine again. As multiple sets of ancestors listened to my pleas and the field clung to the small treasures that I had offered to it, our luck began to change.

First, our city's deputy mayor called and asked to meet me and Doug at the park. When we did, she placed her hands on both my shoulders and said, "I want everyone to know that the mayor's office fully supports this project. That's why I'm here meeting you in public at this park. I want the neighbors to see me," she said.

But the neighbors weren't there that day. Neither were the commissioners. And given the attitudes I had seen from the task-force commissioners and the disconnects I had seen between the Department of Recreation and Parks, our neighborhood advisory councils, our council member, and the mayor, I still was not willing to take only one shot and rely on a single real-world person to successfully finish it, no matter what his or her title was.

Fortunately, the next day, our political consultant, Aaron, called to let us know that the Department of Recreation and Parks had had a sudden change of heart and was reconsidering my original design for Tommy's Field. The one Tommy and I had discussed on our way to San Diego. The one that ran north to south and that I had recently asked Tommy's spirit to help resurrect. The only one that had ever truly felt right.

When Doug and I received this news, we immediately refined our plan A and privately agreed that if the city did not move forward with it, we would look for a plan B somewhere else. Our egos had no problem letting the Dynamic Dozen claim victory if it meant making sure Tommy's Field best accommodated the park it was in and the surrounding community it served. Our intentions behind Tommy's Field had never been clearer.

As plan A crystallized, my anxieties about the future of Tommy's Field diminished and my dreams at night flourished. One evening, I dreamt that my throat was painfully dry. So, in the dream, I rolled out of bed and stumbled into the kitchen to get some water. Dressed in the pink flannel pajamas that I had fallen asleep in that night, I got a glass of water, turned around, and saw a sparkling green humming-bird hovering inches from my face. I lowered myself to the floor, leaned back against our stainless-steel refrigerator door and pressed the soles of my bare feet flat against the wooden floor beneath me. "Hi, Tommy," I said, gazing at the hummingbird, who was gleefully dancing in front of me at eye level.

Then the hummingbird started playing with Ginger, who in my dream had followed me into the kitchen and was politely sitting by my side. The hummingbird darted back and forth between us. Play-ing. Singing. Buzzing with delight.

"Ginger!" I shrieked, as I watched her famous jaws open and try to playfully capture the tiny bird. "That's Tommy! You can play with him, but don't hurt him!"

I looked up at the single bulb shining over our sink and spoke aloud in my dream. "I miss you so much, T. I love you so much."

The instant I finished the "ch" sound in the second *much*, all the lights in the kitchen went dark, except for the one above the sink that blinked on and off as if it were communicating some sort of secret code. Bursting with excitement, I clapped my hands and cried, "Thank you so much, T. I can't believe you are here. Thank you for my sign!"

My clap was so loud it woke me up and prompted me to write every detail down. To this day, the dream is so clear. So real. I can still see that hummingbird. Feel it. And words cannot express how much I miss it.

CHAPTER 21

As I left the future of Tommy's Field in the hands of nature, multiple sets of ancestors, and our mayor, I turned my attention to my next project. The one labeled "Book #1" in velvet-tipped green ink pen that I had drawn on a branch stemming from the right side of my tree.

"We will write a memoir," a message had dropped in during a recent meditation class. I agreed that we would and as I waited for the final meeting on Tommy's Field to get scheduled, I walked up to UCLA to conduct some research on Westwood and start writing my prologue.

When I planted myself in the middle of UCLA's Powell Library at a table full of college students cramming for tests, I clicked into the university's public database and searched historical archives of *LA Times* articles that documented the history of Westwood. I had no idea what I was looking for until, less than an hour later, I found it.

It was an *LA Times* article dated May 12, 1974, titled: "Park Groundbreaking Slated in Westwood." I skimmed it the first time I saw it, not realizing I had struck gold: "The official groundbreaking for the first segment of a 19.2-acre park . . . will be held at 1:30 p.m. Tuesday, May 14."

When my breath stopped short, I examined the details more closely.

". . . the official groundbreaking . . . will be held . . . Tuesday, May 14 . . ."

"Seriously, T?" I whispered, releasing a loud huff.

Heads looked up, and I could feel Tricky Tommy snickering.

"Tommy, the groundbreaking of Westwood Park actually took place on May 14. It could have taken place on any day of the year, but it took place on your birthday?"

Now Tricky Tommy was howling, just the way he and Dono were the night he left and I tickled under his arms.

The facts continued to hit me.

". . . will be held at 1:30 p.m. . . ." *"Tommy, you were born at 1:40 p.m. What are the chances that ceremony started ten minutes late . . . ?"*

Astonished by this discovery, I saved the article and promptly shut down my laptop. While my memoir was only beginning, I knew Tommy's Field was done.

My head started tingling and a clear message dropped in.

"It doesn't matter how you start, Mom. It matters how you finish."

Chills exploded through my chest and lined my arms with goose bumps.

I got to thinking. Maybe my healers had all been real-world people in disguise. Maybe my dreams were all steeped in wishful thinking. Maybe the many spiritual messages I had received were really just purified thoughts. Maybe even all the hummingbirds that graced my presence were just convenient signs of nature that I had conveniently woven into my story. But one thing was fact and finally appeased my practical mind. The groundbreaking of Westwood Recreation Center, which occurred thirty-one years prior to Tommy's birth, had taken place on the very same date and within minutes of the very same time that Tommy had entered our world. When that truth found its edge, I knew for certain that Tommy's Field was destined to be developed in this park and it was time for me to get out of the way.

Elated by this discovery, I visited Healer Christopher to share the news. "Guess what day the groundbreaking of the park originally took place on?" I asked, anxious to test the extent of his superpowers.

"Tommy's birthday," he responded with a knowingness that did not feel human.

"How did you know?" I asked, genuinely surprised.

"Because it makes perfect sense. The universe works with precision. There are no accidents. You can't make this shit up, Nikki."

Without another word, his television turned on in front of us and flashed a bright blue screen just as it had multiple times for me at home. The remote control was sitting on a table across the room.

Christopher smiled at me. "If that's not a sign that Tommy is with you, I don't know what is."

Days later, I got the call I was waiting for. The mayor was ready to meet. Downtown in his office. This was nearly a year and half after my family had made the decision to donate Tommy's Field.

"When are you available?" his office asked me.

"Any time the mayor is," *obviously*.

On that early December day when Doug and I sat down with our mayor, I could feel Tommy's enthusiasm follow me into his office.

"We did it, T," I silently acknowledged. *"We got here."*

Then I clicked into the real world and got down to business.

"Thank you for this gift," the mayor said to us both. "Thank you for honoring Tommy in this beautiful and important way. I know how difficult the NIMBYs in your area can be and I really appreciate how you have not given up."

I gave my spiel again. Doug gave his, and then the mayor assured us that Tommy's Field would not be a problem.

In response, I simply asked, "Do your commissioners know that Tommy's Field won't be a problem? At least one of them seems to have a different opinion on the matter and does not appear very supportive."

I studied him. I had spent my entire first incarnation career working for leaders at the very top of their organizations, like him.

The top was busy. Savvy. Made promises without being fully aware of the many disconnects between the top and the bottom that might derail them. The top was also my specialty. For the sake of our mayor's reputation, the future of our parks, and the sanity of the people who worked for him, I was helping to improve his operations and make him more effective.

"Your commissioners don't like logos. They don't like donor walls. They don't seem to like anything that represents all the love and community behind this field," I pointed out. "They appear to be taking action based on their personal opinions, rather than supporting your own public park strategy."

He smiled and assured me it would all get straightened out.

"Based on how difficult the approval process for Tommy's Field has become," I responded, "who would ever want to create another public-private partnership with our city again? My family is driven by love so we were never giving up, but most people who want to serve and better their communities would never expose themselves to the kind of nastiness and abuse that we've had to endure."

He genuinely apologized for the process and assured us that he would be meeting with Recreation and Parks and his commissioners to clarify his vision for our city's public parks and the way in which he expected them to work together moving forward.

That was all I needed to know.

When Doug and I left the mayor's office that day, we felt some sanity reenter our lives. We still had no idea what the outcome would be, which field design would ultimately be presented and what steps the mayor would actually take after our meeting, but since we were both very clear on plan A, we trusted it to lead Tommy's Field to the right location. It was as if the more we committed to our own selves, the more we trusted the world to commit to us.

CHAPTER 22

ONE MONTH LATER, AT 7:00 A.M. ON JANUARY 16, 2020, I SETTLED into my gray SUV and drove downtown to Expo Park, where the commissioners of the Department of Recreation and Parks were scheduled to vote on Tommy's Field two hours later. The mother in me needed the car ride alone to connect with Tommy. The operator in me wanted to get down there early to make sure logistics like parking were organized. The dreamer in me wanted to verify that the day was actually happening before all of our supporters made the drive.

As I made my way through Westwood, and headed downtown, some of LA's finest landmarks triggered my deepest memories.

There was the tall white Federal building that I passed on my left that reminded me of the once relatively unknown park that sat behind it. The one where Tommy and decades of children had watched the empty field swirl with dust and eventually turn to mud.

There was the journey I took on the 405 Freeway South that reminded me of the last trip Tommy and I took to San Diego and the fateful conversation we had that will forever give me peace.

There was the 10 East Freeway that I merged onto toward downtown, paralleling the train ride Tommy took from his middle school to the Expo Park metro stop where I picked him up on the way to practice.

Every landmark and corresponding memory was stitched into the scar that will forever grace my heart.

When I finally approached Expo Park and its tall black northern gates, I could not simply pass by my surroundings without acknowledging them, as I did in my first incarnation. Instead, I studied them. Dissected them. Tried to reassemble them.

First, I stared at the Los Angeles Memorial Coliseum, adorned with Olympic rings and a torch on the outside and blessed with perfectly groomed blades of Bermuda grass on the inside. Having learned from my research at UCLA that it was built in 1923 to honor our city's Great War veterans, I marveled at the way it had evolved and expanded alongside the city it serves.

When I drove through the park and searched for a parking spot, I wondered what the birds and the trees and the spirit of the park thought about the disparity of its neighbors and what they planned to do about it. USC and the park's fancier neighbors to the north were in stark juxtaposition to the homeless encampments I saw to the south.

The morning of the vote turned out to be full of unexpected highs. There were the hundred or so friends and colleagues who showed up to support us. The generation of elders who came to share their wisdom. The community leaders from adjacent parts of our city who arrived armed with strong political arguments. The passionate public comments that reminded the commissioners that this was about more than just a field. The thorough presentation by the Department of Recreation and Parks that finally explained why no other park in the neighborhood was able to accommodate Tommy's Field as well as Westwood Recreation Center and why the field's design in the north-south direction was the final one being recommended. There were the supportive texts Doug received from our center back, who wasn't able to attend in person but was listening in on a live feed on behalf of the parks' advisory board. And there was the realization that Tennis was nowhere to be seen.

The day also had its lows.

There was the undeniable boredom I saw in the eyes of the commissioners throughout the hour-long public comment period. There was the commissioner who didn't show up because the term of her services had ended, and there was another commissioner who was feeling ill and excused herself in the middle of the meeting, leaving two empty commissioner chairs and only three left to vote. There was the realization that neither the commissioners nor the Dynamic Dozen could empathize with what it was like for a team to pursue victory in the face of incomprehensible loss. There was the flashing red light that cut off heartfelt opinions and stories. There were the hisses from the Dynamic Dozen seated behind me and all the times they called our team liars and bullies under their breath.

"Let's hurry up and finish this already, Mom!" a message dropped in as the commissioners prepared to render their individual votes. Never could I have anticipated how much watching Tommy play would help me in building his legacy.

My thoughts were interrupted by the sharp knock of the president of the commission's gavel as she gave the final vote, unanimously approving Tommy's Field, 3–0. The room erupted. Cell phones started filming. Doug and I embraced and then our community lifted us once again with hugs and cheers.

I slowly made my way toward the exit.

Out of the corner of my eye I saw Pink Lips coming in for a hug. "I will never visit that park again," she said with a smile. We were no longer feuding neighbors. We were friendly acquaintances who agreed to disagree.

Then a woman I did not recognize approached me. I had only vaguely processed the back of her blond head when she stood up at the very end of the public comment period to support Tommy's

Field. "I represent US tennis," she said to me as supporters hugged and cried all around us. "I am so sorry we had to oppose the last design of the field. I felt really bad about that. A lot of the tennis community did as well. But I'm so glad a design was created that works for almost everyone."

"Thank you so much," I said, handing out yet another hug and leaving it at that.

When I entered the hallway that would lead me downstairs and outside, Blue-Suit Stan extended his hand to me. "Congratulations, Nikki."

I looked at him and debated what to say in response.

I considered telling Stan that, as much as Doug and many of our supporters wanted to punch him in the face, I was grateful for the role he played in this drama and specifically appreciated the way his tedious arguments had pulled me out of my grief for minutes at a time and distracted me to the point where I had survived longer than I believed was possible.

When those thoughts evaporated and failed to return, I thought about thanking Stan for always recognizing Donovan, for complimenting all of his public comments, and for encouraging him to become president of the United States.

I also considered thanking him for all the times he greeted me and reached across the aisle.

Most importantly, I almost thanked him for honoring his own close family member who I had only recently learned had lost a child. There was a line Blue-Suit Stan did not cross with me and my family, perhaps because his soul had its own edge and a deeply rooted sense of empathy would not let him.

Unfortunately, when I looked him in the eye, all that my voice could muster without falling apart was, "Thank you, Stan. I really appreciate that." Then I walked downstairs to get some air.

By the time I walked out of the recreation building minutes later, some of the Dynamic Dozen were huddled outside with the Head Honcho, plotting their revenge. Supporters lingered. Ginger, who arrived with a friend of ours in time for the verdict, was sitting in the middle of everyone with a TM23 T-shirt on and a basket full of freshly baked green velvet–tipped pen–colored TM23 cookies by her side. I had been a soccer mom long enough to know that, win or lose, after every match, players need to eat.

Minutes later, Dono and both his and Tommy's friends jetted off to school. Doug took off for the office. And I drove back to Westwood alone with my thoughts, surrounded by Tommy's spirit and protected by my Boss.

As I passed the same landmarks that had triggered deeply emotional memories just hours earlier, the past fell behind as bright possibilities of the present pressed forward.

"I showed you how to play, Mom," Tommy's spirit reminded me during the vote. *"Keep playing hard. I showed you how."*

By the time I neared Westwood, the fog in my brain that rolled in when Tommy departed began to lift as the drama of Tommy's Field came to an end. My ears might forever ring. My head might forever tingle. And messages might forever drop in to guide my way. But just as with Tommy's departure, there was no use rehashing all the whys, questioning all the hows, or pondering all the ifs behind them.

Later that evening, Doug confirmed that he had reached out to the GM of the Department of Recreation and Parks to thank him for all of his efforts and support.

"I've personally learned so much from you and Nikki," he told Doug. "We are a stronger department because of Tommy's Field."

I still couldn't believe this was my life and turned to Doug to ask, "Why Tommy?"

"I never ask myself that question," Doug replied. "All I ever ask myself is why we were so blessed to have him."

It is these words I remember when sadness creeps in and the scar stitched across my heart begins to ache.

Not long after that fateful day, my Boss approached me in my dreams. It had no form. No color. No voice. And yet it gently rippled through the air, introducing itself as the universe and speaking directly to me.

"I'm sorry for taking Tommy," it said. *"Please forgive me."*

"I forgive you," I said, hardly believing my own ears.

Then my mind switched on in the middle of this dream. *"I'm not sure I mean that,"* I said, testing my truth. *"I want to forgive you, but I'm not sure that I do."*

"Tommy and our family were doing good here together."

"We needed him here," the universe immediately responded.

"Maybe one day I will forgive you," I added, knowing that day would have to come. *"I'm not ready yet."*

Then I woke up, wrote my dream down, and fell back to sleep, wishing our conversation would continue. I wanted to ask why Tommy was so needed there. I wanted to get more facts to address my lingering resentments. I wanted another chance to forgive.

But when I woke up in the morning, reread my notes, and replayed the conversation in my mind, I knew that it couldn't have finished any other way. My truth had found its edge, and whenever I was ready to shift and truly forgive, I knew that my Boss would be right there listening and waiting to receive.

CHAPTER 23

TWENTY MONTHS AFTER BEING APPROVED, AND NEARLY THREE-and-a-half years after Tommy left us, Tommy's Field officially opened on September 26, 2021.

Never could I have predicted all that would transpire between the day of the vote and opening day.

There was the COVID pandemic that shut the real world down for over a year and forced everyone in it to experience loss and transformation together. I watched from my dimension as fear divided friends and families, cities and states, and I couldn't help but wonder how people would resolve their growing list of differences, given how hard it was to simply improve a desiccated field in a public park for children to play on.

There were the regular meetings that the Head Honcho's neighborhood council hosted online during the pandemic, which, to my surprise, continued to include Tommy's Field as an agenda item. Meeting after meeting, board members took the opportunity to berate city officials and demand that the development of Tommy's Field be delayed indefinitely. They did not understand, or perhaps did not care, that when our city reopened, both children and adults would need to reengage with their communities and play more than ever.

There was the Westwood Recreation Center's director who was transferred to the park at some point during the ongoing drama of Tommy's Field approval and appeared to have been struck by amnesia when he later appointed three of Tommy's Field's harshest opponents to the park's advisory board, including Slim and the Heckler. The Head Honcho and Blue-Suit Stan stood behind them, expanding their authority over a park that neither of them frequented, much less cared about, prior to the approval of Tommy's Field.

Fortunately, all the insanity was offset by unforgettable moments of magic.

There was the school that contacted Doug and me out of the blue because it had heard about "Tommy's Field" and wanted one of its own. Not only did this school serve our city's most underserved and challenged children, but it offered to open its campus for the first time in its hundred-year history and share the field with its neighbors. A new branch on the left side of my tree drawn in velvet-tipped green ink began to grow.

There was the reading I had with a medium named Rebecca, who told me that a spirit with the initials JR was guiding me. When I didn't recognize these initials, she said I had an album of some sort that was hers. *Jennie Ruben*, I later remembered, my great-great-grandmother who was married to my Hungarian great-great-grandfather, who lost a son Tommy's age, loved to "do art," and whose high school autograph album rested on a shelf in my living room. It was during this reading that Rebecca also told me there was the spirit of a young boy communicating with us that day who loves me, who hears me, and who is soaring higher in his world because of the work we are doing together in this one. "This spirit says hello to his grandfather, 'Pops,'" she said, which was what Tommy called my father, his grandfather. Then Rebecca unexpectedly cut our reading twenty minutes short because this young spirit told her, *"My mom and I don't need you, Rebecca. We are good. We talk all the time."* I agreed and politely hung up.

There was the former teammate of Tommy's from the east side of our city who at the age of fifteen signed his first professional MLS contract; the other former teammate from the south side who signed with a top international agent; the fifteen-year-old girlfriend from the north side with whom Tommy used to train, who already played professionally with women three years older and was a rising star in the US Women's National Team pool of players; the sixteen-year-old goalkeeper from mid-city who landed the Division 1 scholarship of his choice; and there was the growing list of teammates spread across the country, all wearing TM necklaces, bracelets, tattoos, and armbands beneath their jerseys when they played and who continued to be inspired by their flashy friend to pursue the game they loved.

There was the massive shift we saw in Donovan after three years and three months. His smile returned. His blue eyes reverted to their natural color. And our trio could eat together. Drive together. Even travel together. With a TM charm draped around his neck, Dono asked us to drive him across the crowded streets of our city so he could play with the most talented players he could find. Every minute in traffic together was perfection.

There was Ethan's transformation. The decision he made to stop numbing his pain and start addressing the root of it. And the day he committed to a job he found meaningful and reentered the real world on his own terms.

There was the spiritual journey that Doug pursued on his own every now and again. The one he declared was full of crazy signs and "mumbo jumbo" and that he enthusiastically told his real-world friends all about before immediately challenging them in his lawyerly tone: "How do you explain it?"

There was the spirituality my father embraced. The mornings he talked to Tommy while drinking coffee out of a cup Tommy had painted for him. The pictures and text messages he forwarded to assure me that our family would never ever forget the child who left us all too soon.

There was the night when I stopped dreaming that I was in the back of a classroom learning and found myself standing in front of a class teaching. There were also the deeply memorable dreams that continued to fill up my dream journal, including the one during which Tommy assured me, *"Don't worry, Mom. I got the meaning of life before I left."*

There were the eight hours a day that I committed to writing my memoir, and the multiple dozens of green journal notebook inserts that piled high in my bedroom cabinet. There were all the other hours I spent playing Tommy's guitar, writing songs, and singing . . . just as I loved to do as a child. And there was the day Doug started taking guitar lessons and regularly serenaded me before bed at night.

There were the flickers of light in our new home. The wisps of air that made Ginger and me both look up when I wrote to Tommy in my green journal at night. And the high-pitched ringing in my ears that made me feel that Tommy was visiting me. Playing with me. Whispering to me.

And there was the personal realization that I no longer needed mediums to help me connect with my son. Nor did I crave plant-based medicine or actively seek new spiritual modalities on a regular basis. I was creating the world I wanted to see, and when I felt stuck, I trusted both myself and the beautiful game that Tommy loved to play to guide my next move.

EPILOGUE

At 4:00 p.m. on the day of the Tommy's Field grand opening event, Dono, Doug, and I arrived at Westwood Recreation Center and walked past a large wooden park sign that said, tommy's field welcomes you . . . My breath stopped.

You did so good in this world, T, I whispered. *You are still doing so good.*

As I walked through the park and toward Tommy's Field, memories of our family and nearly a thousand friends congregating for Tommy's memorial up at UCLA quickly flashed through my mind. It still felt like yesterday, but now we were all smiling and ready to celebrate.

When guests arrived, many of them painted rocks with beautiful messages and symbols and placed them next to a poster-size rendering of a dedication plaque that included a picture of Tommy celebrating a goal in his jersey number, twenty-three, and was a temporary stand-in for the donor wall that would finally be approved by Recreation and Park commissioners a month later. Two portable wrought-iron gates designed with hummingbirds welded into them were covered with freshly cut roses and served as a cheerful backdrop where we all took a private minute to honor our boy.

Before the opening ceremony began, Eastside and Westside friends and family mingled.

Music played.

Lemonade flowed.

And ice cream carts, hot dog grills, and popcorn stands proudly served Tommy's favorite treats.

When the music stopped, Tommy's friends sat on the sideline of the field with Dono and Ethan, just as they had during Tommy's memorial. Older adults filled up two sets of bleachers behind them, while younger ones scattered themselves in between.

I stood in the middle of the field looking out at everyone and thought, *We have all come a long way together.*

Then Doug kicked off the opening ceremony.

"At the count of three, let's all shout, 'Thank you, Tommy!'"

I could sense Tommy beaming.

Our district's council member proceeded to thank our family for our perseverance.

Our city's GM of Recreation and Parks expressed sincere gratitude for our much-needed gift.

One of our city's park commissioners reinforced the need for more athletic fields across our city, as if Tommy's Field had been a no-brainer to the commission all along.

The LA Galaxy spoke of the importance of prioritizing community over rivalry.

LAFC addressed Tommy's passion for the game; noted that his picture graces its corporate office walls; and cited how his legacy was already inspiring others to play the game he loved.

Speech after speech, I clapped. I smiled. And my spirit buzzed.

When it was my turn to speak, I walked toward the podium and stood in front of everyone just as I had done at Tommy's memorial. Only this time, Dono was not holding my hand. I was not shaking. And my feet were firmly grounded.

I did not stop to look for Tommy, but, knowing his spirit was there, I took the opportunity to plead . . . *Please don't mess with the audio system, T. Not now . . .*

I proceeded to tell everyone about the discussion Tommy and I had driving down to San Diego the weekend before he left. How I had told him that I was thinking about building an adult-size athletic field with lights for this community. How he said our neighborhood didn't have anything like it and he couldn't wait to play on it. How when he departed three days later, my friend Linda convinced me to finish what I'd started.

"Tommy would want to know that his life is continuing to impact others," she told me that very day he left.

"Wouldn't we all?" I posed to everyone.

"Whether you are the one who donated financially to this field," I continued, "or you are the one who supported it by showing up to meetings, writing letters, or simply taking the time to be by our side. Or you are the one who still checks in on our family, sends us pictures of Tommy, and continues to share memories and thoughts of Tommy . . . you have helped build this field. And we thank you."

I smiled thinking about the hundreds of kids who had already jumped the construction fence in the prior weeks to play on the field.

"Tommy would have been one of them," I told everyone, "if not the first."

"I've learned from Tommy," I continued, "that when the world feels too dark, feels overly divided, or we are just downright sad, that it's to our benefit to play more. That's what Tommy would do."

Then one of Tommy's favorite people, who was not only the largest single donor to the field outside of our family, but also embodied the spirit of play that Tommy so deeply valued, led everyone to the ribbon-cutting moment.

Dono, Tommy's close Westside friends and Eastside teammates, along with their siblings, all lined up and ran from the northern end of the field through a massive red ribbon that extended the width of the field and through the center circle where TOMMY'S FIELD was permanently painted in black capital letters just as the head of Recreation and Parks had suggested it be.

Music pumped louder and the celebration officially began.

Field lights turned on. Kids and adults started throwing footballs at one end. Soccer balls got kicked at another. And hundreds of adults stood center circle, taking pictures, and absorbing every inch of love stitched into the field.

Underneath my sneakers, I felt the soul of the field begin to activate.

Healer Sheila, Doug, and I had visited the field months earlier to conduct a private ceremony. We again buried crystals, red roses, and drops of Egyptian oils underneath a small portion of its dirt surface prior to the synthetic turf being installed. Every offering we made to the land was accompanied by a specific intention.

"With this crystal, I activate Tommy Mark's joy and enthusiasm for everyone who plays on this field," I said. Then I buried a clear quartz rock into the dirt and sprinkled some tears along with it.

"With this crystal, Tommy's Field will unite this community and bring more positive energy back to Westwood," Doug continued, dropping his crystal into the ditch next to mine.

Crystal after crystal, rose after rose, we linked beautiful memories of one meaningful life lived to future memories of uncountable lives ahead.

After all the crystals were buried, I gave them a directive.

"When the day comes when our immediate family is no longer living, you are to neutralize and allow this land to be converted into whatever it needs to be to best accommodate the community at that time."

There would be no more drama for this land if I could help it.

Now standing center circle, surrounded by our community on opening day, I celebrated as Tommy would after scoring goals. I hugged my teammates, high-fived our supporters, and cheered with our fans, grateful for the way they had united in tragedy and fought for one small acre of change. I pointed to the sky and gave credit to Tommy, who will forever inspire the way I live and impact the community he loved. And I smiled, thinking about all the children and grandchildren of Tommy's Field opponents who would one day join our community, and many from outside of it, in the spirit of play.

To my surprise, Blue-Suit Stan was already there. Although he showed up uninvited, he was ready to accept and open to receive.

When the event ended and I walked off the field, I felt Tommy, surrounded by our ancestors, shining down on me. We were all one team, and on this day felt like World Cup Champions.

The very next morning, I did what Tommy would do after analyzing his matches.

I reset.

Tommy's Field may have opened, but I still had a mission to complete. A plan to figure out. An ongoing game of life to play.

My tree was ready to grow. The last chapter of my memoir was waiting to be written. A second field was yearning to be built.

"You are so strong," people would tell me.

"It's not about strength," I politely corrected them. "It's about love."

Love for my son in this world. Love for my son in the next. And the firm belief that both worlds impact each other.

Dono once told me, "We are not better off without Tommy, but we are better people."

Yet another gift.

Thank you, Tommy.

ACKNOWLEDGMENTS

I'd like to acknowledge everyone, including Tommy's friends and teammates who showed up for me, my family, and Tommy's Field in any way they could, including the following individuals and organizations who played a special role in bringing this book to life:

My editor, Claire Wachtel; thank you for believing in my story, shaping it with your wisdom, and acknowledging the moment when your lights flickered overhead as we worked.

My agent, Richard Abate, for reading it. Selling it. And not giving up on it.

My mother, father, and brother, Gregg, for giving me a childhood of love and lifetime of support from which I draw upon every single day.

The Ibrahimovic Family, for swooping in and opening your hearts, your home, and your homemade Swedish pancakes to Dono at a time when he needed a miracle.

Mike Shull and the Los Angeles Department of Recreation and Parks for championing Tommy's Field and not giving up on Westwood when you very easily could have.

The Los Angeles Football Club and the Los Angeles Galaxy, for your immediate and unwavering support that gave us a backbone that would not break.

My soul sisters, Diane and Andrea, because we smile at rainbows, lizards, and hummingbirds, and are in this together.

Christopher Lee Maher, Sheila Marie Campbell, Pamela Oslie, Robert Brown, Rebecca Rosen, Joan Hyman, Chris Plourde, and the hundreds of other healers, authors, mediums and teachers whose superpowers helped me heal from the inside out.

Linda Ramsbottom, Rebecca Kaufman, Richard Lewis, and Nicole Field Brzeski, who have taught me the true meaning of friendship and without whom there would be no Tommy's Field or TM23 Foundation.

My Hungarian sister, Tamara, for walking me through a spiritual awakening and never once telling me I was crazy.

Ginger, the best girl in the whole wide world, who has gone above and beyond for our family without saying a word.

My husband, Doug, who grieved with me, transformed with me, and never stopped loving me even when I said I believed in magic and was quitting my day job to tell the world about it.